ROUTLEDGE LIBRARY EDITIONS: ACCOUNTING HISTORY

Volume 8

THE BIRTH OF AMERICAN ACCOUNTANCY

THE BIRTH OF AMERICAN ACCOUNTANCY

PETER L. MCMICKLE AND PAUL H. JENSEN

Routledge
Taylor & Francis Group
LONDON AND NEW YORK

First published in 1988 by Garland Publishing, Inc.

This edition first published in 2021
by Routledge
2 Park Square, Milton Park, Abingdon, Oxon OX14 4RN

and by Routledge
52 Vanderbilt Avenue, New York, NY 10017

Routledge is an imprint of the Taylor & Francis Group, an informa business

© 1988 Peter L. McMickle and Paul H. Jensen

All rights reserved. No part of this book may be reprinted or reproduced or utilised in any form or by any electronic, mechanical, or other means, now known or hereafter invented, including photocopying and recording, or in any information storage or retrieval system, without permission in writing from the publishers.

Trademark notice: Product or corporate names may be trademarks or registered trademarks, and are used only for identification and explanation without intent to infringe.

British Library Cataloguing in Publication Data
A catalogue record for this book is available from the British Library

ISBN: 978-0-367-33564-9 (Set)
ISBN: 978-1-00-304636-3 (Set) (ebk)
ISBN: 978-0-367-53468-4 (Volume 8) (hbk)
ISBN: 978-0-367-53477-6 (Volume 8) (pbk)
ISBN: 978-1-00-308209-5 (Volume 8) (ebk)

Publisher's Note
The publisher has gone to great lengths to ensure the quality of this reprint but points out that some imperfections in the original copies may be apparent.

Disclaimer
The publisher has made every effort to trace copyright holders and would welcome correspondence from those they have been unable to trace.

The Birth of American Accountancy

A Bibliographic Analysis of Works on Accounting Published in America through 1820

PETER J. McMICKLE
PAUL H. JENSEN

GARLAND PUBLISHING, INC.

NEW YORK & LONDON 1988

For a list of Garland's publications in accounting, see the final pages of this volume.

Copyright © 1988
by Peter L. McMickle and Paul H. Jensen

Library of Congress Cataloging in Publication Data

McMickle, Peter L.
The birth of American accountancy : a bibliographic analysis of works on accounting published in America through 1820 / Peter L.. McMickle. Paul H. Jensen.
p. cm. — (Foundations of accounting)
ISBN 0-8240-6128-4 (alk. paper)
1. Accounting—Bibliography. 2. Bookkeeping—Bibliography.
3. Accounting—United States—History—Sources—Bibliography.
I. Jensen, Paul H. II. Title. III. Series.
Z7164.C81M345 1988
[HF5631]
0 16.657—dc 19   88-17578

Design by Renata Gomes

The volumes in this series are printed on acid-free, 250-year-life paper.

Printed in the United States of America

The Birth Of American Accountancy

LIST OF CONTRIBUTORS

Ron Allen
Thomas B. Clevenger
Karen Costley
Carolyn George
Cynthia D. Heagy
John G. Jeakle
Paul H. Jensen
Peter L. McMickle
Laura C. Middleton
Mary Helen Ola
Khursheed Omer
Gregory K. Nelson
Gary John Previts
Lynn M. Rockwell, Jr.
Philip H. Siegel
Stanley D. Tonge
Mark A. Turner
Ming-Ein Wang
Wanpen Wasinarom
Loren A. Wenzel
Ray E. Williams
Steve Ming Wong
Debra A. Wright

ACKNOWLEDGEMENTS

Work on this project has spanned many years and involved the help of many people. Some of these individuals have been acknowledged as contributors. We would particularly like to thank Gary Previts for his encouragement and his generous sharing of his personal investigations and knowledge in this area. Also we owe many thanks to Richard Brief for his support and belief in this project. Steve Wong's help on so many aspects of the project was absolutely invaluable. Karen Costley helped get it all started with her research assistance back in 1981. Many thanks to Joanie Rockwell, Lynn (Rocky) Rockwell, and Carolyn George for their editorial assistance. The librarians and libraries that aided in this endeavor are too numerous to list but to all of them we are humbly indebted. However, we owe a special debt of gratitude to Deborah Brackstone of the Interlibrary Loan Department of John Willard Brister Library at Memphis State University for her efforts on our behalf. Also, particular thanks to a good friend and supporter, Constantine Konstans, Director of Memphis State's School of Accountancy for his strong encouragement. Since we typeset the pages ourselves, we are solely responsible for any typographic errors.

Pete McMickle
Paul Jensen

PREFACE

This book brings together for the first time a comprehensive, annotated bibliography of all American accounting works through 1820. The discussion extends, clarifies, and corrects our knowledge of early American publications on accounting. All known printings are listed including many heretofore overlooked accounting treatments. Each work is reviewed and many illustrations are provided including the title pages of the first printing of every item. The reviews provided represent, in many instances, the first modern analyses of these early accounting writings and the illustrations are often the first ever published.

The Bentley – Leonard Bibliography

What is known and not known up to now regarding early works of American accounting has been strongly influenced by the scholarly efforts of Harry C. Bentley and Ruth S. Leonard published in their definitive: *Bibliography of Works on Accounting by American Authors,* Volume One (of two) 1796-1900, Boston: Published by Harry C. Bentley, 1934.

Bentley was the founder of the Bentley School of Accounting and Finance in Boston which is now Bentley College in Waltham, Massachusetts. He hired and financed Ruth Leonard, a library science graduate, to conduct exhaustive research at the Library of Congress, the American Institute of Accountants, and many other libraries throughout the United States.

<u>Bentley and Leonard's Restrictive Definition of American Works on Accounting</u>

Bentley and Leonard adopted a restrictive definition of "American works on accounting." Only two books qualified for eighteenth century inclusion in their bibliography. Bentley states in their preface (which he alone signed):

> The distinction of being the pioneer American author on accounting falls to William Mitchell, and his work heads the list of titles. His "New and complete system of bookkeeping by an improved method of double entry" was published in Philadelphia in 1796, and William Cobb's "The

country trader's assistant" was published in Brookfield, Massachusetts, in 1799. These two books are the only works on accounting by American authors published prior to the 19th century. (pgs. iii-iv)

The "Must be Published as a Book" Restriction

Bentley and Leonard excluded periodicals, bulletins, yearbooks, and proceedings. They also omitted "government bulletins for the use of departments in municipal, state, and federal administration." (pgs. iv,v) While it can be argued that this is a reasonable and possibly necessary restriction for a "book" bibliography, it did eliminate some early accounting related publications such as the reports of the various Auditors-General on the "Accompts" of the Colonies.

The "Must be Printed in America" Restriction

Printed in America would also seem to be an obvious restriction, but there were a few remote possibilities for inclusion that it eliminated. For example, Benjamin Booth is not listed, but he was an American and also a loyal British subject on the Tory Side of the American Revolution. As a result of the war, his 1789 book on accounting was published in London, England, rather than the United States. On the title page of his *A Complete System of Bookkeeping*, he referred to himself as "late of New York" and in his introduction he explained:

> Being cut off, by the late war, from the friendships formed in my youth; and prevented, by the Peace that succeeded it from pursuing the line of business to which I had long been habituated; it became a duty with me to attempt some other way of rendering my time and talents useful to society: how far I have succeeded in my choice of objects, time will show. (pg. 6)

The "Authored by an American" Restriction

The "American Author" limitation resulted in the exclusion of a number of early books on accounting printed in America but extracted from the writings of foreign authors. Bentley and Leonard did, however, accept some degree of plagiarism:

> All works by American authors which were found to be verbatim copies of works by foreign authors, as the case may be, were eliminated but many works plagiarized in part from foreign or American works were not eliminated. (pgs. v-vi)

In fact, a foreign author is associated with one well known challenge to Bentley's claim of Mitchell (1796) as the first American accounting book. This challenge was lodged by no less an authority than the U.S. Library of Congress. In 1977, the Library purchased for their collections a book which they publicly displayed as the "earliest book on bookkeeping published in America." It is *A course of book-keeping according to the method of single entry*, extracted from the works of Charles Hutton (Philadelphia, printed by Joseph James, 1788). William Matheson, Chief of the Rare Book and Special Collections Division of the Library of Congress, states:

> Although Charles Hutton is English, there is reason to believe Bentley would have included the book, had he known of it. The title page indicates that the information has been "extracted from the work of Hutton, with sundry alterations and additions by the editor." The editor is not named; if he was Joseph James, the printer, the book is a candidate for Bentley. . . . We do not find mention of an American edition of any book on bookkeeping by an English writer as early as this one. (W. Matheson,"Microcosm of the Library of Congress," *A B Bookman's Weekly*, November 28, 1977, p. 3161)

The only other known surviving example of this printing is a damaged copy at Harvard (NUC NH0641321). However, there were several later printings of the same book by other Philadelphia printers (see Item 4).

The Hutton publication, however, would not have qualified for inclusion in Bentley and Leonard's bibliography because it was not "authored by an American." In an advertisement on the second page of the 1801 printing, the "editor" states, "The difference between this and the original may be best known by comparing them, without enlarging here." Taking his advice and making the comparison reveals only one difference – a one word change of London to Philadelphia at the start of the journal example. Otherwise, pound sterling remains as the medium of exchange and there are a number of references to British towns such as Liverpool, York, and Bath. As a matter of fact, Bentley specifically mentioned in the preface that he and Leonard excluded American printings of books by Charles Hutton as well as Thomas Dilworth, William Jackson, Edward Thomas Jones, Patrick Kelly, and Richard Turner (pg. vi).

The "Must be an Accounting Work" Restriction

This requirement eliminated such works as check systems, ready reckoners, keys, charts, diagrams, classifications of accounts, office manuals, account books, and forms (pg. v). Because of this restriction, Bentley and Leonard would not have included in their formal listings Thomas Goddard's large wall chart of 1818 entitled *The trial balance* . . . (Item 26) which contains almost as much accounting instruction as the 1788 Hutton. (They do indicate on pgs. 11-12 that they observed the copyright but couldn't locate an example of this "title" to examine, which they thought was possibly a preliminary part of Goddard's 1821 book.)

The "Devoted Primarily to Accounting" Restriction

This restriction represented Bentley and Leonard's most questionable exclusion – books with sections on accounting but principally devoted to non-accounting topics such as arithmetic and commerce. On an international level, many of the commonly referenced early books on accounting give a majority of their coverage to non-accounting topics. Perhaps the most notable example is the first printed writing on bookkeeping in Frater Lucas de Burgo Sancti Sepulchri (Pacioli) *Suma de arithmetica geometria proportioni et proportionalita* (Venice: Paganinus de Paganinis, 10 November 1494). Only 27 of 616 total pages of the Suma (308 leaves) are devoted to bookkeeping. Most of the book deals with arithmetic, algebra, and geometry.

Another example is E. Hatton's *The merchants magazine* first printed in London in 1695 and listed in all principal bibliographies of early English accounting. In Hatton, only one 46 page chapter in a book totaling 297 pages is devoted to bookkeeping. Many similar examples could be cited.

In adopting this restriction, Bentley and Leonard actually excluded certain writings by American authors that were longer than some of the wholly dedicated works which they listed. Consider, for example, Chauncey Lee's *American accomptant* (Lansingburgh: 1797). Lee's chapter on accounting is entitled "A compendious treatise on book-keeping; or accomptantship reduced to practice." This accounting section is 44 pages of rather fine print and two pages of the introduction are also devoted to bookkeeping. (This 310 page book is famous for being the first work to use the dollar mark ($) in print. Lee may have in fact been the originator of the dollar mark.)

Bentley and Leonard do not list Lee's 46 pages of bookkeeping because his book as a whole is not "primarily devoted to accounting." (Lee is mentioned in their preface, pg. iv.) They do include such authors as Cobb, 1799 (48 pages) and Gale, 1817 (40 pages, only 27 of which are devoted to bookkeeping).

The fourth book listed in Bentley and Leonard is *Bookkeeping by the method of single entry for the use of young persons* printed for Francis Nichols with the preface signed by O. E. (Philadelphia: 1808, 38 pgs.). This work is an expanded version of an earlier unlisted writing contained in *A treatise of practical arithmetic and bookkeeping* by F. Nichols (Boston, July 1797). The 1797 *Treatise* devotes 24 of 103 pages to single entry bookkeeping and it too, like Lee, provides examples of accounts kept in dollars and cents but with no dollar marks. Bentley and Leonard again chose not to give this work a line listing because the book was not primarily devoted to accounting. (They did make a parenthetic note of the work on pg. 8 under the heading of the 1808 version.)

Bentley and Leonard are appropriately remembered for the great contribution of their American accounting bibliography. In order to keep their total effort down to a manageable size, they limited their listings to books that were printed in America, written by American authors, and primarily devoted to accounting. Unfortunately, these limitations have resulted in widely held, but inaccurate, views of the extent of eighteenth century publishing efforts in America dealing with accounting.

A very important example of the impact of Bentley and Leonard's decision is that they made no mention, and were probably unaware, of the first writing on accounting which was published in America 59 years prior to Mitchell. In 1737, the fifth edition of *The secretary's guide, or young man's companion* was compiled, printed, and sold in Philadelphia by Andrew Bradford.

Bradford's *Young man's companion* is a one volume encyclopedia of useful knowledge. The book contains a 14 page section described as "a short and easy method of shop and book-keeping, merchant's accompts, etc." which is more specifically entitled "Rules and directions for bookkeeping, or merchant's-accompts." This work has been completely overlooked by accounting historians even though it went through 15 known eighteenth century American printings. This oversight can be attributed in great part to Bentley and Leonard's view of what constituted American accounting works.

The McMickle – Jensen Bibliography

The present work is an annotated, American accounting bibliography through 1820 that builds on Bentley and Leonard's foundation for this early period. It adds to their listing books that contain sections on bookkeeping, writings authored by or extracted from foreign writers, and accounting broadsides. It also contains publications that were simply overlooked by Bentley and Leonard such as the 1789 *An introduction to the counting house* by the American author Thomas Sarjeant which was recently brought to the attention of accounting historians in an excellent article by Terry Sheldahl (see cite in Item 5). The annotations provide reviews and photographs of all works which bring to the reader a much greater understanding of the beginnings of American accountancy.

Content Restrictions

This bibliography also has content restrictions. Bentley and Leonard's "must be printed in America" and "must be published as a book" restrictions are retained. The latter restriction offers much room for further research. Another fertile area for further study is identification of the foreign accounting books sold in America during the eighteenth century as indicated by the surviving bookseller catalogues of which, surprisingly, there are quite a few.

A significant restriction of this bibliography, **not** imposed consistently by Bentley and Leonard, is that there must be a known surviving copy. Many unlocated American accounting works are thought to have existed because of recorded copyrights, advertisements, and listings in old general bibliographies and library catalogues. A number of listings contained in Evans (see below) have been omitted because surviving copies for verification could not be found. For example, Evans lists a 1790 printing of Hutton (Evans 22582) but no existing copy could be located.

Research Methodology

A research base for this bibliography was laid with the assistance of two graduate accounting history classes at Memphis State University (Development of Accounting Thought, ACCT 8710). The first class, in the Summer of 1983, conducted an exhaustive search for early American accounting works that might have been "lost" by contemporary accounting authorities. The focus of this search was upon the comprehensive cataloging of early

American imprints which Library Scientists have been assembling since before the turn of the century. Two key bibliographies in this effort are Charles Evans' life work entitled *American Bibliography* (reprinted in a complete collection by New York: Peter Smith, 1942) and the successor work by Ralph R. Shaw and Richard H. Shoemaker entitled *American Bibliography: A Preliminary Checklist 1801 to 1819* (New York & London: The Scarecrow Press, Inc., 1958). These bibliographies are organized first by date, then by author, and finally by title. They are not organized by subject.

The more than 100,000 entries were divided among the researchers who then reviewed the works for titles that "sounded" as if they might contain writings on accounting. Approximately 250 possible books were identified in this fashion.

About half of these possibilities were then examined by using the American Antiquarian Society's microprint collection entitled *Readex Early American Imprints*. This collection is not complete and many key accounting works were only identified after copies were obtained and inspected through inter-library loan. Reviews of some of these works were begun in 1983. The second class, in the Summer of 1984, continued the effort collecting more works on inter-library loan and developing additional reviews.

Later research has principally consisted of obtaining the scarcest works for study, identifying the many printings, and tying down loose ends. Key references that aided in this effort were: *The National Union Catalog pre-1956 Imprints* (London: Mansel Information and the American Library Association, 1971), Louis C. Karpinski's classic *Bibliography of Mathematical Works Printed in America Through 1850* (Ann Arbor: The University of Michigan Press, 1940), and *A Dictionary Catalog of American Books Pertaining to the 17th through 19th Centuries* (Library of the American Antiquarian Society, Westport, Conn.: Greenwood Publishing Corp., 1971).

Conventions Used

The old spellings of key words have been retained in the reviews. Depending upon the work, for example, "ledger" can also be found spelled "leidger," "leiger," and "leger." Original letter capitalizations which often varied at the whim of the printer have not been retained either in the listings or the reviews. Instead, the first letter of the first word of the old book title is capitalized and the remaining words are uncapitalized. Nor have full book titles been provided which in some cases run into several paragraphs. Full titles and original capitalization can be easily discerned by reference to the illustration of the original title page of every first printing which is found to the left of each bibliographic listing.

The height of each book is given in centimeters when known. Many of the early book printers did an incomplete job of page numbering. Unnumbered pages before and after the main numbered body of the text are indicated in brackets [ ]. When paging is particularly confusing, the phrase (Various pagings) is often used. Evans, Shaw-Shoemaker (SS), and National Union Catalogue (NUC) numbers are provided if known. If they are known to not exist this is also indicated, *viz* (Not in NUC). Inconsistencies in presentation are often the result of incomplete information.

Undoubtedly, errors both factual and typographical will come to light over time. The authors would appreciate anyone discovering such errors to be good enough to bring them to their attention.

Peter L. McMickle
Paul H. Jensen

March 19, 1988

TABLE OF CONTENTS

ITEMS   Pg.

Item 1. The George Fisher Series beginning 1737.

    1737. [No author listed]. *The secretary's guide, or young man's companion . . .* Fifth edition. Philadelphia: Printed and sold by Andrew Bradford. [2] [8] 248 pgs. 16.5 cm. (Fifth edition is first occurrence of book-keeping) Evans 4127, NUC NB0729644   3

Item 2. 1774. Elie Vallette. *The deputy commissary's guide, within the province of Maryland . . .* Annapolis: Printed by Ann Catharine Green & Son. [2] [1] 248 pgs. 20 cm. Evans 13742, NUC NF0023044   21

Item 3. 1776. Arthur Young. *Rural oeconomy, or essays on the practical parts of husbandry . . .* From the second London edition. Philadelphia: Reprinted and sold by James Humphreys, Jr. 154 pgs. 20.5 cm. (*The rural socrates* is not included, though mentioned on the title page) Evans 15226, NUC NY0024098   29

Item 4. The Charles Hutton Series beginning 1788.   35

    Philadelphia imprints: *Course of book-keeping*, single entry series.

    1788. Charles Hutton. *A course of book-keeping, according to the method of single entry . . .* Philadelphia: Printed by Joseph James. [8] 30 [46] pgs. 19.5 cm. (Not in Evans) NUC NH0641321   38

Table of Contents Con't

ITEMS	Pg.

Crukshank, et al printers: *American tutor's assistant*, single entry series.

1809. [No author listed]. *The American tutor's assistant revised ... to which is added a course of book-keeping by single entry.* Originally compiled by sundry teachers in and near Philadelphia. Philadelphia: Printed by Joseph Crukshank. [4] 180 [28] 17.5 cm. (Not in SS) NUC NJ0090400 (Earlier printings had no bookkeeping.) ... 39

New York imprints: *A complete treatise*, double entry series.

1809. Charles Hutton. *A complete treatise on practical arithmetic and book-keeping both by single and double entry....* Corrected, enlarged, and adapted ... by D. P. Adams. New York: Sold by Samuel Campbell (and others), W. Elliot printer. [8] 228 pgs. 18 cm. SS 17794 NUC NH0641316

1810. Charles Hutton. *A complete system of practical arithmetic and book-keeping both by single and double entry ...* New York: Printed and sold by Smith & Forman. [9] 224pgs. 17.5 cm. SS 20420 NUC NH0641307 ... 41

Item 5. 1789. Thomas Sarjeant. *An introduction to the counting house ...* Philadelphia: Printed by Dobson & Lang. 52 pgs. 16 cm. Evans 22127, NUC NS0134249 ... 50

Item 6. 1791. Samuel Freeman. *The town officer* .. Portland: Printed by Benjamin Titcomb. 178 [2] pgs. 17.5 cm. Evans 23389 NUC NF0357711 ... 63

Table of Contents Con't

ITEMS Pg.

Item 7. The Thomas Dilworth Series beginning 1794.

[1794? No date shown]. Thomas Dilworth. *The young book-keeper's assistant* ... Twelfth edition. Philadelphia: Printed by Benjamin Johnson. 162 pgs. 21.5 cm. Evans 26889 NUC ND0274221 — 75

Item 8. 1794. Richard Turner. *A new introduction to book keeping* ... First American Edition. Boston: Printed by I. Thomas and E. T. Andrews. 24 [3] [17] [3] pgs. (various pagings) 16 cm. Evans 27824 NUC NT0397210 — 81

Item 9. 1796. [Edward T. Jones, No author listed]. *Jones's English system of book-keeping, by single or double entry* ... First American edition. New York: Printed by William A. Davis for Thomas Allen. (Various pagings) 26.5 cm. Evans 30644, NUC NJ0148079 — 97

Item 10. 1796. William Mitchell. *A new and complete system of book-keeping, by an improved method of double entry* ... Philadelphia: Printed by Bioren and Madan. [8] 454 pgs. 21.5 cm. Evans 30802 NUC NM0654391 — 101

Item 11. 1797. Chauncey Lee. *The American accomptant* ... Lansingburgh, New York: Printed by William W. Wands. [8] 254 [15] pgd. 17.5 cm. Evans 32366, NUC NL0196251 — 109

Item 12. 1797. F. [Francis] Nichols. *A treatise of practical arithmetic and bookkeeping* ... Boston: Printed by Manning & Loring for David West. [5] 108 pgs. 17.2 cm. Evans 32583 NUC NN0244931 — 117

Table of Contents Con't

ITEMS	Pg.

Item 13. 1798. Samuel Temple. *A concise introduction to practical arithmetic; in which all the rules that occur in common business are applied to the federal currency* . . . Second edition. Boston: Printed and sold by Samuel Hall. 118 pgs. 18 cm. (Not in Evans) NUC NT0089286 (1796 first edition had no bookkeeping.) — 123

Item 14. 1799. William Cobb. *The country trader's assistant* . . . Brookfield, Massachusetts: Printed for the author. 46 pgs. Evans 35315 NUC NC0501740 — 129

Item 15. 1801. William Jackson. *Book-keeping in the true Italian form* . . . Philadelphia: Printed by John Bioren. [8] 296 pgs. 22 cm. SS 706 NUC NJ0008040 — 133

Item 16. 1803. Patrick Kelly. *The elements of book-keeping* . . . Philadelphia: Printed by James Humphreys. [14] [1] 203 pgs. SS 4470 NUC NK0084487 — 139

Item 17. 1804. Thomas Turner. *An epitome of book-keeping by double entry* . . . Portland, Maine: Printed by Jenks & Shirley for Thomas Clark. 148 pgs. 17.5 cm. SS 7396 NUC NT0397559 — 141

Item 18. 1807. [William Kinne, no author's name on first edition]. *A short system of practical arithmetic, compiled from the best authorities, with demonstrations of the rules, to which is annexed a short plan of bookkeeping* . . . Hallowell, Maine: Published and sold by Ezekiel Goodale. Printed by: N. Cheever. 173 pgs. 17.2 cm. SS 12869 NUC NK0152979. — 147

Table of Contents Con't

ITEMS	Pg.

Item 19. 1808. O. E. *Book-keeping by the method of single entry. for the use of young persons.* Philadelphia: Printed for F. Nichols by T. & G. Palmer. [38] pgs. 24 cm. (Shaw-Shoemaker misclassifies the author as O. D. see SS 14817) (Not in NUC) ... 153

Item 20. 1810. [No author given]. *The mercantile manual, or, accountant's guide* ... New Haven: Printed by Oliver Steele and Co. (Only a 15 page fragment of a much larger book survives.) 24 cm. (Not in NUC) ... 157

Item 21. 1815. John Blake. *The private instructor* ... Trenton, New Jersey: Published by D. Fenton. [7] [1] [4] 232 pgs. 18.5 cm. SS 34144 NUC NB0532002 ... 161

Item 22. 1815. B. [Briant] Sheys. *The American book-keeper; part the first. comprising a system of book-keeping by single and double entry* ... New York: Printed by N. Van Riper. [7] 153 pgs. 21 cm. SS 35925 NUC NS0504501 ... 167

Item 23. 1817. Edmund Gale. *An epitome of book-keeping by single entry* ... Nantucket: A. G. Tannatt. 40 pgs. 17.5 cm. SS 40883 NUC NG0015875 ... 171

Item 24. 1817. Charles Gerisher. *Modern book-keeping, by double entry* ... New York: Printed by E. Conrad. 158 pgs.(Various pagings) 23.5 cm. SS 40908 NUC NG0146264 ... 175

Item 25. 1817. James Maginness. *The family clerk and student's assistant* ... Harrisburg, PA: Printed by Wm. Greer. [4] 190 [2] pgs. 21.5 cm. SS 41330 NUC NM0112634 ... 181

Table of Contents Con't

ITEMS	Pg.
Item 26. 1818. Thomas H. Goddard. *The trial balance, or the book keeper's directory; showing a complete system of book keeping, commenced, carried on, and closed, and new books opened, upon a clear and experimental plan.* New York: Printed by J. Seymour. 1 page broadside 73 x 49.5 cm. (Not in SS) (Not in NUC)	185
Item 27. 1819. Zachariah Jess. *The American tutor's assistant, improved* . . . Twelth edition. (Copyright 1818.) Philadelphia: Published and sold by McCarty and Davis. 188 [2] [23] pgs. 17 cm. SS 48375 NUC NJ0090410 (Earlier printings had no bookkeeping.)	189
Item 28. 1818. D. C. Roscoe. *A new and compendious system of book-keeping; by double entry* . . . Hagers-Town, MD: Printed by William D. Bell. [4] [7] [9] [18] [16] pgs. 20 cm. SS 45579 NUC NR0420035	195
Item 29. 1818. B. [Briant] Sheys. *The American book-keeper; comprising a complete system of book-keeping* . . . New York: Printed and sold by Collins and Co. [8] 333 [1] pgs. 22 cm. SS 45709 NUC NS0504502	201
Item 30. 1818. Daniel Staniford. *Staniford's practical arithmetic* . . . Boston: Printed by J. H. A. Frost for West, Richardson & Lord. [7] 324 pgs. 19 cm. SS 45789 NUC NS0860884	205
Item 31. 1819. Benjamin Davies. *A new and concise system of book-keeping* . . . Second edition. Philadelphia: Benjamin Johnson. 66 pgs. (Various pagings) 21.5 cm. SS 47793 (No first edition is known)	213

Table of Contents Con't

ITEMS	Pg.
Item 32. 1820. I. [Israel] Alger. *The young merchant's manual, or practical book-keeper* . . . Boston: Printed for the author. [48] pgs. (Various paging) 32.5 cm. NUC NA0168009	219
Item 33. 1820. James Bennett. *The American system of practical book-keeping* . . . New York: Printed by Abm. Paul. [20] 72 pgs. (Various pagings) 24 cm. With broadside bound in. NUC NB0313008	223

LIST OF ILLUSTRATIONS

ILLUSTRATIONS	Pg.
ILLUSTRATION 1. Title page from Andrew Bradford's 1737 printing of *Young man's companion*.	2
ILLUSTRATION 2. Waste-Book and journal entries from Andrew Bradford's 1737 printing of *Young man's companion*.	18
ILLUSTRATION 3. Waste-Book and journal entries from Andrew Bradford's 1737 printing of *Young man's companion*.	19
ILLUSTRATION 4. Title page from 1774 Elie Vallette's *The deputy commissary's guide* (note Francis Scott Key's autograph).	20
ILLUSTRATION 5. Discussion of probate accounting in 1774 Elie Vallette's *The deputy commissary's guide*.	25
ILLUSTRATION 6. Discussion of probate accounting in 1774 Elie Vallette's *The deputy commissary's guide*.	26
ILLUSTRATION 7. Discussion of probate accounting in 1774 Elie Vallette's *The deputy commissary's guide*.	27
ILLUSTRATION 8. Title page from Arthur Young's 1776 *Rural oeconomy*.	28
ILLUSTRATION 9. Ledger example for farm accounting in Arthur Young's 1776 *Rural oeconomy*.	33
ILLUSTRATION 10. Title page from Harvard's damaged 1788 copy of Charles Hutton's *A course of book-keeping*.	34

List of Illustrations Con't

ILLUSTRATIONS	Pg.
ILLUSTRATION 11. Day-book entries from 1801 copy of Hutton's *A course of book-keeping, according to the method of single entry.*	43
ILLUSTRATION 12. Ledger entries from 1801 copy of Hutton's *A course of book-keeping, according to the method of single entry.*	44
ILLUSTRATION 13. Title page of printer Joseph Crukshank's 1809 Hutton based *The American tutor's assistant revised.*	45
ILLUSTRATION 14. Title page from 1809 Hutton *A complete treatise . . . both by single and double entry.*	46
ILLUSTRATION 15. Wastebook example from 1809 Hutton *A complete treatise . . . both by single and double entry.*	47
ILLUSTRATION 16. Title page from 1810 Hutton *A complete system . . . . both by single and double entry.*	48
ILLUSTRATION 17. Wastebook example from 1810 Hutton *A complete system . . . . both by single and double entry.*	49
ILLUSTRATION 18. Title page from 1789 Thomas Sarjeant's *An introduction to the counting house.*	50
ILLUSTRATION 19. Waste book example from 1789 Thomas Sarjeant's *An introduction to the counting house.*	60
ILLUSTRATION 20. Journal example from 1789 Thomas Sarjeant's *An introduction to the counting house.*	61

List of Illustrations Con't

ILLUSTRATIONS	Pg.
ILLUSTRATION 21. Title page from 1791 Samuel Freeman's *The town officer.*	62
ILLUSTRATION 22. Beginning of the accounting section in 1791 Samuel Freeman's *The town officer.*	72
ILLUSTRATION 23. Example of town accounts from 1791 Samuel Freeman's *The town officer.*	73
ILLUSTRATION 24. Title page from the first American printing of Thomas Dilworth's *The young book-keeper's assistant*.	74
ILLUSTRATION 25. Journal example in 1794 Thomas Dilworth's *The young book-keeper's assistant.*	78
ILLUSTRATION 26. Title page from the 1803 *Dilworth's Book-keepers assistant improved.*	79
ILLUSTRATION 27. Title page from 1794 Richard Turner's *A new introduction to book keeping.*	80
ILLUSTRATION 28. Title page from 1820 *A new introduction to book-keeping . . . on the plan of R. Turner, LL.D.*	93
ILLUSTRATION 29. Waste-book example from 1820 *A new introduction to book-keeping . . . on the plan of R. Turner, LL.D.*	94
ILLUSTRATION 30. Journal example from 1820 *A new introduction to book-keeping . . . on the plan of R. Turner, LL.D.*	95
ILLUSTRATION 31. Title page from 1796 *Jones's English system of book-keeping, by single or double entry.*	96

List of Illustrations Con't

ILLUSTRATIONS	Pg.
ILLUSTRATION 32. Table of contents page from 1796 William Mitchell's *A new and complete system of book-keeping*.	99
ILLUSTRATION 33. Title page from 1796 William Mitchell's *A new and complete system of book-keeping*.	100
ILLUSTRATION 34. First page of Preface in 1796 William Mitchell's *A new and complete system of book-keeping*.	106
ILLUSTRATION 35. Final page of Preface in 1796 William Mitchell's *A new and complete system of book-keeping*.	107
ILLUSTRATION 36. Title page from 1797 Chauncey Lee's *The American accomptant*.	108
ILLUSTRATION 37. Description of dollar mark $ characteristics in 1797 Chauncey Lee's *The American accomptant*.	113
ILLUSTRATION 38. First page of book-keeping section in 1797 Chauncey Lee's *The American accomptant*.	114
ILLUSTRATION 39. Journal entries from 1797 Chauncey Lee's *The American accomptant*.	115
ILLUSTRATION 40. Title page from 1797 Francis Nichol's *A treatise of practical arithmetic and bookkeeping*.	116
ILLUSTRATION 41. Day book example from 1797 Francis Nichol's *A treatise of practical arithmetic and bookkeeping*.	119

List of Illustrations Con't

ILLUSTRATIONS | Pg.

ILLUSTRATION 42. Ledger example from 1797 Francis Nichol's *A treatise of practical arithmetic and bookkeeping.* — 120

ILLUSTRATION 43. Balancing entry example from 1797 Francis Nichol's *A treatise of practical arithmetic and bookkeeping.* — 121

ILLUSTRATION 44. Title page from 1798 Samuel Temple's *A concise introduction to practical arithmetic.* — 122

ILLUSTRATION 45. Account for goods and services provided to Samuel Thornton from Walter Underwood in 1798 Temple. — 126

ILLUSTRATION 46. Account for goods and services received by Walter Underwood from Samuel Thornton in 1798 Temple. — 127

ILLUSTRATION 47. Title page from 1799 William Cobb *The country trader's assistant.* — 128

ILLUSTRATION 48. Ledger example from 1799 William Cobb *The country trader's assistant.* — 131

ILLUSTRATION 49. Title page from 1801 William Jackson *Book-keeping, in the true Italian form.* — 132

ILLUSTRATION 50. Waste-book example in 1801 Jackson's *Book-keeping, in the true Italian form.* — 136

ILLUSTRATION 51. A journal example in 1801 Jackson's *Book-keeping, in the true Italian form.* — 137

List of Illustrations Con't

ILLUSTRATIONS	Pg.
ILLUSTRATION 52. Title page from 1803 Patrick Kelly's *The elements of book-keeping.*	138
ILLUSTRATION 53. Title page from 1804 Thomas Turner's *An epitome of book-keeping by double entry.*	140
ILLUSTRATION 54. Steps for closing the books explained in the 1804 Turner's *An epitome of book-keeping.*	143
ILLUSTRATION 55. First half of quarterly statement and trial balance in 1804 Turner *An epitome of book-keeping.*	144
ILLUSTRATION 56. Second half of quarterly statement and trial balance in 1804 Turner *An epitome of book-keeping.*	145
ILLUSTRATION 57. Title page from 1807 William Kinne's *A short system of practical arithmetic.*	146
ILLUSTRATION 58. Example problem in 1807 William Kinne's *A short system of practical arithmetic.*	151
ILLUSTRATION 59. Title page from O. E.'s 1808 *Book-keeping by the method of single entry. for the use of young persons.*	152
ILLUSTRATION 60. Preface from 1808 O. E. *Book-keeping by the method of single entry: for the use of young persons.*	155
ILLUSTRATION 61. Title page from 1810 *The mercantile manual, or, accountant's guide.*	156

List of Illustrations Con't

ILLUSTRATIONS	Pg.
ILLUSTRATION 62. Bookkeeping discussion from 1810 *The mercantile manual, or, accountant's guide.*	159
ILLUSTRATION 63. Title page from 1815 John Blake *The private instructor.*	160
ILLUSTRATION 64. Preface from 1815 John Blake *The private instructor.*	164
ILLUSTRATION 65. First page of bookkeeping section in 1815 John Blake *The private instructor.*	165
ILLUSTRATION 66. Title page from 1815 Briant Sheys *The American book-keeper; part the first.*	166
ILLUSTRATION 67. Error correcting discussed in 1815 Briant Sheys *The American book-keeper; part the first.*	169
ILLUSTRATION 68. Title page from 1817 Edmund Gale's *An epitome of book-keeping by single entry.*	170
ILLUSTRATION 69. Preface from 1817 Edmund Gale's *An epitome of book-keeping by single entry.*	173
ILLUSTRATION 70. Title page from 1817 Charles Gerisher's *Modern book-keeping, by double entry.*	174
ILLUSTRATION 71. Cash book example from 1817 Charles Gerisher's *Modern book-keeping, by double entry.*	178
ILLUSTRATION 72. Financial "sheets" from 1817 Charles Gerisher's *Modern book-keeping, by double entry.*	179

List of Illustrations Con't

ILLUSTRATIONS	Pg.
ILLUSTRATION 73. Title page from 1817 James Maginness' *The family clerk and student's assistant*.	180
ILLUSTRATION 74. Day book example from 1817 James Maginness' *The family clerk and student's assistant*.	183
ILLUSTRATION 75. Leger example from 1817 James Maginness' *The family clerk and student's assistant*.	184
ILLUSTRATION 76. Top of Thomas H. Goddard's 1818 broadside entitled *The trial balance*... (greatly reduced).	186
ILLUSTRATION 77. Bottom of Thomas H. Goddard's 1818 broadside entitled *The trial balance*... (greatly reduced).	187
ILLUSTRATION 78. Title page from 1819 Zachariah Jess *The American tutor's assistant, improved*.	188
ILLUSTRATION 79. First page of book keeping section in 1819 Zachariah Jess *The American tutor's assistant, improved*.	192
ILLUSTRATION 80. Day book example in 1819 Zachariah Jess *The American tutor's assistant, improved*.	193
ILLUSTRATION 81. Title page from 1818 D. C. Roscoe's *A new and compendious system of bookkeeping; by double entry*.	194

List of Illustrations Con't

ILLUSTRATIONS	Pg.
ILLUSTRATION 82. Journal example from 1818 D. C. Roscoe's *A new and compendious system of book-keeping; by double entry.*	198
ILLUSTRATION 83. Leger example from 1818 D. C. Roscoe's *A new and compendious system of book-keeping; by double entry.*	199
ILLUSTRATION 84. Title page from 1818 Sheys *The American book-keeper; comprising a complete system of book-keeping.*	200
ILLUSTRATION 85. Error correcting discussed in 1818 Sheys *The American book-keeper; comprising a complete system.*	203
ILLUSTRATION 86. Title page from 1818 Daniel Staniford's *Staniford's practical arithmetic.*	204
ILLUSTRATION 87. First page of single entry book-keeping section in 1818 *Staniford's practical arithmetic.*	208
ILLUSTRATION 88. Single entry journal example from 1818 *Staniford's practical arithmetic.*	209
ILLUSTRATION 89. First page of double entry book-keeping section in 1818 *Staniford's practical arithmetic.*	210
ILLUSTRATION 90. Double entry journal example from 1818 *Staniford's practical arithmetic.*	211
ILLUSTRATION 91. Title page from 1819 Benjamin Davies *A new and concise system of book-keeping.*	212

List of Illustrations Con't

ILLUSTRATIONS	Pg.
ILLUSTRATION 92. Journal example from 1819 Benjamin Davies *A new and concise system of book-keeping.*	216
ILLUSTRATION 93. Two ledger pages from 1819 Benjamin Davies *A new and concise system of book-keeping.*	217
ILLUSTRATION 94. Title page from 1820 Israel Alger's *The young merchant's manual, or practical book-keeper.*	218
ILLUSTRATION 95. Waste book example in 1820 Israel Alger's *The young merchant's manual, or practical book-keeper.*	221
ILLUSTRATION 96. Title page from 1820 James Bennett's *The American system of practical book-keeping.*	222
ILLUSTRATION 97. Table of contents from 1820 first printing of Bennett's *The American system of practical book-keeping.*	229
ILLUSTRATION 98. Day-book and journal example from 1820 James Bennett's *The American system of practical book-keeping.*	230
ILLUSTRATION 99. Broadside from 1820 Bennett's *The American system of practical book-keeping . . .* (greatly reduced).	231
ILLUSTRATION 100. Title page of *Jackson's book-keeping* bound in some printings of Bennett's first edition of 1820.	232

The Birth Of American Accountancy

Item 1. The George Fisher Series beginning 1737.

THE Secretary's GUIDE, OR Young Man's Companion.

In FOUR Parts: CONTAINING,

PART I. Directions for Spelling, Reading and Writing true ENGLISH, with the Pronunciation, &c.

PART II. How to write Letters of Compliment, Friendship, or Business; with proper directions for external and internal Superscriptions, and other Things necessary to be understood in that Affair.

PART III. Arithmetick made Easy, and the Rules thereof explained and made familiar to the Capacities of those that desire to Learn. With a short and easy Method of SHOP and BOOK-KEEPING, MERCHANT'S ACCOMPTS, &c. And TABLES, how to lay out and measure Land, Gauging Vessels, Measuring Boards, Glass, round or square Timber, Buying or Selling any thing by the Hundred: Also a Table of Interest at 6 or 8 per Cent.

PART IV. Forms of the most useful Writings, such as, Bills, Bonds, Letters of Attorney, Indentures, Bonds of Arbitration, Awards, Umpirages, Deeds of Sale, Deeds of Gift, Assignments, Leases and Releases, Counter Securities, Declarations of Trust, with many other useful Writings, Bills of Exchange, &c. With Monthly Observations in Gardening, Planting, Grafting, and Inoculating Fruit Trees, and the best time to prune them.

To which is added, The FAMILY COMPANION:

Containing Rules and Directions, how to make *Cyder, Mead, Wines* of our own Growth, &c. With a Collection of choice and safe Remedies, very useful in Families.

The Fifth Edition, greatly Enlarged and carefully Corrected.

Philadelphia: Printed and Sold by ANDREW BRADFORD, at the Sign of the *BIBLE.* MDCCXXXVII.

ILLUSTRATION 1. Title page from Andrew Bradford's 1737 printing of *Young man's companion*.

Item 1. The George Fisher Series beginning 1737.

1737. [No author listed]. *The secretary's guide, or young man's companion* . . . Fifth edition. Philadelphia: Printed and sold by Andrew Bradford. [2] [8] 248 pgs. 16.5 cm. (Fifth edition is first occurrence of bookkeeping) Evans 4127, NUC NB0729644

1738. [No author listed]. *The secretary's guide, or young man's companion* . . . Fifth edition. Philadelphia: Printed and sold by Andrew Bradford. [5] 248 pgs. 16.5 cm. (Not in Evans) NUC NB0729646

1748. George Fisher. *The American instructor: or, young man's best companion* . . . Ninth edition. Philadelphia: Printed by B. Franklin & D. Hall. [5] 378 pgs. 10.5 cm. (Not in Evans) NUC NF0162586

1753. George Fisher. *The American instructor: or, young man's best companion* . . . Tenth edition. Philadelphia: Printed by B. Franklin & D. Hall. [5] [2] 384 pgs. 17 cm. (Not in Evans) NUC NF0162589

1760. George Fisher. *The American instructor: or, young man's best companion* . . . New York: Twelfth edition, printed by H. Gain. [5] 378 pgs. 17 cm. (Not in Evans) NUC NF0162591

1770. George Fisher. *The American instructor: or, young man's best companion* . . . Fourteenth edition. New York: Printed by H. Gain. [5] [1] 390 pgs. 16.2 cm. Evans S432 NUC NF0162593

1770. George Fisher. *The American instructor: or, young man's best companion* . . . Fifteenth edition. Philadephia: Printed by John Dunlap. [5] 390 pgs. (Not in Evans) (Not in NUC)

1775. George Fisher. *The American instructor: or, young man's best companion* . . . Fifteenth edition. Burlington, N. J.: Printed by Issac Collins. [12] 372 pgs. (Not in Evans) (Not in NUC)

1779. George Fisher. *The American instructor: or, young man's best companion* . . . Boston: Printed by John Boyle and J. D. McDougall. [6] 354 pgs. 16.5 cm. (Not in Evans) NUC NF0162597

Item 1. The George Fisher Series beginning 1737.

1785. George Fisher. *The instructor: or, American young man's best companion* . . . Thirteenth edition. Worchester & Boston: Printed by Isaiah Thomas and others. 384 pgs. (Not in Evans) (Not in NUC)

1786. George Fisher. *The instructor: or, American young man's best companion* . . . Thirteenth edition. Worchester & Boston: Printed by Isaiah Thomas and others. (Not in Evans) (Not in NUC)

1786. George Fisher. *The American instructor: or, young man's best companion* . . . Philadelphia: Printed and sold by Joseph Crukshank. [12] 372 pgs. (Not in Evans) (Not in NUC)

1787. George Fisher. *The American instructor: or, young man's best companion* . . . Philadelphia: Printed and sold by Joseph Crukshank. (Not in Evans) (Not in NUC)

1794. George Fisher. *The instructor: or, American young man's best companion* . . . Walpole, N. H. & Boston: Printed by Isaiah Thomas and David Carlisle. 384 pgs. (Not in Evans) (Not in NUC)

1797. George Fisher. *The instructor: or, young man's best companion* . . . Wilmington, Delaware: Printed by Peter Brynberg. [12] 360 pgs. (Not in Evans) (Not in NUC)

1801. George Fisher. *The instructor: or, young man's best companion* . . . Philadelphia, Baltimore, & Washington City: Printed by John Bioren for John Conrad & Co. and others. [12] [13] 346 pgs. SS 498-499 NUC NF0162673

1810. George Fisher. *The instructor: or, American young man's best companion* . . . Philadelphia: Printed and sold by John Bioren. [11] [13] 300 pgs. 18.5 cm. SS 20118 NUC NF0162681

1812. George Fisher. *The instructor: or, American young man's best companion* . . . Philadelphia: Printed by John Bioren. 300 pgs. 19 cm. SS 25429 NUC NF0162682

1833. George Fisher. *The young man's best companion, improved* . . . Philadelphia: Printed by T. L. Bonsal. [12] [15] 370 pgs. 18.5 cm. NUC NF0162692

Introduction

This bibliography begins with the first accounting work published in America: "Merchant's-Accompts" in Bradford's printing of the *Young man's companion* (Philadelphia, 1737). There are fifteen known eighteenth century American printings of the *Young man's companion.* "Merchant's-Accompts" presents a short, but fairly sophisticated, double-entry instruction. Research reveals a tangled bibliographical history involving an incorrect attribution and a double plagiarism. The republication in 1748 by Benjamin Franklin gave credit to the proper author, George Fisher, who was once thought to be a woman. Knowledge of the *Young man's companion* adds an important dimension to our understanding of the development of accounting in America.

The secretary's guide, or young man's companion . . .

In 1737, the fifth edition of *The secretary's guide, or young man's companion* (hereafter referred to simply as *Young man's companion*) was printed and sold in Philadelphia by Andrew Bradford "at the Sign of the Bible." No author's name was given. Bibliographers of early American imprints such as Evans (1903) and Sabin (1868) attributed this and all other editions to William Bradford. This choice was undoubtedly influenced by a letter to the reader contained in the fourth edition of 1728.

> To the Reader
> It is now above thirty years since I first compiled this short manual, during which time several impressions have sold off, and each time it has been reprinted, it has been enlarged, and now (in) this fourth edition, thou wilt find many additions, in order to make it more useful than heretofore (signed) W.B.

W. B. was most likely William Bradford of New York who printed this edition in conjunction with Andrew Bradford of Philadelphia. A first edition of this was printed in New York in 1698 by William Bradford alone (Evans, #818).

Bradford's *Young man's companion* was a one volume encyclopedia of useful knowledge. Similar works of this type had been successfully published in England. A 1695 version describes its contents as "Plain Directions for a Young Man" (Mather, 1695). A later edition states that it is written ". . . in a plain and easy style, that a young-man may both readily and easily improve and qualify himself for business without the help of a master" (Mather, 1734).

It should be remembered that books were an expensive luxury in the New World. Some of the American purchasers of these manuals may have owned only one other book - a Bible. Their pride of ownership is evidenced by inscriptions in many of the surviving copies boldly proclaiming the purchaser's name and sundry other facts like important dates and events in the owner's life. (This comment is based on contents of volumes in the author's collection and elsewhere.) Thus, a book containing a collection of practical subjects probably sold better than one devoted to a single topic. Many such manuals on various topics were published and sold in America in the 18th century.

Bradford's fifth edition of 1737 was the first printing in the series to contain a section on bookkeeping. It was also the last edition of the publication. A final reprinting was made in 1738. The book is divided into four parts as described on the title page which is reproduced as Illustration 1. Part III contains a section described as "a short and easy Method of Shop and Book-keeping, Merchant's Accompts, etc." This section is specifically entitled on page 126 as "Rules and Directions for Bookkeeping, or Merchant's-Accompts." This section is only 14 pages long out of a total book size of 258 pages.

Description of "Merchants-accompts" in *Young man's companion* of 1737

The accounting technique explained in the *Young man's companion* is double entry. The author explains:

> This Art of Italian Bookkeeping, is called Bookkeeping by Double Entry, because there must be two Entries; the first being a Charging of a person, Money, or Goods; and the second, a Discharging of a Person, Money, or Goods. (p. 139)

The importance of knowing both the profit and the state of affairs of a business was recognized.

> It is not without good Reason that most People of Business and Ingenuity are desirous to be Masters of this Art, if we consider the Satisfaction that naturally arises from an Account well kept; the Pleasure that accrues to a Person by seeing what he gains by each Species of Goods

he deals in, and his whole Profit by a Year's Trade; and thereby also, to know the true State of his Affairs and Circumstances; so that he may, according to his Discretion, retrench or enlarge his Expenses, etc. as he shall think fit. (p. 126)

Three books of principal use are described: the waste-book, the journal, and the leidger (sic). The discussion begins with some short examples of waste-book and journal entries. However, there are no leidger examples, and the discussion of the leidger is very brief.

William Mitchell, in 1796, published the first book listed in Bentley which was partially entitled *A new and complete system of bookkeeping by an improved method of double entry*. Mitchell's "Improved method" was the elimination of one of the two books of original entry. (In Mitchell's case, the elimination of the journal in preference to the waste-book). Back in 1737 the author of the *Young man's companion* casually recognized the basis around which Mitchell developed a whole book.

> From these few Examples of Entry, it may be observed, That an experienced Person in Accompts, and a good Writer, may keep a Journal without a Waste-Book, or a Waste-Book without a Journal, since they both impart one and the same Thing, though they differ a little in Words or Expression: For the Leaves of both are numbered by Pages, or Parcels. (p.130)

Another interesting comment cryptically implies the possible early stages of a lower of cost or market concept (p. 137).

> Cast up all your Goods Bought and those Sold, of what Kind soever, in each Accompt of Goods; and see whether all Goods Bought, be Sold, or not; and if any remain Unsold, value them as they cost you, or according to the present Market Price, ready Money; and bear the Nett Rest to balance Dr. (p. 137, emphasis added).

The author also gives space to a description of "pricking marks":

> Note, By pricking over the Books is meant an Examining every Article of the Journal, against the Leidger, and marking it thus, - or thus +; and upon a second Examination thus; and upon a third Examination thus-or any other Marks. (p. 138)

Several other "Books used by Merchants" are briefly discussed. These are the cash-book, book of charges of merchandise, invoice book or book of factories, bill book, book of household expenses, book to copy all letters sent abroad, receipt book and a note or memorandum book (pp. 133, 134).

The narrative further provided a list of rules for debit and credit under various circumstances. For example: "Goods bought for ready Money, make the Goods Dr. to Cash, and Cash Cr. by the Goods." (p. 135)

The discussion concludes with instructions of how to: (1) "balance or clean an Accompt when full written" (p. 136), (2) "remove an Accompt full written to another Folio" (p. 136), and (3) "Balance at the Year's End, and thereby to know the state of your Affairs and Circumstances." (p. 137)

While the discussion of bookkeeping in the *Young man's companion* of 1737 is fairly brief, it is considerably more sophisticated than that found in Hutton (1788) which the Library of Congress has designated the "earliest book on bookkeeping published in America." The Hutton book has more pages devoted to bookkeeping (86 v. 14), but a direct comparison of the works reveals that the Bradford writing clearly has more words.

Thus "Merchant's-Accompts" in Bradford's *Young man's companion* is a strong candidate for the claim of "first accounting work published in America." It also offers some interesting aspects from the standpoint of content. However, to bibliophiles a much more interesting story attaches to the *Young man's companion*, namely: "Who was the real author of the work?"

Was Andrew or William Bradford the Compiler of *Young man's companion*?

As mentioned earlier, Charles Evans (1903) and other bibliographers of early American imprints attribute all editions of the *Young man's companion*, including the 1737 edition, to William Bradford.

In his day, William Bradford (1663-1752) was Colonial America's most prominent printer. He learned his trade in London and emigrated to Pennsylvania in 1682 with William Penn where he introduced printing into the middle Colonies. In 1690 he helped establish the first paper mill in America. In 1693 he moved to New York when he was appointed royal printer for the colony, a position which he held for more than 50 years (Britannica, 1910).

William Bradford began the publication of the *Young man's companion* in 1698. The second edition of 1710 and the fourth edition of 1728 were produced jointly with Andrew Bradford (1686-1742) of Philadelphia who was William's son. Andrew had moved from New York to Philadelphia in 1712 to establish himself independently in the printing trade. By the time of the printing of the fifth edition in 1737, William (who died in 1752) was 74 years old and in the final years of his active life (Britannica, 1910). The title page of this edition gives printing credit solely to Andrew Bradford.

William's age and the fact that he is not mentioned on the title page of the 1737 printing implies that Andrew was more likely responsible for this final edition. Also the title page of the 1728 publication states that the book is "much enlarged" while the 1737 work is said to be "greatly enlarged and carefully corrected." One of these enlargements was, of course, the addition of the section on bookkeeping. Therefore, Andrew, not William, is more appropriately attributed to the 1737 printing, particularly with regard to the bookkeeping addition. But was Andrew Bradford in fact the author, or...?

Was William Mather the Author of *Young man's companion*??

In his 1728 edition, William Bradford stated that he had only "compiled" his manual. Louis Karpinski, writing in 1924, demonstrated that William Bradford relied heavily upon William Mather's *The young man's companion* (note the similarity in the name) and William Leybourne's *Arithmetick* both published in England (Karpinski, 1924). Could Andrew Bradford have also relied upon these sources for his bookkeeping section in the 1737 "Merchant's-Accompts"? Various editions of Mather and Leybourne were examined to explore this possibility.

No instance of bookkeeping could be found in Leybourne's *Arithmetick*. In the process of researching Mather, however, an unusual discovery occurred. In 1975 the Institute of Chartered Accountants in England and Wales produced a catalogue of their extensive accounting collection containing a section on books prior to 1750 not in the Institute's Library. Listed in this section is a copy of Mather's fourth edition bookkeeping or "merchants accompts" (ICA, 1975, p. 237). [My thanks to R. H. Parker for his clarification to me of this matter.]

It seemed that a review of a copy of this edition was in order. The only known American holding of this printing is at the University of California, Los Angeles (NUC, Vol. 369, p. 141). When UCLA's copy was examined, it was found to have no section on bookkeeping and no mention of bookkeeping in the title.

Examination through the twelfth edition of Mather (1723) also failed to produce a section on bookkeeping. A key to the puzzle was the thirteenth edition of 1727, but no copies were known to be in the United States. A way around this problem was discovered.

In 1939, Scott, Foresman, and Company reprinted portions of the 1727 Mather as a Christmas gift to their clients. This unusual reprint is held by several libraries (NUC, Vol. 369, p. 141). Examination of the title page of the reprint, which has a content's listing, revealed no section on bookkeeping.

The last opportunity for Andrew Bradford to have "borrowed" from Mather was from Mather's fourteenth edition of 1734. The only example of this printing known to be in the United States is held by the New York Public Library (NUC, Vol. 369, p. 141). This copy was examined and was found to have a section on bookkeeping, while further comparison revealed that it corresponded in every particular to Andrew Bradford's 1737 bookkeeping section (except for the general change of the date 1734 to 1736). Thus, Andrew had followed the family practice of checking the latest edition of Mather before reprinting the manual, and his section on bookkeeping was totally plagiarized from Mather's 1734 edition.

Mather, like Bradford, had after many years of publication abruptly added a section on bookkeeping. Could he, too, have obtained the idea and contents of his bookkeeping section from someone else? Could the first American printing on accounting be a double plagiarism?

George Fisher's *Young man's best companion*

In 1727, William Mather's book was in its thirteenth edition. That year it received some new competition. George Fisher, Accomptant, authored *The instructor: or, young man's best companion* (1727). The word "best" would seem to have been directed toward the Mather series.

Harvard has America's only reported copy of Fisher's first edition (NUC, Vol. 173, p. 620). An examination of this volume reveals that Mather's 1734 bookkeeping section was indeed extracted from Fisher. There is a general change of dates in the Mather narrative from 1726 to 1734, but the contents are practically identical to Fisher. Fisher alone notes that the waste-book is "by some called the Memorial" and also includes the following paragraph omitted in Mather:

> This art of Bookkeeping, or Merchants Accompts, is talked of by many, but truly understood but by very few: For every petty school-Master in any By-corner, will be sure to have Merchants Accompts expressed on his sign, as a principal article of his ability in teaching, though strictly speaking for want of the Practical Part, knows hardly any thing of the Matter, and consequently is uncapable of teaching it. (Fisher, 1727, p. 198.)

Since Andrew Bradford also omitted the preceeding paragraph and the waste-book comment, it would seem that he must have copied Mather rather than Fisher. Thus, the probable chain is that Bradford plagiarized Mather who, in turn, had plagiarized Fisher. Whether Fisher plagiarized from still another source is still not known.

The last printing of Bradford's manual was in Philadelphia in 1738. Andrew died four years later in November 1742 (Evans, 1903, A#2011). In 1748, Benjamin Franklin and David Hall reintroduced to America the same writing on bookkeeping when they published an American version of Fisher entitled *The American instructor or young man's best companion*.

Franklin, in his autobiography, describes William Bradford as "a cunning old fox". When Franklin first visited New York about 1723, he applied to William for work. William, who was apparently the only printer in New York at the time, referred Franklin to his son Andrew in Philadelphia. Franklin went on to Philadelphia but Andrew was unable to hire him. He later went to work with a rival printing house and then into his own printing business. However, Andrew allowed him to stay in his home for some time and was apparently quite friendly to him. Despite this, Franklin states that Andrew was poorly qualified for his profession and very illiterate. This has been disputed by later authorities (Thomas, 1970, pp. 362, 460).

When Fisher's work was published in 1748, Franklin had just gone into partnership with David Hall and was in the process of withdrawing from active participation in the printing business in order to pursue his public life. Hall, a master printer who had recently arrived from London, may well have been the one responsible for the American publication of Fisher (Thomas, 1970, pp. 368, 379). Thus, the writing on bookkeeping in its original form, attributed to the original author, came into widespread popularity in America (see title page illustrated in Figure 3).

Franklin and Hall began the American printing of Fisher in 1748 with the "ninth" edition. They printed a tenth edition in 1753. Then H. Gaine of New York City published a twelfth edition in 1760 and a fourteenth edition in 1770. Other printers published the volume throughout the remainder of the eighteenth century and well into the nineteenth, resulting in at least 15 American printings by the end of the 1700s. The last known American edition was published in 1833 by T. L. Bonsal of Philadelphia (see Table 2 for a printing history of Fisher in America).

The mathematical historian, Karpinski, stated that Fisher's *Young man's best companion* "became the most popular American work on arithmetic up to the end of the American Revolution and was second only to *Dilworth's Assistant*" in number of editions printed before 1800 (Karpinski, 1935, p. 339). Thus, the little article on bookkeeping, first printed by Andrew Bradford in 1737, became one of America's most widely circulated printings of the 18th century.

Who was George Fisher?

Unlike William and Andrew Bradford, relatively little information is currently available concerning the lives of George Fisher and William Mather. Even the approximate dates of their birth and death are unknown.

In addition to the *Young man's companion*, Mather is believed to be the author of a few short writings criticizing the

Quaker religion. Interestingly, the title of one of these tracts provides some clues to Mather's life. This particular work of a little more than 100 pages was published in London in 1701 and is entitled: A vindication of William Mather and his wife, who having lived about forty years professed Quakers, have now renounced that persuasion, and are returned to the Communion of the Chuch of England (NUC, Vol. 364, p. 140).

It would seem from this title that Mather in his youth "professed" Quakerism but later "returned" to the Church of England. If he were a Quaker for about 40 years, he was probably at least 60 years of age or older in 1701 when the tract was printed. If this presumption is correct, he would have been about 40 when the *Companion* was first published in 1681 and in his late 60s when his last recorded religious writing was published in 1708 (NUC, Vol. 369, p. 140). It is, therefore, unlikely that he was still alive when the 1734, fourteenth edition of the *Companion* was published with a section on bookkeeping "borrowed" from Fisher. Mather apparently sold the rights to the *Companion* many years earlier to a woman publisher.

When the fourth edition of the *Young man's companion* was published in 1695, it was printed for Sarah Hawkins in Georgeyard, Lombard Street (Mather, 1695). Sarah Hawkins was probably a bookseller who published selected works. Later editions through the thirteenth of 1727 were printed for S. Clark (or S. Clarke) which might have been a married name of Sarah Hawkins (NUC, Vol. 364, p. 141). The bookkeeping edition of 1734 was printed for:

> R. Ware at the Bible and Sun in Amen Corner, S. Clarke at the Golden-Ball in Duck-Lane, and S. Osborne at the Golden-Ball in Pater Naster-Row. (Mather, 1734)

R. Ware continued as the primary British publisher of the work through the twentieth edition of 1755 (NUC, Vol. 364, p. 141). He was probably responsible for the addition of the bookkeeping section. When he joined S. Clarke in 1734, the new edition was said to have "large additions and improvements". (The previous edition only had "many additions and alterations".)

Unlike Mather, George Fisher was most likely alive at the time of the publication in 1727 of his *Young man's best companion* with the section on bookkeeping (Fisher, 1727). George Fisher also authored *Arithmetick in the planest and most concise method hitherto extent* first published in 1719 by Eben. (Karpinski, 1935, p. 338.) Tracy had published many editions of *Cocker's arithmetick* between 1696 and 1722 (Cocker died just before the printing of his first edition in 1675). Somewhere between the thirty-fourth edition of Cocker in 1716 (NUC, Vol. 113, p. 542) and the thirty-ninth edition of 1722 (Karpinski, 1935, p. 338), he added George Fisher's name to the title page of Cocker as "Carefully corrected and amended by George Fisher, Accomptant".

From 1725 to 1742, all three books with Fisher's name on them were published by the same series of Booksellers - first Edw. Midwinter (the first publisher of the *Young man's companion*) then, A. Bettesworth and C. Hitch and J. Hodges in publishing *Cocker's Arithmetick* with Fisher still acknowledged for his corrections (NUC, Vol. 113, p. 542). Karpinski compared the three writings of Fisher and found that they "are largely quite distinct, with enough verbal similarities to show that the author felt free to use the material but chose to make new versions" (Karpinski, 1935, p. 338).

At one time bibliographers thought that George Fisher was a woman. The British Museum Catalog of Books in the 1930s stated that Fisher was a pseudonym of Mrs. Ann Fisher Slack (Karpinski, 1935, p. 339). Other authorities also credited the writings to Mrs. Slack, who, as A. Fisher, wrote in 1770 *A new english exercise book*, printed and published by her husband Thomas Slack. Louis Karpinski has demonstrated that Fisher could not have been Mrs. Slack. "This Ann Fisher was born in 1719 which is the indisputable date of the first edition of George Fisher's *Arithmetick* . . . her marriage with the printer (Slack) is well established." (Karpinski, 1935, p. 339)

So Fisher was not Ann Slack, but who Fisher might have been and any details of his or her life are presently unknown.

Conclusions

The history of accounting published in America begins at a much earlier point than heretofore believed. Hutton's work of 1788 and Sarjeant's of 1789 are pre-dated by "Merchant's-Accompts" which is found in the fifth edition of the *Young man's companion* published by Andrew Bradford in 1737.

Whether this work should be considered "America's First Book on Accounting" is a matter of interpretation. It certainly contains what appears to be the first printing in the British

American Colonies of directions on bookkeeping. Partially dedicated works such as this are commonly listed in many early accounting bibliographies. For example, the original British editions of Fisher are listed in Yamey, Edey, and Thompson's Bibliography: Books on Accounting in English, 1543-1800 (Yamey, 1963, p. 213).

The failure to previously recognize this early accounting work is particularly surprising in light of the fact that it was so widely circulated with nineteen American printings spanning a period of almost one hundred years. Knowledge of the *Young man's companion* adds an important dimension to our understanding of the early development of accounting in America.

Written by Peter L. McMickle (based in part on an article written by him in *Abacus,* Vol. 20, No. 1, June 1984, pp.34-51)

References

Bentley, H. C. and R. S. Leonard. *Bibliography of Works on Accounting by American Authors* (2 Vols), Boston: Harry C. Bentley, 1934, 1935.

Bradford, Andrew. *The Secretary's Guide, or, Young Man's Companion,* The Fifth Edition, Philadelphia: Printed and Sold by Andrew Bradford, 1737.

Bradford, William. *The Secretary's Guide, or Young Man's Companion*, The Fourth Edition, New York: Printed and Sold by W. Bradford and Philadelphia: A. Bradford, 1728.

Bradford, William and Andrew. *The Young Man's Companion*, The Second Edition, New York: Printed and Sold by William and Andrew Bradford at the Bible, 1710.

The Encyclopedia Britannica, Eleventh Edition, Volume IV, New York: The Encyclopedia Britannica Company, 1910.

Evans, Charles. *American Bibliography*, 14 Volumes, New York: Peter Smith, 1903.

Fisher, George (Accomptant). *The Instructor: or Young Man's Best Companion,* Ninth Edition, Philadelphia: Printed by B. Franklin and D. Hall, 1748.

Item 1. The George Fisher Series beginning 1737.

―――. *The American Instructor: or, Young Man's Best Companion*, Twelfth Edition, New York: Printed and Sold by H. Gaine, Bookseller, 1760.

Institute of Chartered Accountants in England and Wales, *Historical Accounting Literature*, London: Mansell, 1975.

Karpinski, Louis C. 'Colonial American Arithmetics.' In *Bibliographical Essays, A Tribute to Wilberforce Eames*, Boston: Harvard University Press, 1924.

Karpinski, Louis C. 'The Elusive George Fisher, "Accomptant" - Writer or Editor of Three Popular Arithmetics,' *Scripta Mathematica*, III October 1935.

Karpinski, Louis C. *Bibliography of Mathematical Works Printed in America Through 1850*. Ann Arbor: The University of Michigan Press, 1940.

Mather, William. *The Young Man's Companion: or, Arithmetick made Easie*, Fourth Edition, London: Printed for Sarah Hawkins, 1695.

Mather, W. *The Young Man's Companion: or, Arithmetick made Easie.* Tenth Edition, London: Printed for S. Clarke, 1717.

Mather, W. *The Young Man's Companion: or, Arithmetick made Easy.* Twelfth Edition, London: Printed for S. Clarke, 1723.

Mather, W. *The Young Man's Companion: or Arithmetick made Easy*, Thirteenth Edition, London: Printed for S. Clarke, 1927. This is a partial reprint made in 1939 for Christmas presents by Scott, Foresman & Company.

Mather, W. *The Young-Man's Companion: or Arithmetick made Easy*, Fourteenth Edition, London: Printed for R. Ware, S. Clarke, and S. Osborne, 1734.

The National Union Catalog: Pre-1956 Imprints, 700 Volumes, London: Mansell and the American Library Association, 1971.

Paciolo, (Frater Lucas de Burgo Sancti Sepulchri). *Suma de Arithmetica Geometria Proportioni et Proportionalita*, Venice: Paganinus de Paganinis, 10 November 1494.

Sabin, Joseph, *Bibliotheca America: A Dictionary of Books Relating to America, from its Discovery until the Present Time*, Begun by Joseph Sabin, continued by Wilberforce Eames and completed by R. W. G. Vail, 29 Volumes, New York: Bibliographical Society of America, 1868-1936.

Thomas, Isaiah. *The History of Printing in America,* Edited by Marcus A. McCorison from the Second Edition of 1874 for the American Antiquarian Society, New York: Weathervane Books, 1970.

Yamey, B. S., H.C. Edey, and Hugh W. Thomson. 'Bibliography: Books on Accounting in English, 1543-1800,' *Accounting in England and Scotland: 1543-1800*, London: Sweet & Maxwell, 1963.

Item 1. The George Fisher Series beginning 1737.

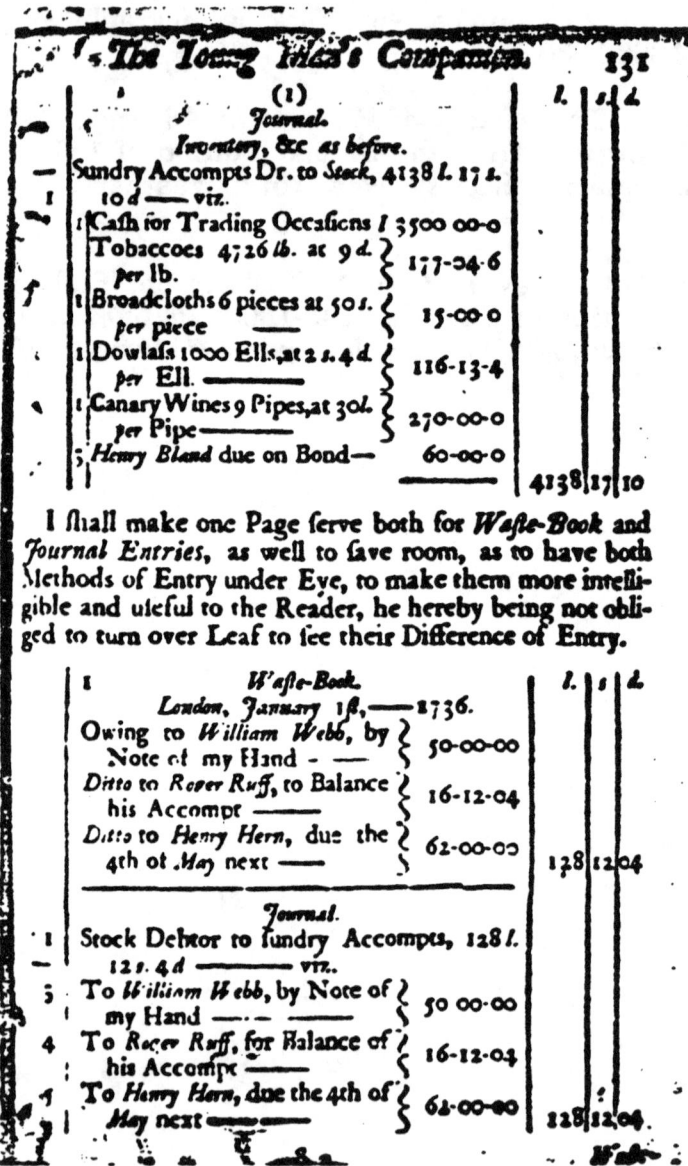

ILLUSTRATION 2. Waste-Book and journal entries from Andrew Bradford's 1737 printing of *Young man's companion*.

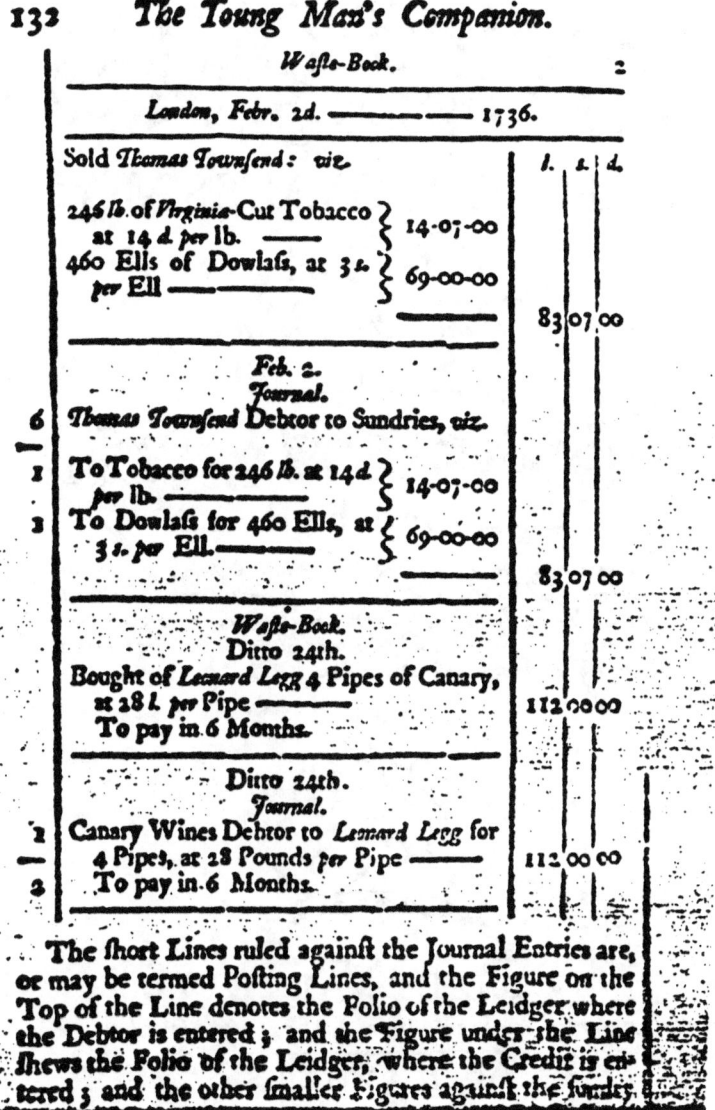

ILLUSTRATION 3. Waste-Book and journal entries from Andrew Bradford's 1737 printing of *Young man's companion*.

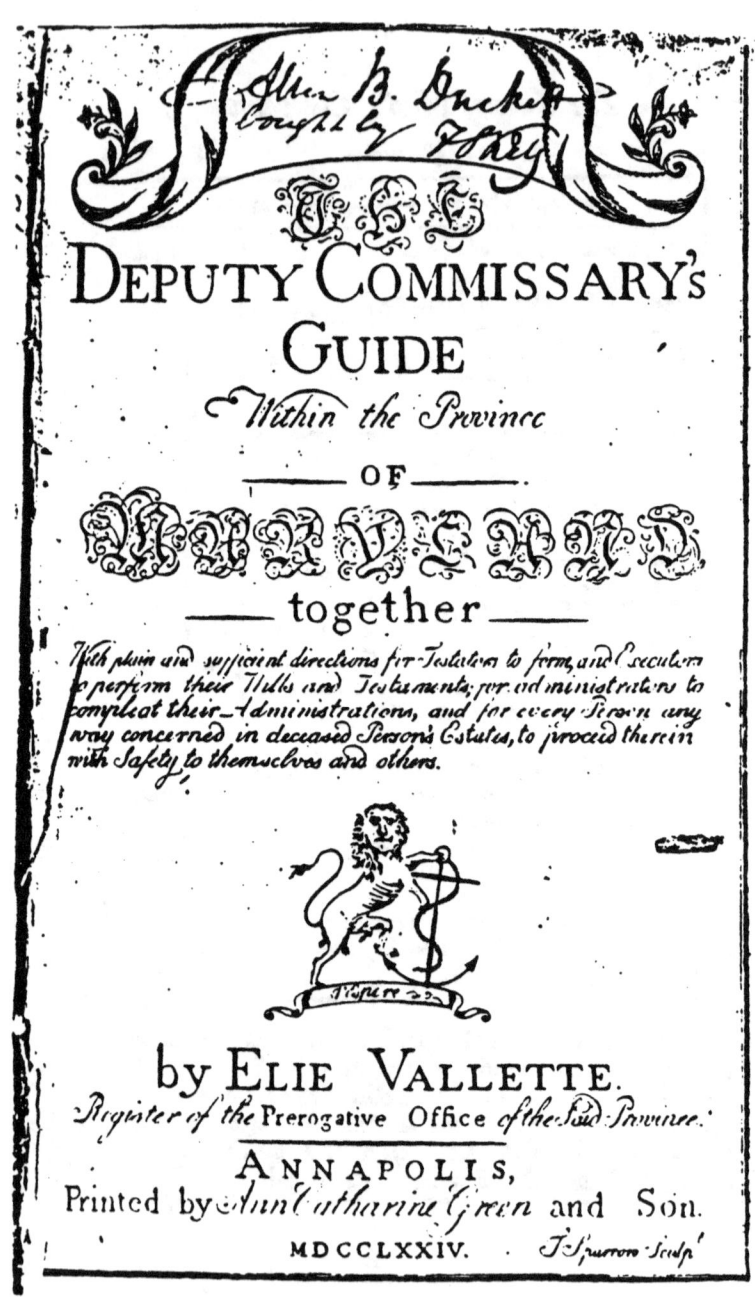

ILLUSTRATION 4. Title page from 1774 Elie Vallette's *The deputy commissary's guide* (note Francis Scott Key's autograph).

Item 2. 1774. Elie Vallette. *The deputy commissary's guide, within the province of Maryland* ... **Annapolis: Printed by Ann Catharine Green & Son.** [2] [1] 248 pgs. 20 cm. Evans 13742   NUC NF0023044

Other American Printings: No other known printings.

Introduction

This book is written to introduce a general uniformity in the proceedings of deputy commissaries and to assist executors and administrators in the performance of their duties. Having been in the office of register for ten years, the author claims to have gained general knowledge of the business. He points out the duties and functions of deputy commissaries in the various cases of administration. After explaining the procedures for taking inventory of the deceased, he discusses the deputy commissary's "passing accounts," which in today's terminology is the function of the probate court in "approving the accounting" filed by the executor or the administrator. This is the section that is especially important to accountancy since the author talks of the debits and the credits to the estate account.

Description of *The deputy commissary's guide* ...

The inventory is taken in the presence of two next of kin and two creditors. An appraisal is made of all the decedent's goods, chattels, wares, merchandise, such as ready money, household furniture, clothing, negroes, stock of cattle, corn, crop on hand, every sort of property in and about the house (apparel of the widow excepted), and all leases however long the term.

Houses, lands, and real estate are liable to and chargeable with all just debts and shall be assets for the satisfaction of these debts. The inventory must be cast in one total sum and signed by two sworn appraisers, the two next of kin, and the two creditors who certify they were present at the appraisal and approve of it. The inventory is then probated.

The passing of accounts is the most material part of the administration and requires the utmost attention and care of the deputy commissary. He must have competent knowledge of the legality of the procedure for each class of debts since the class determines the order wherein executors or administrators pay the debts due from the estate. The four classes are:

Item 2. 1774. Elie Vallette.

1. Judgments, or decrees of a court of record. These must be attested by the clerk of the court and require a deposition of the creditor taken before a magistrate.

2. Recognizances. These must be under seal and attested by the clerk of the court.

3. This class takes in all debts payable for rent and specialties, that is, bonds, bills of exchange, and every writing with a seal to it. These also require a deposition of the creditor.

4. This class includes all sorts of debts on simple contracts such as accounts and all others not included in any of the foregoing classes.

Since the propriety of a legally proved account [accounting] is not generally understood, the author explains one. Every account must consist of enumerated articles without ambiguity. The truth of the account must be probated within twelve months after the first article therein charged becomes due. Therefore, if an account contains dealings for only one year and the first article charged is dated April 15, 1766, then the account must be proved before April 15, 1767. After the deputy commissary certifies that he has examined the probate and accounts with the books from which it is taken and finds it truly extracted, the "account may be safely paid" [estate may be distributed].

The allowance for funeral expenses ought not exceed three or four pounds currency except where the rank and opulence of the deceased may require a larger allowance and the claims of creditors and the convenience of the deceased's family may not suffer by it. But for small estates, such part should be allowed that will defray the costs of the coffin and interment of the deceased without any allowance for vain pomp and ostentation. When the testator directs an expensive funeral, if the claims of the creditors should not be affected by the performance, the directions ought to be pursued.

Executors and administrators are entitled to the same compensation for their pain and trouble, hazards and adventures in administering the estate. The allowance is as follows: For every sum or sums of money, quantity or quantities of tobacco or other goods or chattels paid by them, for debts due from the deceased, and for charges of administration, they are allowed a commission of 10 percent. Testators frequently bequeath a legacy to their executors as compensation for their trouble. Such a bequest excludes their claiming the 10 percent commission.

In cases where there are no known relatives of someone who dies intestate, the administrator is directed to pay the balance into the hands of the visitors of the public school of the county wherein the deceased resided.

Instructions are then given by the author for drawing up the account. Being fully satisfied of the legality of every voucher produced, the executor or administrator is then styled an accountant and is made debtor with the whole amount of the deceased's personal estate. The sum total of the inventory must be charged. Debts and monies are next charged. If debts are received in wheat or tobacco, then the amount of the charge is according to the net current price of the commodity received. All of these constitute the debit part of the account and are cast into one total sum. Under this, mention must be made by way of memorandum of the amount of the list of debts to be charged thereafter. The inventory and debts received being thus charged, all payments are to be deducted out of that sum.

In constructing the account, every voucher should be listed with its amount in tobacco or money properly cast in the several columns taking care to enumerate the properties of each voucher, such as what the debt is for, so that at anytime the whole transaction appears plain. The several vouchers being thus credited, the next allowance is for funeral expenses, officer's fee, and for finishing the crop. Extravagant demands are often made by executors and administrators for finishing the crop but that allowance is not to be made for more than what appears to have been necessarily expended by them and nothing at all for their personal trouble. The 10 percent commission concludes the account.

The whole amount must be brought into current money. The whole credit of the account will then appear which is to be deducted out of the amount of inventory and lists of debts debited. The balance is so much current money in the executor's or administrator's hands to be accounted for in an additional account. When the executor or the administrator declares he has no more accounts to pass, then the last account is the final account.

The final account must mention at the foot of it the names of the sureties on the administration with their places of abode, and in all accounts of intestate estates, particular mention must be made of the names of the kindred entitled to a distributive share thereof and in what degree they are related. Then the executor or administrator takes an oath that the foregoing account is just and true as stated. The finished account is recorded in the prerogative office and the balance is transmitted to the county court with a distribution of surplus among the representatives of the deceased.

The book then covers the following subjects:
Issuance of letters of administration.
Issuance of letters of ad colligendum.
Nature of and method used in proving wills and testaments.
Payment of legacies.
Rules of descent.
Distribution of intestate's estate.
Directions for executors and administrators.
Directions for guardians.
Rules of office for deputy commissaries.

The appendix contains precedents of letters, bonds, writs, and other instruments together with an approved form for drawing wills and codicils and tables for the reduction of sterling money into common currency.

Elie Vallette served as Register of the Prerogative Office of the Province of Maryland for a period of ten years.

Written by Cynthia Heagy and Carolyn George.

INVENTORY. 23

Probate to a lift of defperate debts, viz.

―― county, to wit. the ― of ―― 1773.
Then came A. B. adminiftrator of C. D. late of ―― county, deceafed, and made oath, that the aforegoing is a juft and true lift of debts defperate, which have come to his knowledge, that he hath not received any part thereof, and that he will well and truly charge himfelf, with all and every fuch debt or ..... as fhall hereafter come to his hands or poffeffion.

Probate lift debts defperate.

Certified by ―― ―― deputy commiffary of ―― county.

Thus far the inventory: The next thing in courfe to be confidered of, being returnable within twelve months from the date of the letters of adminiftration, is

THE ACCOUNT.

Every deputy commiffary may, and is by virtue of his commiffion fully authorifed, and empowered, to audit, pafs, and allow all fuch accounts as fhall come before him, within his county,

Extent of the deputy commiffary's power in paffing accounts.

B 4

ILLUSTRATION 5. Discussion of probate accounting in 1774 Elie Vallette's *The deputy commissary's guide.*

36   ACCOUNT.

them yearly) and as such endorsed on the account, they must, together with the account, and books out of which they were severally taken, be produced before a magistrate, or before the deputy commissary of that county, who then certifies at the foot of the account, that he hath examined the several probates and accounts with the books from which they were taken, and finds them truly extracted.

At the same time the creditor must take such another probate for the latter part of the account, commonly remaining unproved in the books, by reason of the twelve months, in which such part is to be proved remains as yet unexpired, or where the deceased died after the date of the last probate to the account: thus executed the account is compleat, and may safely be paid and allowed.

It is to be understood, that the above regulates only the accounts of creditors then living, against the estate of the debtor deceased; for if the creditor be dead, then the executors or administrators of such deceased creditor, must to every account they draw off, as due to their deceased, besides the aforementioned probate, make one themselves, to be endorsed on the account, in the following words, viz.

That

ILLUSTRATION 6. Discussion of probate accounting in 1774 Elie Vallette's *The deputy commissary's guide.*

ACCOUNT. 37

That the creditor deceased, (to the knowledge of the deponent, or by any books, writings, account or other thing, appearing to him) hath not received any part or parcel, security or satisfaction for the same, (save what is credited) and likewise that he this deponent hath not received any part of the debt, or any thing else towards satisfaction thereof, more than he hath given an account of. — Probate to an account, where the creditor is dead.

The credits given in as received by the executor or administrator, if any, must be particularly mentioned in such oath, as to time and quantity, and deducted from the principal debt.

Where persons in this province act as factors for merchants beyond seas, under the firm of their principals and not their own, the following probate must be taken by such factor, before the account can pass the commissary, viz. *Came A. B. sole factor and book-keeper for C. & D. merchants in ———, at their store kept by him this deponent at ———, and made oath, &c. that this account is just and true as stated, and that he hath not, nor that, to the best of his knowledge, his principals, or any other factor or person for them, have not received any part or parcel, security or satisfaction for the same, more than credit given.* — Probate to an account taken by factors.

Vide factor's probate to a bond in fol. 28.

C 3   And

ILLUSTRATION 7. Discussion of probate accounting in 1774 Elie Vallette's *The deputy commissary's guide.*

Item 3. 1776. Arthur Young.

RURAL OECONOMY

Or ESSAYS on the

Practical Parts of Husbandry.

Designed to explain several of the most important Methods of conducting FARMS of various kinds; including many Useful Hints to GENTLEMEN FARMERS, relative to the œconomical Management of their Business.

CONTAINING, among other ENQUIRIES,

Of that Proportioned Farm, which is of all others the most profitable.

The best Method of conducting Farms that consist all of Grass, or all of Arable Land.

The Means of keeping the most Cattle the Year round on a given Quantity of Land.

The cheapest way of manuring Land.

Considerations on the œconomical Conduct of Gentlemen Farmers.

The comparative Profit of farming different Soils.

Of Experimental Agriculture.

Of the New Husbandry.

Of the Management of Borders of Arable Fields.

Of periodical Publications concerning Rural Oeconomics.

TO WHICH IS ADDED,

The RURAL SOCRATES,

Being MEMOIRS of a COUNTRY PHILOSOPHER.

By the AUTHOR of the FARMER'S LETTERS;

Hoc Opus, hoc Studium parvi properemus et ampli;
Si Patriæ volumus, si nobis vivere cari.

THE SECOND EDITION.

LONDON, PRINTED:

PHILADELPHIA: RE-PRINTED AND SOLD

BY JAMES HUMPHREYS, JUNR.

M,DCC,LXXVI.

ILLUSTRATION 8. Title page from Arthur Young's 1776 *The Rural oeconomy* . . .

Item 3. 1776. Arthur Young. *Rural oeconomy, or essays on the practical parts of husbandry* ... From the second London edition. Philadelphia: Reprinted and sold by James Humphreys, Jr. 154 pgs. 20.5 cm. (*The Rural Socrates* is not included, though mentioned on the title page) Evans 15226 NUC NY0024098

Other American Printings:

1776. Arthur Young. *Rural oeconomy, or essays on the practical parts of husbandry* ... From the second London edition. Philadelphia: Reprinted and sold by James Humphreys, Jr. 245 pgs. 20.5 cm. (This printing includes the Rural Socrates) (Not in Evans) NUC NY0024100

1792. Arthur Young. *Rural oeconomy, or essays on the practical parts of husbandry* ... Third edition. Burlington, N. J.: Printed by Issac Neale. [1] 299 pgs. Evans 25061 NUC NY0024092

Introduction

Rural oeconomy ... is not listed in any previous bibliography of American accountancy. It was written by the British writer, Arthur Young, in 1770 and was reprinted in Philadelphia by James Humphreys in 1776. Rural oeconomy ... was primarily a book on agriculture. Young's works are considered for the period to be the "finest English writing on agriculture, which did for farming what the industrial revolution had done for industry" (Kunitz & Haycraft, 1952).

Young's desire to find the most profitable farm left him well traveled and in debt. His attention to detail can be surmised in his lengthy expense accounts – constantly striving to find the most profitable combination of farm stock and land utilization.

Young was quite an interesting individual. He corresponded with George Washington and Lafayette and was well recognized for his work in agriculture. He held the post of Secretary of the Board of Agriculture in London until he became blind. An operation for his cataracts failed when he began to weep due to the plight of agriculture (Kunitz and Haycraft, 1952).

In *Rural oeconomy* ... , Young is emphatic about the absolute necessity of detailed bookkeeping. He states that ". . . accounts may be said to be the foundation of good husbandry. . . ."

Item 3. 1776. Arthur Young.

According to Young, the gentleman farmer's greatest advantage over the common farmer is his understanding of the importance of good account keeping. He says that the common farmer guesses at profit and losses but the gentleman farmer has a good idea because of his record keeping.

Young's interest in bookkeeping and awareness of its significance has been attributed to his father's desire to make him a bookkeeper (Kunitz & Haycraft, 1952). His father apprenticed him in 1758 to a mercantile firm which is where Young attained his accounting knowledge. He says the gentleman farmer should "have a minute-book of work laid before him every evening." This minute-book should contain all of the farm's transactions. He also requires a cash book which is to be balanced every Saturday night. There is no need for a general journal. The transactions should be posted directly from the minute and cash books into the ledger. At year end an account should be taken of all the stock and a valuation taken of all the implements to determine wear and tear. He then explained how the profit and loss could be determined.

Following are some selected quotes from the book that pertain to bookkeeping.

> All money matters should go through the hands of the bailey, who must keep an open book in the most regular manner, to which the master can have recourse at any time; (a room, for instance, with each a key); this book should be balanced every Saturday night; and whenever much money is in hand, which the master must always know by the minute-book of transactions, he should order the bailey to bring to him such sums as he thinks proper, to be charged to his own account. . . .
> This mention of accounts reminds me of the vast importance of regular accounts to a gentleman farmer. This is one of the advantages he has over the common farmer; and, I think, one of the greatest. The latter knows whether his business is, upon the whole, profitable or not, but only guesses the particulars. . . .
> When a man turns over his books, and finds a regular balance of profit and loss on every article, he is enabled to review his business, to consider what have probably been his errors, and wherein he has been most successful. The result of such reflections is true experience, not the random notions that are carried in the memory. . . . Nor should fugitive notes and memorandums be called accounts; nothing can effect this great end

but a ledger regularly kept. . . .

The first book to be mentioned that a gentleman farmer should open is *A Minute Book*. This should be a regular journal of all the transactions of the farm. The bailey should keep this. . . .

. . . there can be no transaction of any sort but what should be thus registered. I recommend the short lines between each article, to keep the bailey from crowding his writing close together. . . .

Next comes the *Cash Book* to be balanced every Saturday night; this is only for a check upon the person who keeps it, and that the disbursements and receipts may be regularly known. If a gentleman keeps his own books, it is not necessary.

The Ledger comes next; in which an account, debtor and creditor, is opened and every field, by name, in the farm; also for every article of livestock: one for wear and tear, &c. &c. &c. so as no money can be paid or received, no exchange of commodity made on the farm, without an account there being open for it. Two of them should be kept, one the bailey should post the cash book into; that is, enter each article of cash expended or received, in its proper account, and one also to substitute for a Journal, the use of which book is too complex for a bailey to keep.

What I mean by this, is the carrying of transactions that have an amount in value, without any money being paid or received, to their regular account. For instance, an account is opened in the Ledger for the *Six-acre grass field*. On one side all the expenses, on the other the receipts for hay sold; but, instead of selling this hay, suppose it delivered from the stack to the horses, how is this to be carried to account? In regular bookkeeping, a merchant would enter this in his Journal, *Horses debtor to six acres grass* for so much hay delivered; and then post the sum to both accounts in the Ledger. But the gentleman farmer turns at once to the account of horses in his Ledger and writes on the debtor side, *To six acres grass*, so and so; and then, in the field account, on the creditor side, *By horses*, so and so.

In a word, he skips the Journal, and at the same time that he simplifies his account, keeps them perfectly regulated.

All this I suppose to be done by the bailey and all is so very plain, that any ingenious fellow would form a clear idea of it in half an hour. But the master should keep the fair Ledger, in which he enters everything in the same manner as in the other; but reduces them to distinct headings. In the first ledger they stand in confusion; many small sums of cash, and parcels of hay, corn, &c.

&c. delivered at different times, his business therefore, is to throw them, at the end of the year, into one view, under distinct headings. For instance, he finds a corn field account, with a great number of sums of cash; and corn sold, and some delivered at home for cattle. He consolidates all the expenses into a few totals . . .

Now the advantage of having such a view as this of every crop is immense. By looking over the particulars of the expenses, he sees which run the heaviest, and knows from thence, the proper channel, in the like cases for the future, for his chief expense to flow in.

At the end of every year an account must be taken of all the stock; the implements of all kinds valued, and carried to the new year's account accordingly; and, as the article of *wear and tear* includes everything relative to implements, the annual valuation will throw into that account the *decrease of value* as well as articles of new expenditure. The same observation is applicable to the accounts of horses and draught oxen, which being valued in that manner, give the expense of horses &c. declining in worth; an article that is never dreamed of in common; and yet the sinking of a horses value is as much a part of the expense of tillage as the reparation of a plough. By these general methods, a gentleman every year knows, to a shilling, the year's profits or loss, and the sum of money he has employed in agriculture.

Written by Cynthia Heagy, Peter McMickle, and Paul Jensen.

Reference

Kunitz, Stanley J. and Howard Haycraft, *British Authors Before 1800*, New York: The H. W. Wilson Company, 1952.

[91]

the receipts for hay sold; but, instead of selling this hay, suppose it delivered from the stack to the horses, how is this to be carried to account? In regular book-keeping, a merchant would enter this in his Journal, *Horses' debtor to six acres grass* for so much hay delivered; and then post the sum to both accounts in the Ledger. But the gentleman farmer turns at once to the account of horses in his Ledger, and writes on the debtor side, *To six acres grass,* so and so; and then, in the field account, on the creditor side, *By horses,* so and so.

In a word, he skips the Journal, and, at the same time that he simplifies his account, keeps them perfectly regular.

All this I suppose to be done by the bailey; and all is so very plain, that any ingenious fellow would form a clear idea of it in half an hour. But the master should keep the fair Ledger, in which he enters every thing in the same *manner* as in the the other; but reduces them to distinct heads. In the first Ledger they stand in confusion; many small sums of cash, and parcels of hay, corn, &c. &c. delivered at different times, his business therefore, is to throw them, at the end of the year, into one view, under distinct heads. For instance; he finds a corn field account, with a great number of sums of cash; and corn sold, and some delivered at home for cattle. He consolidates all the expences into a few totals thus;

Debtor———	Six acres	——Creditor.		
	l. s. d.		*l. s. d.*	
To cash for expence of tillage	8 6 0	By hogs for 30 qrs. of barley deliver'd	24 0 0	
Ditto seed	3 0 0			
Ditto rent	6 0 0			
Ditto labour (*Exclusive of tillage*)	4 0 0	Loss	7 7 6	
Ditto manure	8 0 0			
Ditto sundry small articles	2 1 6			
	31 7 6		31 7 6	

ILLUSTRATION 9. Ledger example for farm accounting in Arthur Young's 1776 *Rural oeconomy* . . .

A

COURSE OF

Book-Keeping,

According to the Method

SINGLE ENTRY;

With a description of the Books, and directions for using them: very useful either for young Book-keepers going into Business, or for Teachers in their Schools, &c. &c.

Extracted from the Works of
CHARLES HUTTON, L.L.D. F.R.S.
And Professor of the Mathematics in the Royal military Academy, Woolwich.

With sundry Alterations and Additions, by the Editor.

PHILADELPHIA,
BY JOSEPH JAMES IN CHESNUT STREET.
M.DCC.LXXXVIII.

ILLUSTRATION 10. Title page from Harvard's damaged 1788 copy of Charles Hutton's *A course of book-keeping* ...

Item 4. The Charles Hutton Series beginning 1788.

<u>Philadelphia imprints: *Course of book-keeping*, single entry series.</u>

1788. Charles Hutton. *A course of book-keeping, according to the method of single entry* . . . Philadelphia: Printed by Joseph James. [8] 30 [46] pgs. 19.5 cm. (Not in Evans) NUC NH0641321

[Evans lists a 1790 printing of Hutton (Evans 22582) but no existing copy could be located.]

1801. Charles Hutton. *A course of book-keeping, according to the method of single entry.* . . . Philadelphia: Printed by Robert Johnson. [8] 30 [46] pgs. 19.5 cm. SS 691 NUC NH0641322

1806. Charles Hutton. *A course of book-keeping, according to the method of single entry.* . . . Philadelphia. (Various pagings) 19.5 cm. SS 10605 NUC NH0641323

1809. Charles Hutton. *A course of book-keeping, according to the method of single entry.* . . . First improved edition. Philadelphia: Printed for Bennett & Walton, Dickinson printer. 86 pgs.(Various pagings) 19.5 cm. SS 17795 (Not in NUC)

1815. Charles Hutton. *A course of book-keeping, according to the method of single entry.* . . . Second improved edition. Philadelphia: Printed for Bennett & Walton, James Stackhouse printer. [7] [46] 30 pgs. 19.5 cm. SS 34982 NUC NH0641324

1829. Charles Hutton. *A course of book-keeping, according to the method of single entry.* . . . Third improved edition. Philadelphia: Bennett & Walton. [7] [46] 30 pgs. 20 cm. NUC NH0641326

<u>Crukshank, et al printers: *American tutor's assistant*, single entry series.</u>

1809. [No author listed]. *The American tutor's assistant revised . . . to which is added a course of book-keeping by single entry.* Originally compiled by sundry teachers in and near Philadelphia. Philadelphia: Printed by Joseph Crukshank. [4] 180 [28] 17.5 cm. (Not in SS) NUC NJ0090400 (Earlier printings had no bookkeeping.)

Item 4. The Charles Hutton Series beginning 1788.

1810. [No author listed]. *The American tutor's assistant revised .... to which is added a course of book-keeping by single entry.* Originally compiled by sundry teachers in and near Philadelphia. Philadelphia: Printed and sold by Joseph Crukshank (and several other booksellers listed). [4] 180 [32] 17.5 cm. (Not in SS) NUC NJ0090402

1813. [No author listed]. *The American tutor's assistant revised .... to which is added a course of book-keeping by single entry.* Originally compiled by sundry teachers in and near Philadelphia. Philadelphia: Printed and sold by Joseph Crukshank. [4] 180 [32] 17.5 cm. SS 27718 NUC NJ0090404

1824. [No author listed]. *The American tutor's assistant revised .... to which is added a course of book-keeping by single entry.* Originally compiled by sundry teachers in and near Philadelphia. Philadelphia: Printed and sold by Joseph Crukshank. NUC NJ0090415

1824. [No author listed]. *The American tutor's assistant revised ... to which is added a course of book-keeping by single entry.* Originally compiled by sundry teachers in and near Philadelphia. Charleston: Printed and sold by John Grigg (and others). [2] 180 [32] 18cm. NUC NJ0090413

1824. [No author listed]. *The American tutor's assistant revised .... to which is added a course of book-keeping by single entry.* Originally compiled by sundry teachers in and near Philadelphia. Philadelphia: Printed and sold by John Grigg (and others). [2] 180 [32] 18cm. NUC NJ0090416

1825. [No author listed]. *The American tutor's assistant revised .... to which is added a course of book-keeping by single entry.* Originally compiled by sundry teachers in and near Philadelphia. Philadelphia: Marot and Walter. [2] 180 [32] 18cm. NUC NJ0090413

1830. [No author listed]. *The American tutor's assistant revised .... to which is added a course of book-keeping by single entry.* Originally compiled by sundry teachers in and near Philadelphia. Philadelphia: Printed and sold by Joseph Crukshank. NUC NJ0090421

See related single entry series: Item 27. 1818. Zachariah Jess, which is altered enough from Hutton to warrant separate listing.

New York imprints: *A complete treatise, double entry series.*

1809. Charles Hutton. *A complete treatise on practical arithmetic and book-keeping both by single and double entry* .... Corrected, enlarged, and adapted . . . by D. P. Adams. New York: Sold by Samuel Campbell (and others), W. Elliot printer. [8] 228 pgs. 18 cm. SS 17794 NUC NH0641316

1810. Charles Hutton. *A complete system of practical arithmetic and book-keeping both by single and double entry* . . . New York: Printed and sold by Smith & Forman. [9] 224pgs. 17.5 cm. SS 20420 NUC NH0641307

Introduction

Apparently there is no known surviving copy of a first Engish edition of Charles Hutton's *A complete treatise on practical arithmetic and book-keeping both by single and double entry.* As a result, the date of the first edition is also unknown. The earliest printing presently known to survive is described as the fifth edition (London: 1778). The work was quite popular in England and it continued through the 19th edition of 1849 (and a new edition of 1858).

Hutton also proved to be quite popular in America as can be seen from the preceeding bibliographic listing. In an attempt to clarify the multiple American printings of Hutton, they have been divided into three series: (1) Philadelphia imprints: *Course of book-keeping,* single entry series, (2) Crukshank, et al printers: *American tutor's assistant,* single entry series, and (3) New York imprints: *A complete treatise,* double entry series. These are related by the fact that every book listed contain the same series of single entry journal entries and postings extracted from the English edition of Hutton. In some cases, American dollars have been substituted for English pounds. The two works in the double entry category contain, in addition to the common set of single entry examples, double entry examples also taken from the English Hutton.

Thought was given to including an additional work under Hutton: Item 27, 1818, Zachariah Jess, *The American tutor's assistant improved.* However, this work was altered enough from the English Hutton to warrant a separate listing. The Jess series, which was first published without bookkeeping in Wilmington in 1799, has been confused by several bibliographers with a series of almost the same name first published in Philadelphia in 1797 and printed mostly in later years by Joseph Crukshank of Philadelphia.

The Crukshank work originally included a preface signed by Jess and three other teachers. No author's name was shown on the title page but there was the comment "compiled by sundry teachers in and near Philadeplphia." This series did not contain bookkeeping until 1809. In the 1809 edition, Crukshank included Hutton's single entry examples, apparently revised the arithmetic section, and dropped the preface signed by the four teachers. From then until the last printing in 1830, the title stated "originally compiled by sundry teachers in and near Philadelphia, now revised."

By 1818, the separate Zachariah Jess series, which had always given Jess's name as compiler on the title page, had gone through its 11th edition without a section on bookkeeping. With the tweflth edition in 1819, a section on bookkeeping was added whose relationship to the English Hutton was reminiscent of the similarities between many of today's principals of accounting texts. These different publications with practically the same name continued to compete until Crukshank's last edition in 1830.

About the Author

Charles Hutton's fame was gained primarily in the area of mathematics where he was largely self-educated. Living between 1737 and 1823, Hutton taught math at the Royal Military Academy at Woolwich for thirty-four years. Most of his writings were in math and included such items as *The compendious measure* (1790) and *An astronomical dictionary* (1817). Hutton was very active in his profession, writing textbooks for his pupils, papers and commentary for scientific periodicals, and editing many almanacs.

Philadelphia Imprints: *Course of book-keeping*, **Single Entry Series**

In 1977, the Library of Congress purchased for their collections the 1788 Hutton which they have publicly displayed as the "earliest book on bookkeeping published in America." However, a comparison of the American edition with the British reveals the change of only one word, *Philadelphia* for *London*. This work was originally a section of Hutton's *A complete system of practical arithmetic.* The section on bookkeeping was published as a separate work both in England and the United States. The only other known example of this printing is a mutilated copy at Harvard (NUC, Vol. 262, p. 184). However, there were several later printings of the same book by other Philadelphia printers. The 1801 version has the same number of pages as the 1788 and appears to be identical. An explanation of the contents of the book can be found under the next heading.

Crukshank, et al Printers: *American Tutor's Assistant,* **Single Entry Series**

The single entry bookkeeping section of this book includes four pages describing the daybook, the ledger, posting, balancing, the memorandum book, and the expense book. The remainder shows illustrations of various transactions and entries.

During the period 1801-1824 in Philadelphia there existed three Crukshank's. Listed in the *American bibliography* are Joseph, James, and "J." Crukshank. It would seem plausible that this was a family printing shop, and of some size. In the Crukshank series, although Hutton was not given any title page recognition, Crukshank did gave Hutton credit at the beginning of the bookkeeping section. The Crukshank series states that the work is "altered from C. Hutton." However, when analyzed, Hutton's work is used intact except for currency and date changes.

The currency alteration is explained by providing a two-page section giving a table of foreign monies with a cross-reference to United States Federal Currency. It is explained that the proper use of dollars and cents is to separate the two with a "point" in the accounts. The abbreviation to be used for dollars is "Dols.," and for cents "Cts." It must be remembered that the dollar sign ($) as we now commonly use it was not yet in existence.

The entire bookkeeping section covers 30 pages of which only one and one-half are devoted to written text. The remainder of the pages are examples of entries in the journal and the ledger.
There are, however, gems of wisdom and candid comment in these few lines. The author feels that everyone should learn this method, because it is used in almost every business.

The feeling about the use of the single entry system as a teaching tool was also presented where the author stated, "and even supposing a boy is intended for a business which requires the Italian method alone, I would, notwithstanding, have taught him this method first, if it were only to facilitate his acquisition of the other." To save space, approximately one page of written explanation is given regarding the "books" as it was felt that "the forms of the books may be sufficiently known by inspection." In other words, here are the examples, follow them and I will not have to waste more paper. Further instructions follow for the student with the implication that the teacher is to lead the exercise. After copying the correct format and examples correctly, they are to be "placed according to the teacher's mind. . . ." The remaining 28 pages are of day book and ledger examples.

The Day Book

The day book is wherein the accounts are written by date (i.e. 1st Month 1, 1810). These entries are then to be posted to the Ledger. These accounts are those of persons and are to be identified as such. If multiple entries are included, the use of To or By Sundries is recommended. This example given is straightforward and easy to follow. However, it is implied that the teacher may prepare examples for the student where calculations will have to be made and checked.

Ledger A

This is to be the first ledger; following ledgers are to be consecutively lettered through the alphabet for proper reference. The first page, the index, is called "The Alphabet". In this index, names from the day book are to be entered along with the pages referenced to where they stand in the ledger. It should be noted that the ledgers are opened in order of the transactions from the day book; no pages are to be left blank. Only one ledger should exist for any one person until the page is completely filled, then another can be opened and entered to the index. Once the ledger is full, at the end of the ledger draw out a balance account placing debits on one side and credits on the other.

Entry Examples and Explanation

The content of selected entries is rather interesting. First, on the 1st Month 27th, 1810, one James Wilson, Schoolmaster, purchased sundry items including six copies of the *American tutor's assistant* at 56 cents each. This same James Wilson on the 9th Month 3d, 1810, purchased six copies of Hutton's *Arithmetic* at 30 cents each.

Another entry to the account of Aaron Ableman on the 2d Month 5th, 1810, shows also sundry school supplies so one would presume him also to be a schoolmaster, or at least a teacher of sorts. However, later in the year on 12th Month 1st, 1810, Aaron Ableman had an entry to his account for one pipe of wine. (A pipe is 2 hogsheads; a hogshead is 63 gallons.) So here we have a teacher who has 126 gallons of wine for the holiday season.

The final comparison between Mr. Wilson and Mr. Ableman was made at the close of the books, when a balance was struck. The 1810 December balance shows that Mr. Wilson and Mr. Ableman both have paid for their school supplies, but Mr. Ableman has not paid the 167 dollars for the pipe of wine.

New York Imprints: *A complete treatise,* **Double Entry Series**

Hutton's double entry bookkeeping was included in the 1809 and 1810 books mentioned earlier. Hutton's *A complete system of practical arithmetic* was originally published in London and went through thirteen editions before being printed in the United States in 1809. The first edition published in the United States in 1809 was apparently not an authorized version. It gives Hutton full credit as author but lists D. P. Adams as the one responsible for the adaptation "to the use of Schools and men of business in the United States." It was printed in New York, sold by S. Campbell and printed by W. Elliot and entitled: *A complete treatise on practical arithmetic.* The following year, 1810, the "First American, from the latest London edition" was published in New York, printed and sold by Smith and Foreman. This was apparently the first authorized publication in the United States.

The arithmetic portion of *A complete system* is much the same as other textbooks of the times. Subjects included were, simple and compound addition, subtraction, multiplication, division, fractions, tare and tret, decimals, compound interest, discount, and single and double fellowship. On page 141 of the 1809 edition, the section "Book-keeping by Single Entry" begins, followed by a section on "Book-keeping by Double Entry" on page 173.

The section of "Book-keeping by Double Entry, or According to the Italian Method", begins by saying "this method is said to be by double entry because every article is twice entered into the ledger, viz., on the debit side of one account, and on the credit side of another account. And it is called the Italian method because of it having been invented in Italy." Three books are considered with this method, the wastebook, the journal, and the ledger, a short account of which is given of each. The perspective of the instruction is given as that of the teacher to the pupil. Following various illustrations is a list of rules identifying what accounts are to be debited and credited under varying circumstances. A wastebook then illustrates how those items are recorded.

Written by Peter McMickle, Paul Jensen, Mark Turner, and Thomas Clevenger

Reference

Matheson, W. 'Microcosm of the Library of Congress', *A B Bookman's Weekly*, 28 November 1977.

(27)

		£	S	D
Twelfth Mo. 3d, 1801.				
3	ABLE ABLEMAN, Dr.			
	To a Pipe of Wine	25	0	0
———— 6 ————				
3	WILLIAM WINTON, Cr.			
	By 30 Gallons Brandy at 7s 6	11	5	0
	By Cash in full	9	6	0¼
		20	11	0¼
———— 8 ————				
10	THOMAS HUNTER, Dr.			
	To 3 Chaldrons of Coals at £. 1 15	5	5	0
———— 10 ————				
3	WILLIAM WATSON, Cr.			
	By Cash in full	3	17	0

K

ILLUSTRATION 11. Day-book entries from 1801 copy of Hutton's *A course of book-keeping, according to the method of single entry.*

Item 4. The Charles Hutton Series beginning 1788.

(3)

1801			ABEL ABLEMAN,	Dr.	£.	S.	D.
2 Mo	5		To Sundries		15	17	6
12 Mo	3		To a Pipe of Wine		25	0	0

1801			WILLIAM WINTON,	Dr.			
2 Mo	12		To Sundries		2	3	6¼
8 Mo	1		To Sundries		18	7	6
					20	11	0¼

1801			WILLIAM WATSON,	Dr.			
2 Mo	20		To Sundries		3	17	0
12 Mo	31		To 1 Year's Rent		40	0	0

ILLUSTRATION 12. Ledger entries from 1801 copy of Hutton's *A course of book-keeping, according to the method of single entry.*

THE

American Tutor's Assistant

REVISED;

OR,

A COMPENDIOUS SYSTEM OF

PRACTICAL ARITHMETIC;

CONTAINING

THE SEVERAL RULES OF THAT USEFUL SCIENCE

CONCISELY DEFINED, METHODICALLY ARRANGED, AND
FULLY EXEMPLIFIED.

THE WHOLE

PARTICULARLY ADAPTED TO THE EASY AND REGULAR

INSTRUCTION OF YOUTH IN OUR AMERICAN SCHOOLS

Originally compiled by sundry Teachers in and near Philadelphia; now Revised and an additional number
of Examples given in money of the
United States.

TO WHICH IS ADDED A COURSE OF

Book-keeping by Single Entry.

PHILADELPHIA:
PRINTED BY JOSEPH CRUKSHANK.

1809.

ILLUSTRATION 13. Title page of printer Joseph Crukshank's 1809 Hutton based *The American tutor's assistant revised.*

Item 4. The Charles Hutton Series beginning 1788.

A COMPLETE TREATISE

on

PRACTICAL ARITHMETIC

AND

BOOK-KEEPING,

BOTH BY

SINGLE AND DOUBLE ENTRY.

BY CHARLES HUTTON, L.L.D. & F.R.S.

Corrected, enlarged, and adapted to the Use of Schools and Men of Business in the

UNITED STATES.

BY D. P. ADAMS.

NEW-YORK:

Sold by Samuel Campbell, William Falconer, T. & J. Swords, Ezra Sargeant, Evert Duyckinck, Inskeep & Bradford, M. & W. Ward, Robert M'Dermut, Williams & Whiting, Thomas A. Ronalds, Stephen Stephens, John Tiebout, and Samuel Wood.

W. Elliot, Printer.
1809.

ILLUSTRATION 14. Title page from 1809 Hutton *A complete treatise . . . both by single and double entry.*

184 BOOK-KEEPING BY DOUBLE ENTRY. (1)

THE

WASTE-BOOK.

NEW-YORK, *January* 1, 1807.

		dol	c
	AN INVENTORY *Of the money, goods, and debts due to and by me,* W———— M————	dol	c
1	I have in ready money	25000	00
	300 yards of superfine broad cloth, at 3 dol 24 cts per yd	972	00
	1200 yards of linen, at 56 cents per yard	672	00
	800 pieces of lead, weighing in all 44 tons, at 71 d⁵ per ton	3124	00
	25 puncheons of rum, at 168 dol per puncheon	4200	00
	12 hogsheads of sugar, containing 140 cwt, cost	1352	50
	¼ of the ship Endeavour	1333	00
	William Johnson owes me per note, due the first of March	888	88
	James Gibson, per bond, with interest at 7 per cent from the 1st of November last	2222	22
		39764	60
3	I owe as follows: To Edward Young on demand	533	33
	Charles Wilson, Esq. due the 12th instant	32	00
	William Mercer, per account	269	00
		834	33

ILLUSTRATION 15. Wastebook example from 1809 Hutton *A complete treatise . . . both by single and double entry.*

Item 4. The Charles Hutton Series beginning 1788.

COMPLETE SYSTEM

OF

PRACTICAL ARITHMETIC;

AND

Book-keeping,

BOTH BY

SINGLE AND DOUBLE ENTRY

ADAPTED TO THE USE OF SCHOOLS.

BY CHARLES HUTTON, LL.D. AND F.R.S. &c.

First American, from the latest London Edition.

New-York:

PRINTED AND SOLD BY SMITH & FORMAN,

No. 195 and 213 Greenwich-street,

1810.

ILLUSTRATION 16. Title page from 1810 Hutton *A complete system . . . both by single and double entry.*

(2)	WASTE-BOOK.		123	
		l	*s*	*d*
	———— Jan. 4, 1789 ————			
2	Bought 400 yards shalloon, at 1s 3d a yard	25	0	0
	———— 7 ————			
2	Paid Edward Young in full - - -	20	0	6
	———— 12 ————			
2	Bought of Isaac Onslow 18 hhds. Oporto wine, at 9l. a hhd. - - - -	162	0	0
	———— 17 ————			
2	Paid to Charles Wilson, Esq. in full -	87	4	0
2	Sold 150 yards linen, at 3s 2d a yard -	23	15	0
	———— 24 ————			
2	Bought of Timothy Clarkson 12 bags hops qt. 40 cwt. 2 qr. at 46s a cwt. payable in months - - - - - -	93	3	0
	———— 30 ————			
2	Bartered 5 puncheons rum, at 40l a puncheon, for 20 hogsheads Lisbon wine, at 10l a hogshead. - - - -	200	0	0
	———— Feb. 2 ————			
2	Sold Thomas Draper 100 yds of broad cloth, at 18s a yard. - - - - -	90	0	0
	———— 6 ————			
2	Shipped on board the Diligence, Captain Tempest, for Jamaica. the following goods, addressed to Abel Factor, on my account, viz.			
	800 yds linen, at 2s 6d a yard - - 100 0 0			
	200 .. broad cloth, at 15s. - - 150 0 0			
	8 pieces of Holland, bought of ⎫ Tho. Draper, at 19l a piece ⎭ 152 0 0			
	Paid duty, fees, &c. - - - - 21 4 2			
	Ditto for insurance of 400l. by ⎫ Hazard and Co. at 5 per cent ⎭ - 20 0 0			
		443	4	2

ILLUSTRATION 17. Wastebook example from 1810 Hutton A complete system ... both by single and double entry.

Item 5. 1789. Thomas Sarjeant.

AN INTRODUCTION TO THE COUNTING HOUSE;

OR,

A SHORT SPECIMEN OF MERCANTILE PRECEDENTS,

ADAPTED

TO THE PRESENT SITUATION OF THE TRADE AND COMMERCE

OF THE

UNITED STATES OF AMERICA.

FOR THE USE OF SCHOOLS AND PRIVATE EDUCATION.

BY *THOMAS SARJEANT.*

INTENDED AS A SUPPLEMENT TO THE ELEMENTARY PRINCIPLES OF ARITHMETIC.

PHILADELPHIA;
PRINTED BY DOBSON AND LANG FOR THE EDITOR;
AND SOLD BY T. DOBSON AND W. POTHTELL IN SECOND STREET; AND W. PRITCHARD, T. SEDDON,
AND RICE & Co. IN MARKET STREET.
M DCC LXXXIX.

ILLUSTRATION 18. Title page from 1789 Thomas Sarjeant's *An introduction to the counting house.*

Item 5. 1789. Thomas Sarjeant. *An introduction to the counting house...* **Philadelphia: Printed by Dobson & Lang. 52 pgs. 16 cm. Evans 22127 NUC NS0134249**

Other American Printings: No other known printings.

Introduction

This text is the earliest known book written by an American and published in America that is totally devoted to bookkeeping. It has been overlooked by American accounting historians partially because it was not included in H.C. Bentley's bibliography (1934, 1935), and also because of its limited circulation, brevity, and lack of originality (admitted by Sarjeant). As noted by Sheldahl (1985, p. 4), *An introduction to the counting house* was also overlooked by the following historical collections: Goldsmith's Library of Economic Literature (University of London); Kress Library of Business and Economics (Harvard); Herwood Library of Accountancy (housed in Baltimore); and, the Library Company of Philadelphia (a major rare book center).

The book was written as a supplement to Sarjeant's *Elementary principles of arithmetic* (1788). An advertisement in the preface to *An introduction to the counting house* mentions that the two above books could be purchased, bound together, for half a dollar. *An introduction to the counting house* is a brief description of double-entry bookkeeping with relatively little detail as to commercial transactions.

Author's Teaching Environment: Protestant Episcopal Academy

On the title page of *Elementary principles of arithmetic*, Sarjeant refers to himself as the "Late Master of the Mathematical School in the Academy of the Protestant Episcopal Church, in the City of Philadelphia." An academy is defined by Good's *Dictionary of education* (1959) as "an independent secondary school not under public control." Sarjeant's books are aimed for the "American Youth" and he talks of the "Young Men" and "Young Ladies" in his prefaces. The early academies apparently were more adaptable to the early colonial needs than the Latin grammar schools or the colleges. They offered a general education, some vocational training, college-preparatory instruction, religious education and elementary-school teacher training (Smith, Krause, Atkinson, 1961). Concern for adequate education was increasing in the late eighteenth century. The 1776 Pennsylvania constitution states that "a school or schools shall be established in each county by the legislature, for the convenient instruction of youth, with such salaries to masters, paid by the public as may enable them to instruct the youth at low prices" (Callahan 1959). This does indicate an emphasis towards more public education, and the concern for education at this time in Pennsylvania probably contributed to the 1785 beginning of the Academy of the Protestant Episcopal Church.

The Academy of the Protestant Episcopal Church was established in 1785 under the guidance of Dr. William White. The academy is still in existence today as The Episcopal Academy and has become one of the larger Episcopal day schools (Sargent 1983). The Academy was incorporated as a non-profit organization in 1787, and was granted a charter and 10,000 acres of land by the state legislature (Sargent 1983). Sarjeant taught at the Academy for 2-3 years and published his above mentioned books after leaving the school. Sheldahl (1985, p. 8) states that Sarjeant was the Academy's first mathematics teacher and left the Academy in 1787. Further research has uncovered little about his occupation after his departure from the Academy.

In 1786, the English Parliament passed an act authorizing consecration of American Bishops. Dr. William White went to England and was consecrated on February 4, 1787 by John Moore, Archbishop of Canterbury and others (Cross 1964, p. 266). In 1777, while White was rector of the Christ Church in Philadelphia, three signers of the Declaration of Independence were members of his church: Robert Morris, a financier of the American Revolution and brother-in-law of White; Francis Hopkinson, the rector's warden and organist; and, Benjamin Franklin, a vestryman (Albright 1964, p. 84). This was during the time the British troops were occupying Philadelphia. Rev. White was also a friend of George Washington and was elected chaplain to Congress at Yorktown in 1777 (Drake 1872). What has now become known as the Protestant Episcopal Church in the United States of America, emerged from plans for the organization designed by White (Kunitz 1938). Rev. White was the first Protestant Episcopal Bishop in Pennsylvania, presided at the first Episcopal convention in 1785 and wrote the constitution of the church (Drake 1872).

The 'Counting House'

Sarjeant states in his preface to *An introduction to the counting house* that it was suggested by "some gentleman that an abstract of the Court of Mercantile Instruction" would make a good supplement to his book *Elementary principles of arithmetic* (1788). The "Court of Mercantile Instruction" was commonly known as the 'Counting House,' 'Compting House,' or other synonyms.

In England, the term 'counting house' designated the business offices of the industrial firms during the early industrial period; in many instances they were separate buildings. In early Colonial America a countinghouse and a warehouse were the facilities of a merchant business. Apparently, the facilities did not have to be located together (Previts & Sheldahl 1977). On-the-job training was the primary feature of the countinghouses. Up to the American Revolution there were two means of entry into the merchant business. Sons of wealthy families could graduate from college and then enter the countinghouse of wealthy merchants. One could also graduate from a good academy and then enter the countinghouse (Previts & Sheldahl 1977). The countinghouse was a significant force in the progress of account keeping in America. Throughout the latter half of the 19th Century, the 'counting house' operated as the nucleus of accounting functions. It was the 'records center' of the merchant and the educational center for young businessmen. Training in the 'counting houses' was prevalent. John Hancock and Henry Laurens, two signers of the Declaration of Independence were both trained in the 'counting houses' (Previts and Merino 1979, p, 25).

Efforts were continually being made in the counting houses to simplify and routinize the accounting system. The format, style, system, and books of the period all attempted to simplify and improve the methods used (Previts and Merino 1979). Sarjeant was no exception to this claim, as he notes in his preface that "his principal object is, to furnish a Compendium for American Youth, in which the Fundamental Principles of a Mercantile Education are communicated in a More Concise and Intelligible Manner, than in any other Introductory Treatise in the English Language" (Sarjeant 1789, p. iii). As business and commercial transactions increased during the nineteenth century, the counting houses became less practical as a place of learning and apprenticeship. Textbooks and the teaching of accounting grew in importance (Previts and Merino 1979, p. 26).

Item 5. 1789. Thomas Sarjeant.

Description of *An introduction to the counting house*

The book is a rather small book consisting of only 52 pages, including the title page and preface. Sarjeant defends the book's brevity by explaining that examples of the invoices, subsidiary books, etc., "would have been added, but they were inadmissible in a first Course of Instruction" and would have inappropriately increased its size and cost for the intended users (1789 p. ii). He also plainly declares that he "lays no claim to Originality" and that he used other published works as his resources (1789 p. iii). He claims that the "Editor has less ambition to be Original than Useful" (1788 p. ii). Sarjeant speaks of himself as the "Editor." Possibly this could be attributed to his admitted lack of originality and therefore in a real sense he claims the title "Editor".

However, to think of his books as void of any ingenuity or originality is to do a disservice to his works and to disregard his own words. He makes note of his attempt to communicate in a more concise and intelligent manner. He also makes note of the numerous advantages to his *Elementary principles of arithmetic*.

The Contents of *An introduction to the counting house*

Title Page	Page 1
Preface	Page 2
Advertisement for *Elementary Principles of Arithmetic* and others	Page 3
Section the First Bills of Parcel; Book Debts; Receipts; Promissory Notes; Bills of Exchange; Application	Page 5
Section the Second Description of Single Entry; Specimens of Day Book and Ledger	Page 19
Section the Third Description of Double Entry and particular accounts ; Specimens of Day Book, Journal and Ledger Alphabet, Errors	Page 27
Advertisement	Page 52

I. Section the First

In this section, Sarjeant defines various items that are to be used further in the book. These items, including portions of their definitions, are provided below.

Bills of Parcel is "an Account given by the Seller to the Purchaser, of the Goods purchased, their Quality, Quantity, Value, etc."

Bills of Book Debts are "taken from the Ledger, or other Books of the Seller; giving an account of the several Articles, with their value, and the Date when each Parcel was sold and delivered."

Receipts are defined as "a written acquittance, or discharge from a debt, given by the Receiver to the Payer; and is either in full, or in part, on a Person's own account, or on that of another." He separates receipts as to Bills of Parcels or Book Debts, Separate Receipts of various kinds, and Separate Receipts given on another person's account. The receipts are in memorandum form.

Promissory Notes are "a writing given as a Security for some valuable consideration as Money, Goods, etc., promising to pay the Sum, etc. mentioned, at a time appointed."

Bill of Exchange "is an Order for Money to be received in one place, for the Value paid in another."

In the final part of this section entitled "Application," Sarjeant saves a number of exercises for the student to complete pertaining to the above documents and entries.

II. Section the Second - Bookkeeping by Single-Entry

In this section, Sarjeant states that "Bookkeeping is an Art, which teaches the Methods of recording, and disposing the Accounts of transactions in a course of trade." He also says that "Bookkeeping by Single Entry is principally made use of by Retail Traders, Store-keepers, etc., and requires only a Waste or Day Book, and a Ledger -- It contains an Account of all Cash lent or borrowed, Debts discharged or contracted, and Goods sold or bought on Credit." He then adds as a note that "a Course of Bookkeeping of this kind is requisite, because in many trades it is entirely sufficient. In others, the Italian Method is wholly unapplicable. It is also necessary as Introductory to that Method and to facilitate its Acquisition."

The day book, according to Sarjeant, "contains a plain narrative or Memorandum of every occurrence in Trade, as it happens in the ordinary course of business." The day book is ruled with a marginal line at the left hand, for a reference to the folio of the ledger, and three columns at the right for pounds (f), shillings (s), and pence (p).

The ledger page is ruled with a column at the left for the month and day, and two sets of columns for pounds, shillings, and pence in "Debtor and Creditor" with a space between for a reference to the day book.

III. Section the Third - Bookkeeping by Double-Entry

Sarjeant says that this method of bookkeeping requires these principal books: waste book; journal; and, ledger. He defends this method of bookkeeping by stating that "this method of Bookkeeping is the most perfect ever invented. It contains Accounts of the Merchant's Stock in Trade, of every person he deals with, and every Commodity he deals in, his Proft and Loss by any branch of Trade, his Income, Expenditures, etc."

Sarjeant describes the waste book as "exactly familiar to the Day Book in the Course by Single Entry."

He describes the journal by stating that it "rules as the Day Book. In this, every Circumstance of the Waste Book is expressed in a more methodical and Commercial Form, as preparatory to the Ledger." He also notes that "almost the whole mystery of Bookkeeping consists in the Art of Journalizing; and writers on the subject have usually burdened the learner with a multitude of particular Rules for every circumstance which occurs in business." These rules may, however, be reduced to the following:

Rule 1. Whatever the Merchant possesses, or receives, or whoever is accountable to him, is Debtor; and if he asks on what account, the answer shows the Creditor.
Rule 2. Whatever he parts with, and every person to whom he is accountable is Creditor; and if he asks on what account, the answer shows the Debtor.

The Ledger is composed of the following accounts: The Account of Stock - "Merchant's account of himself;" The Account of Cash; The Account of Goods - "Debtor side shows what is on hand and what has been purchased, and Creditor side shows what has been sold, and what the sales have produced;" The Account of Persons; The Account of Profit and Loss - "Debtor side shows the Loss by any Article of Merchandise, and also all incidental expenses; the Creditor side shows the Gain, etc.;" and, The Account of Balances - "The Debtor side shows the several branches of the Merchant's property when the Books are closed; and the Creditor side shows the Debts he owes." Sarjeant explains further that other accounts are sometimes inserted depending upon circumstances.

Description of the *Elementary principles of arithmetic*

As in the previous book, Sarjeant refers to himself as the "Editor" and claims no originality. He describes this book "as a Specimen of the Mathematical Form of Instruction..." and his audience is "actually drawn up for the Use of the Young Noblemen and Gentlemen educated in the Royal Grammar School of Kingston upon Thames, while the Editor conducted the Mathematical branches of Education, in that Seminary." As mentioned earlier, to consider his books as void of any ingenuity or originality would be a disservice. Although he does say that his book of "Instruction, will certainly be found defective," he also admits that "this little work will be found to contain the following advantages:" more concise; more methodical, more original matter dispersed throughout the book, and more portable and convenient.

The favorite English arithmetic books used in early America were *Hodder's arithmetic* 1661; *Cocker's Arithmetic* 1677; and, Dilworth's, *The schoolmaster's assistant* 1776. These were then superseded by *A new and complete system of arithmetic* by Nicholas Pike, 1788 (Littlefield 1965). Pike's arithmetic book was the recognized American arithmetic book from 1788 well into the nineteenth century (Karpinski 1925). Pike's book was written in 1788 as was Sarjeant's. However, Pike's book was of considerable more detail consisting of 8 volumes and 512 pages. Karpinski also notes that an interesting feature of the earlier edition of Pike was a lengthy recommendation of the book by George Washington. Sarjeant's book was intended as an introductory course in arithmetic and certainly did not enjoy the circulation that Pike's book enjoyed.

Conclusions

The significance of Sarjeant's *An introduction to the counting house* is not found in its content or style, but in its publication date. One of the aims of historians is to give credit for first events. Accounting historians have the same aims as historians in other areas and engage in the same kinds of challenges. *An introduction to the counting house* is the earliest known book written by an American and published in America that is totally devoted to bookkeeping. [Note: for further reading refer to the excellent 1985 article by Terry Sheldahl entitled *An introduction to the counting house.*]

Written by Paul Jensen

References

Albright, Raymond W. *A History of the Protestant Episcol Church,* New York: The McMillan Company, 1964.

Cajori, Florian, *A History of Mathematical Notations,* LaSalle, Illinois: The Open Court Publishing Company, 1928. Reprinted by Open Court Publishing Company, 1974.

Callahan, Raymond E., *An Introduction to Education in American Society,* New York: Alfred A. Knopf, 1959.

Cross, Arthur L., *The Anglican Episcopate and the American Colonies,* Hamden, Conn: Archon Books, 1964.

Drake, Francis S., *Dictionary of American Biography,* Boston: James R. Osgood and Company, 1872.

Good, Carter V., Editor, *Dictionary of Education,* New York: McGraw-Hill Book Company, Inc., 1959.

Karpinski, Louis Charles, *The History of Arithmetic,* New York; Rand McNally and Company, 1925.

Kunitz, Stanley J., and Howard Haycraft, Editors, *American Authors 1600-1900: A Bibliographical Dictionary of American Literature,* New York: The H. W. Wilson Company, 1938.

Previts, Gary John, and Barbara Dubis Merino, *A History of Accounting in America: An Historical Interpretation of the Cultu-*

ral Significance of Accounting, New York: John Wiley and Sons, Ronald Press Publication, 1979.

Previts, Gary John, and Terry K. Sheldahl, "Accounting and 'Countinghouses': An Analysis and Commentary." *Abacus,* Vol. 13, June, 1977, pp. 52-59.

Sargent, Martha, Editor, *The Handbook of Private Schools,* Boston: Porter Sargent Publishers, Inc., 1983.

_____, *The Elementary Principles of Arithmetic,* Philadelphia: Dobson and Lang, 1788.

Sheldahl, Terry K., "America's Earliest Recorded Text in Accounting: Sarjeant's 1789 Book," *The Accounting Historians' Journal,* Vol. 12, No. 2, Fall, 1985.

Smith, Edward W., Stanley Krause Jr., and Mark M. Atkinson, *The Educator's Encyclopedia,* Englewood Cliffs, New Jersey: Prentice-Hall, Inc. 1961.

Item 5. 1789. Thomas Sarjeant.

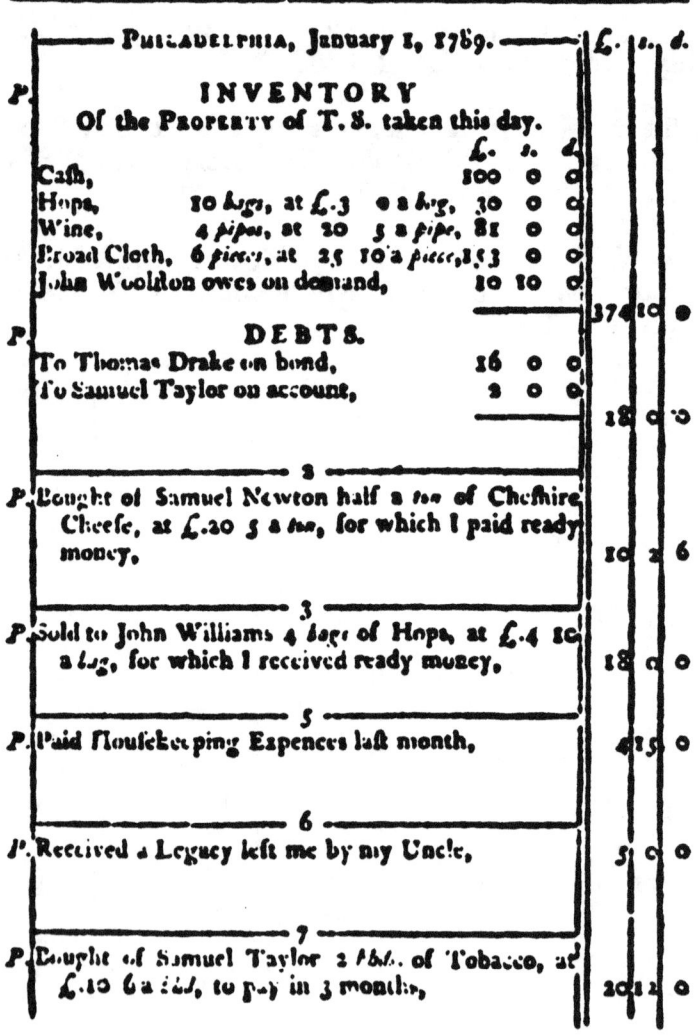

ILLUSTRATION 19. Waste book example from 1789 Thomas Sarjeant's *An introduction to the counting house.*

(Fol. 1)

Specimen of the JOURNAL.

	PHILADELPHIA, January 1, 1789.	£	s.	d.
	Sundry Accounts Drs. £.374 10 to Stock.			
	£ s. d.			
1	Cash, 100 0 0			
2	Hops, 10 bags, at £.3 0 a bag, 30 0 0			
3	Wine, 4 pipes, at 20 5 a pipe, 81 0 0			
4	Broad Cloth, 6 pieces, at 25 10 a piece, 153 0 0			
5	John Woolston, by note on demand, 10 10 0			
		374	10	0
	Stock Dr. £.18 to Sundry Accounts.			
1/2	To Thomas Drake on bond, 16 0 0			
3	To Samuel Taylor on account, 2 0 0			
		18	0	0
	———————— 2 ————————			
	Cheese Dr. £.10 2 6 to Cash.			
3/1	Paid for half a ton of Cheshire,	10	2	6
	———————— 3 ————————			
	Cash Dr. £.18 to Hops.			
1/1	Received for 4 bags,	18	0	0
	———————— 4 ————————			
	Profit and Loss Dr. £.4 15 to Cash.			
3/1	For Household Expences,	4	15	0
	———————— 6 ————————			
	Cash Dr. £.5 to Profit and Loss.			
1/3	Received my Uncle's Legacy,	5	0	0
	———————— 7 ————————			
	Tobacco Dr. £.20 10 to Samuel Taylor.			
4/3	For 2 hhds. at £.10 6, to pay in 3 months,	20	12	0

ILLUSTRATION 20. Journal example from 1789 Thomas Sarjeant's *An introduction to the counting house.*

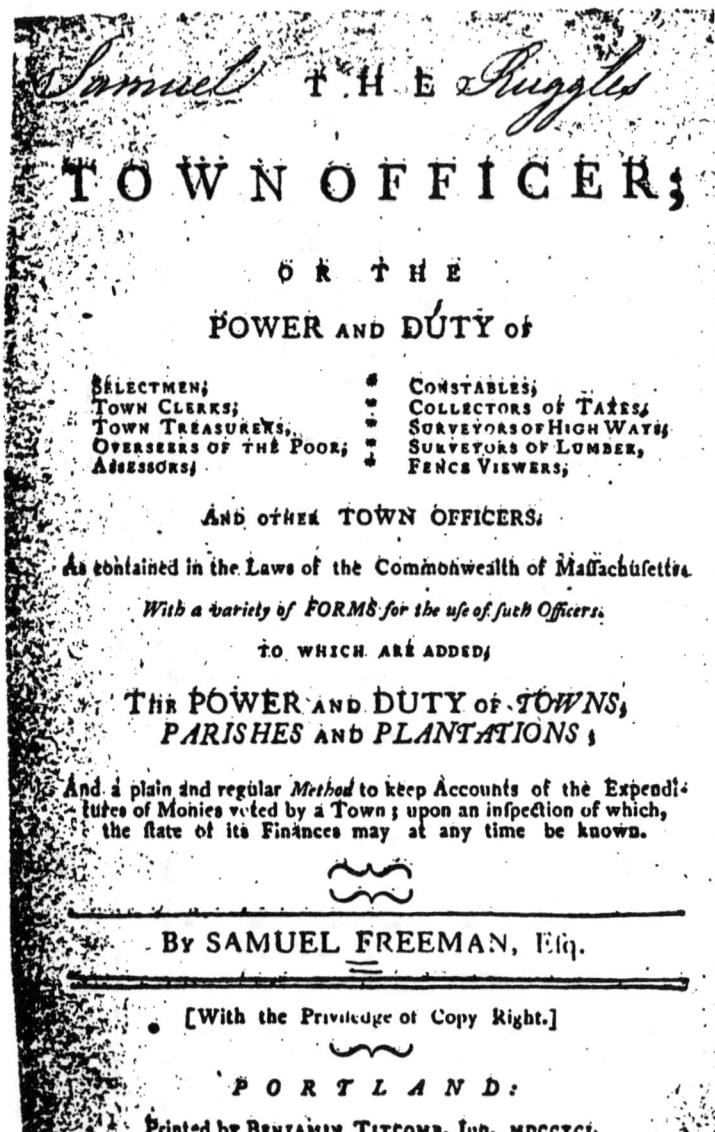

ILLUSTRATION 21. Title page from 1791 Samuel Freeman's *The town officer . . .*

The Birth of American Accountancy 63

Item 6. 1791. Samuel Freeman. ***The town officer*** **... Portland: Printed by Benjamin Titcomb. 178 [2] pgs. 17.5 cm. Evans 23389   NUC NF0357711**

Other American printings:

1792. Samuel Freeman. *The town officer* ... Third edition. Boston: I. Thomas and E. T. Andrews. 240 pgs. (Not in Evans) NUC NF0357712

1793. Samuel Freeman. *The town officer* ... Second edition. Boston: Printed by I. Thomas and E. T. Andrews. [4] [3] 232 [1] pgs. (various pagings) Evans 25512   NUC NF0357713

1794. Samuel Freeman. *The town officer* ... Third edition. Boston: Printed by I. Thomas and E. T. Andrews. [4] [4] 232 pgs. 17.5 cm. Evans 27016   NUC NF0357715

1799. Samuel Freeman. *The town officer* ... Fourth edition. Boston: Printed by I. Thomas and E. T. Andrews. [4] [2] 281 pgs. 18 cm. Evans 3551   NUC NF0357716

1802. Samuel Freeman. *The town officer* ... Fifth edition. Boston: Printed by I. Thomas and E. T. Andrews. [6] 304 pgs. 17.5 cm. SS 2259   NUC NF0357718

1805. Samuel Freeman. *The town officer* ... Sixth edition. Boston: Published by Thomas & Andrews and printed by J. T. Buckingham. [6] 342 pgs. 18 cm. SS 8462   NUC NF0357720

1808. Samuel Freeman. *The town officer* ... Seventh edition. Boston: Printed by J. T. Buckingham for Thomas & Andrews. [4] [2] 366 pgs. 18 cm. SS 15049   NUC NF0357722

1815. Samuel Freeman. *The town officer* ... Seventh edition. Boston: Printed by J. T. Buckingham for Thomas & Andrews. [6] 366 pgs. 17.5 cm. SS 34727   NUC NF0357724

1815. Samuel Freeman. *The town officer* ... Eighth edition. Boston: Printed by J. T. Buckingham for Thomas & Andrews. [6] 366 pgs. 17.5 cm. SS 34728   NUC NF0357724

Introduction

Accountants have much to learn about the history of their profession with the area of governmental accounting no exception. This first edition of *The town officer* is possibly America's first work on municipal accounting.

In order to gain a perspective of the significance of this work, a brief biography of the author is given. This is followed by a history of this popular publication. An analysis of the book is limited to the examination of the one section that concerns itself with the keeping of town accounts. These accounts are analyzed and compared briefly to modern municipal accounting practices. Finally, some topics of historical significance to accounting for municipalities are examined in an attempt to gain further insight into the origin of accounting for municipalities.

Samuel Freeman, Esq.

The author of *The town officer*, Judge Samuel Freeman, was born on June 15, 1743 to Judge Enoch Freeman. His birthright, it appears, was to be a public servant and a politician. The fact that he was a prolific writer who wrote and edited many works, including *The town officer*, is a benefit that not only enabled people of early Massachusetts to understand the rights and obligations of their citizenship, but also adds to our knowledge of accounting in early America.

Freeman zealously supported the American revolution and was active in early revolutionary struggles. He became the Secretary of the Cumberland County convention in 1774. In 1775 he was an "industrious and useful" member of the Provincial government [Drake, 1872]. Freeman's political motivation and connection, whether through his father or his own activity, was further evidenced in 1775 by his appointment as clerk to the newly reorganized court. He continued in this position for forty-five years. In 1775 Freeman was also appointed a Register of Probate in which capacity he served until he was appointed judge in 1804. He served as judge until 1820. His political activity included membership in the House of Representatives in 1776 and 1778. Freeman served as Postmaster of Portland from 1776 to 1805.

Freeman's political activity did not prevent him from publishing. In fact, his tenure in public office may have inspired his publications. One gets the impression, when scanning the titles of these works, that his purpose was to educate the town officers concerning the responsibilities and obligations of local government while, at the same time, informing his constituency, the local citizens, about the intricacies of exercising their rights using local government. Some of his publications include: *The town officer*; "American Clerk's Magazine;" *The massachusetts justice*, of which there where eight volumes, 1803; and,"Probate Directory," twelve months, 1803. He also edited the "Journal of Reverend Thomas Smith" published in 1821.

There is some confusion in the reference books concerning the date of Samuel Freeman's death, although all agree that he died in 1831. One reference [Wallace, 1829] marks the date as September 2, 1831 while another [Drake, 1872] has June 15, 1831 as the day he died. It should be noted that there is some coincidence concerning both of these dates. Samuel Freeman was born on June 15. Is it probable that he also died on June 15? Samuel's father, Judge Enoch Freeman is reported [Drake, 1872] to have died September 2, 1788, at the age of 81. Although it was in a different year, did Samuel Freeman die on the same day as his father? All of the references that were checked, however, place the year of death as 1831 at the age of 88.

Review of *The Town Officer*

The purpose of *The Town Officer* was to propagate a knowledge of the laws of government to both the public servants and the citizenry of Massachusetts because, "Perhaps the evils existing in society from an inattention to its laws, arise more from the want of knowing them, than from the want of a disposition to observe them: And when it is considered, that everyone who sustains an office is not able to furnish himself with the laws at large, it is not to be wondered at that a neglect of them should any where prevail" [Freeman, 1793].

The significance of *The town officer* to accounting historians and accountants in general is that this may very well have been the first American book that addressed accounting for a governmental entity of any type. The title clearly states that part of the content of *The town officer* is devoted to "...a plain and regular method to keep accounts of the expenditures of monies voted by a town: upon an inspection of which, the state of its finances may at any time be known." [Freeman, 1793, p. 170]. The title not only states its purpose as accounting for the governmental entity of a town but also that the accounts should be in such order as to provide for an audit or an inspection such that the financial condition of the Town may be determined at any time.

Freeman's first edition of 1791 was the first in a series of editions to contain a section on accounting for the finances of a town. It contained 178 pages, 23 of which dealt with town accounts. Due to heavy sales, a second edition of *The town officer* was distributed. Because the full text of the 1791 first edition could not be obtained, and because the 1793 second edition is practically identical to the first edition in terms of content, quoting has been extensively from the 1793 edition. This edition had 239 pages and 31 dealt with accounting. Freeman by this time had sold the copy right to I. Thomas and E.T. Andrews of Boston in order that the book "be sold by them" [Freeman, 1793]. The second edition also contained new government forms and an update of laws. The town accounting section was basically unchanged.

A third edition was published in 1794. It was again updated to take into consideration some recently passed laws "respecting town affairs" [Freeman, 1815]. This edition contained 240 pages. Freeman considered the 1799 fourth edition of *The town officer* to be a very improved edition. In addition to including the law changes, he decreased the size of the "part of the work which respects accounts, and which has been considered by some rather complex." The fourth edition still had 22 pages of examples of accounts, but much of the verbal explanation was deleted. Freeman probably cut this portion to enable him to keep *The town officer* to a manageable size because with the addition of the new laws, the book was becoming very thick and expensive. He intimates this in the advertisement when referring to the fourth edition. "These improvements, and the consequent enlargement of the work, although it in some degree enhances the price, make it more valuable than any of the former editions" [Freeman, 1815, p. VI.]. Another important feature of Freeman's 1799 fourth edition is that it is the first time he used dollars instead of pounds sterling in labeling the amounts.

The reduction of the section on town accounts made in the fourth edition remained approximately the same through the eighth edition. There were few changes in the accounting section, footnotes notwithstanding, subsequent to the fourth edition, although the number of pages that dealt with accounting decreased from 22 pages of 287 total in the fourth edition to 19 pages of 372 in the eighth edition.

The remainder of this paper will describe Freeman's "plain

and regular method" and evaluate whether this first book on keeping town accounts resembles the method used by today's municipalities.

Description of town accounts in *The town officer* of 1793

The importance of keeping town accounts is explained by Freeman:

> As one of the great objects of government is to guard and defend the property of its subjects; as no publick (sic) measures engage the attention of a people more than those which affect their interest, and require by way of taxes a part of their property for publick use; and as nothing will ensure a cheerful acquiescence in such measures but an assurance that the monies thus taken from them are applied to the uses for which they were designed; it is of importance in all communities, that proper regulations should be established, whereby it may clearly appear, that such monies are faithfully expended, and regularly accounted for. Too much care cannot be taken in this business, as it relates to the raising and applying of taxes required for the support of the government, and the exigencies of a state; and it must be happy for the people of any state to have such a plan established, as shall provide effectual checks upon the several officers through whose hands their monies are to pass; and as shall exhibit at any time, such a state of the expenditures thereof, as will satisfy every reasonable person who may inspect the same.
>
> Whether such a plan has been adopted, or is now wanted in this state or not, is not for me to enquire. My design is to form a regular plan for keeping the accounts of a Town, by which its inhabitants may at any time know whether the monies which they may have voted at any meeting, be raised, collected, and expended, agreeably to their views in voting them. To these ends it will be necessary for the town to establish the following regulations. (Freeman, 1793, p. 170)

Freeman's regulations, one through five, state in part that subsequent to a vote at a town meeting to raise money, the town clerk should make out three lists or accounts, expressing the sums and the purposes of raising the money. He should give one list to the selectmen (representatives), one to the treasurer, and one to the assessors. The regulations basically provide for control over the money appropriated. Procedures are also set out to account for the money appropriated but not expended. An interesting footnote suggests that "an estimate of the sums proposed to be raised, should be laid before the town, that the town may have opportunity to consider the same, and judge whether. . . ." [Freeman, 1793, p.171]. This statement implies that a budget be presented to the citizens of the town for their approval.

Regulations six and seven state that at every annual meeting the selectmen should present to the town the state of their accounts. These regulations, if not calling directly for an audit, certainly paved the way for an audit of the accounts and the financial affairs of the town. Another interesting footnote recommends that a law be passed that provided for a Town Accountant to keep the financial records of the town rather than the selectmen, whose responsibility for the accounts was previously stated. It appears that Freeman had second thoughts about the selectmen's ability or time to keep accounts, thus the recommendation for a Town Accountant. Freeman's regulations, which were general in nature and provided system controls, laid the foundation on which Freeman built his specific set of rules of accounting for the monies voted by the town.

Freeman's suggested rules were present in the first three editions, 1791, 1793, and 1794 of *The town officer*, where he verbalized the prescribed accounting treatment shown in the examples that followed. In an apparent effort to keep subsequent editions to a manageable size, he omitted this section and showed the examples directly following the regulations. This practice started with the fourth edition in 1799 and remained in effect through the eighth edition published in 1815.

Freeman's plain and regular method

The first and second editions of *The town officer* (1791 and 1793) explained the entries that were to be made prior to exhibiting the accounts. It is clear upon examination of these accounts that Freeman was aware of the fiduciary nature of government. His purpose in describing [inventing?] municipal accounting was certainly to enable better control and to help assure that the monies voted by the town and collected through taxes were expended for the purposes for which they were intended.

Freeman's rules in the 1791 and 1793 editions begin with entering into the Account of the Forms (Journal), the Account of Monies voted by the town, the amount voted to be expended on each specific item. This was to be balanced by the Account of Monies Assessed. The Account of the Monies Assessed were in turn balanced by the Accounts of the Collectors.

Collectors' accounts were to be charged for the amount of the bills and any additions for which each collector was responsible. Freeman then suggested that the collectors' accounts be balanced by the Treasurer's account when the collectors bestow upon the Treasurer their receipts, the account of the unappropriated monies voted by the town, and the account of expenditures voted for the commissions of each.

The account of monies unappropriated contained: 1) the money covered in the tax bills; 2) unexpended money (surplus); 3) money acquired by the town in other ways. This account was to be balanced in turn by the Collectors' accounts for payments made on their bills and the accounts of the expenditures subsequent to appropriation of those monies.

Each authorized expenditure was to have its own account. All of these accounts were to be balanced by the account of orders drawn by the Treasurer upon the Selectmen which was an accounting of the tax collected and specification of the tax that was to be paid for expenditures. The account of orders was balanced by the Town Treasurer's account where it would be charged with the sums he received from the Collectors.

In all, Freeman recommended the use of fifteen accounts, two of which were subsidiary expenditure accounts. The general fund in modern municipal accounting bears a resemblance to the "plain and regular method" set up by Freeman in 1791. The general fund is one of eight classes of accounts recommended by the National Committee on Governmental Accounting [1951]. The general fund of a governmental unit is made up of the resources segregated for the purpose of carrying on the unit's operating activities. It is an independent fiscal and self-balancing accounting entity used to account for the flow of these resources. The general fund entity contains, as a minimum, asset, liability, surplus (fund-balance), revenue and expenditure accounts. It often contains budgetary accounts for estimated revenue and appropriations. Freeman's accounts were also used to account for the resources segregated for the purpose of carrying on the town's operating activities consisting of revenue, surplus and expenditure accounts. More interpretation is required to determine whether this set of accounts contained assets and liabilities of the town. "A plain and regular METHOD" contained budgetary accounts for estimated revenue and appropriations. *The town officer* of 1793 was remarkable in that it included many items of historical significance to accounting in the earliest days of accounting literature.

Significant contributions

Freeman recognized the fiduciary relationship of government to its citizens in his opening paragraph of the section on town accounts. This section was quoted in full above, therefore it will not be repeated here. He made provision in the accounts for a budget (estimate) and an extraordinary amount of control over the town monies. With the system recommended by Freeman an interested party could tell if the appropriations and the assessments were equal and whether or not the assessments were collected. Freeman also recommended that subsidiary accounts be kept for specific expenditures. Finally there are two places in *The town officer* where he recommends an audit of the town accounts. He also refers to a "committee of the town as may be appointed to examine and adjust said accounts" [Freeman, 1793, p. 192]. And states in a footnote, "The treasurer's account should be settled by the selectmen, and settled annually, previous to the March or April meeting" [p. 193]. The significance of the first edition of *The town officer* is clearly evident, as it was apparently the first work on municipal accounting in America.

Conclusion

Judge Samuel Freeman's *The town officer* was a most useful book to eighteenth century Americans. It provided civil servants with a handbook of duties and powers. It informed the citizens of their rights and responsibilities under the law; indeed, one of its stated purposes was to protect the public by imparting to them certain knowledge of the law of the time. Later editions also included the Constitution of the United States as well as that of the Commonwealth of massachusetts. However, the main purpose of this paper is to examine *The town officer* for its contributions to municipal accounting. It appears that Freeman's concept of town accounts resembles that of the modern day general fund. His method was complete concerning the idea of the fiduciary role of government when accounting for its citizens' monies. Freeman recommended annual audits and provided for budgetary control. That many of Freeman's recommendations still pervade modern municipal accounting proves it to be a significant writing in the early history of accountancy.

Written by Peter McMickle, Loren Wenzel, and Paul Jensen

[The authors owe a debt of gratitude to the late William Holmes of Boston, a friend and great accounting historian, who brought this work to their attention in 1976. An abbreviated version of this review was previously published in Peter L. McMickle and Richard Vangermeersch, *The Origins of a Great Profession*, Memphis: The Academy of Accounting Historians, 1987.]

References

Drake, F. S. (1872), *Dictionary of American Biography*, Boston: Osgood & Co., 1872. Detroit: Reprinted by Gale Research Co., 1974.

Municipal Finance Officers Association of the United States and Canada, *Municipal Accounting and Auditing*, Chicago: 1951.

Shipton, D. K. & Mooney, J. E. (1969), *National Index of American Imprints*, Vol. One: A-M, American Antiquarians Society and Barre Pub., 1969.

Wallace, W. S., *A Dictionary of North American Authors Deceased before 1950*, Toronto: Ryerson, 1829. Detroit: Reprinted by Gale Research Co., 1968.

A

PLAIN AND REGULAR METHOD TO KEEP

ACCOUNTS

OF THE EXPENDITURES OF MONIES VOTED BY A TOWN;

Upon an Inspection of which, the State of its Finances may at any time be known.

—+—

As one of the great Objects of Government is to guard and defend the Property of its Subjects; as no public Measures engage the attention of a People more than those which affect their Interest, and require by way of Taxes a part of their Property for public Uses; and as nothing will ensure a cheerful acquiescence in such measures but an Assurance that the Monies thus taken from them are applied to the Uses for which they were designed; it is of importance in all Communities, that proper Regulations should be established, whereby it may clearly appear, that such Monies are faithfully expended, and regularly accounted for. Too much care cannot be taken in this Business, as it relates to the raising and applying of Taxes required for the support of Government, and the Exigencies of a State; and it must be happy for the People of any State, to have such a Plan established, as shall provide effectual Checks upon the several Officers

ILLUSTRATION 22. Beginning of the accounting section in 1791 Samuel Freeman's *The town officer* . . .

> 140   ACCOUNTS.
>   (Brought over)   620
>   For building a Work-House ———   300
>   For building a Bridge over ——— River,   303
>   For future appropriations   100
>
>   Amounting in the whole to   £1123
>   Whereupon, Voted, that the Sum of £423 be appropriated for
> the following purposes, viz.
>   To make up the deficiency for Commissions £20
>   For building a Work-House   300
>   For building a Bridge over ——— River   103
>   423
> and that the Sum of £700 be raised upon the Polls and Estates of the
> Inhabitants of said Town, for the other purposes mentioned in said Es-
> timate.*
>
>   ACCOUNTS.
>
>   I.
>   ACCOUNT of MONIES voted by the Town.   Dr.
>   See page
>   1791. | 134 | To sundry Accounts of the Expenditures of
>   Monies voted Ap. 4, 1791. (See No. VI,   £
>   VII, VIII, IX, X, XI, XIV, XV,) the a- 1000
>   mount whereof is
>
>   CONTRA   Cr.
>   1791. | 134 | By Account of Monies assessed (No. II.) 1000
>
>   II.
>   ACCOUNT of MONIES Assessed.   Dr.
>   1791. | 134 | To Account of Monies voted by the Town 1000
>   (No. I.)
>   (Carried over.)
>
>   * If the Estimate be not agreeable to the Inhabitants of the Town, they
>   will before they vote the same, amend it as they see fit.

ILLUSTRATION 23. Example of town accounts from 1791 Samuel Freeman's *The town officer* . . .

THE YOUNG
BOOK-KEEPER's ASSISTANT
SHEWING HIM
In the moſt plain and eaſy Manner,
THE ITALIAN WAY OF STATING
DEBTOR *and* CREDITOR;
WITH

Proper and inſtructive Notes under every Entry in the WASTE-BOOK, where neceſſary, by which the Method of Journalizing is rendered more eaſy and intelligible; and alſo the like Notes in the JOURNAL and LEDGER, inſerted by way of Information, how to poſt the JOURNAL, and correct Errors in the LEDGER: Wherein there is a great Variety of Examples, not only in the common and ordinary Way of buying and ſelling, but in that of trading beyond the Seas, both for a Merchant's Self and in Company. All which is contained in two Setts of Books, directing the Learner, not by Precept only, but by Example, how to draw out a new Inventory from the old Books, and inſert it in the new ones; and the Trade continued as if it were in the real Shop or 'Compting Houſe.

TO WHICH IS ANNEXED

A SYNOPSIS OR COMPENDIUM

OF THE

Whole Art of ſtating DEBTOR and CREDITOR,

In all the Circumſtances of BOOK-KEEPING, both in Proper, Factorage and Company Accompts, Domeſtic and Foreign.

THE TWELFTH EDITION.

By THOMAS DILWORTH,
Author of the NEW GUIDE to the ENGLISH TONGUE
SCHOOLMASTERS ASSISTANT, &c. &c.

PHILADELPHIA:
PRINTED BY BENJAMIN JOHNSON,
No. 147, Market-Street.

ILLUSTRATION 24. Title page from the first American printing of Thomas Dilworth's *The young book-keeper's assistant* ...

Item 7. The Thomas Dilworth Series beginning 1794.

[1794? No date shown]. Thomas Dilworth. *The young book-keeper's assistant* . . . Twelfth edition. Philadelphia: Printed by Benjamin Johnson. 162 pgs. 21.5 cm. Evans 26889 NUC ND0274221

1798. Thomas Dilworth. *The young book-keeper's assistant* . . . Thirteenth edition. Wilmington: Printed by Peter Brynberg. 82 pgs. 21 cm. Evans 33640 NUC ND0274230

1803. Thomas Dilworth. *Dilworth's book-keeper's assistant improved* . . . New York: T. B. Jansen & Co. 145 [14] pgs. NUC ND0274046

1822. Thomas Dilworth. *Dilworth's book-keeper's assistant . . . Improved and adapted to the currency of the United States, by R. Wiggins.* New York: J. C. Totten. [1] [8] 128 [16] pgs. (various pagings) 22 cm. NUC ND0274047

Introduction

Dilworth was a British author and the 1794 printing was the first American publication. The significance of this book to accounting history is that it has been acclaimed by some as the first substantive book published in America that was totally devoted to accounting. While not as successful as some of his other works, Dilworth's *Young book-keeper's assistant* is a noteworthy contribution to early American accounting literature. It provided useful illustrations and helped further the education of the youth in the art of bookkeeping.

There has been considerable confusion over the numbering of editions, dates of publication, and duplication of publishers relating to this book. *The National Union Catalogue Pre-1956 Imprints* shows Thomas Dilworth's *The young bookkeeper's assistant* as being published in Philadelphia in 1789 and several publications have picked up on this date. However, the title page does not include a publication date. It appears that this first American reprint was not published in 1789, but was probably published in 1793 or 1794. The reason this has been identified as a 1789 publication is because the journal and ledger examples have a 1789 heading. However, the English 1790 eleventh edition and two English twelfth edition printings dated 1792 and 1793 also utilized the 1789 headings. Benjamin Johnson apparently obtained one of these twelfth editions and reprinted it in America as the twelfth edition without dating the title page. Both Evans and the New York Public Library date the work as 1794.

The 1803 edition published in New York included an additional section on currency exchanges between various states. The remainder of the book is basically unchanged.

Very little mention is made by history about Thomas Dilworth. Other than his noted success in writing books and his role as a schoolmaster, little else is known. He did enjoy considerable success in the publications of his *Schoolmaster's assistant, Federal calculator,* and *New guide to the english tongue.*

A review of *The young book-keeper's assistant*

In his preface, Dilworth comments "I write not so much for the Advancement of the Art itself. . . as for the ease of the Teacher, and to save him both Trouble and Time, as well as for the greater improvement of the learner. . . ." His approach to teaching is primarily by example as a five page preface and fourteen page synopsis of the rules for "stating Debitor or Creditor in all the cases" is the primary text for explanation. The remainder of the 162 page book consists of examples displaying the waste book, journal, and posting to the ledger. The body of the book contains two main examples. Each begins with the wastebook, then the journal and posting to the ledger. In addition, various notes are included with the ledger accounts, providing further instruction. Two other items are included; the cash book showing the various debits and credits to that account, and the book of house-expenses identifying items purchased for household use. At the end of the ledger, Dilworth provides an example of a trial balance.

One aspect that is unique to Dilworth's text is the purposeful inclusion of errors in the books. This is done to show the proper method of correcting such errors. Rather than erase the error, a reversing entry eliminates the effect of the error and the correct entry is then entered.

While not illustrated, several other books are mentioned in the preface. The debt-book lists "the day wherein all sums become due whether paid or received." The invoice-book contains an "Accompt of all the Goods which a merchant ships off," and the Factorage-Book contains "an account of what a merchant received to sell in Commission for others." The acquaintance or receipt-book lists everyone to whom money is paid, the book of charges of merchandize shows charges for goods bought or sold, and the letter-book contains copies of the types of letters that a merchant sends in the course of his business. Finally, the remembrance or note-book serves as a "Help of the Memory." Each of these are called "auxiliary" books while the wastebook, journal, and ledger are "necessary" books.

The final section is entitled: "A Synopsis or Compendium of Merchant's Accounts Containing Particular Rules for the True Stating of Debitor and Creditor, In all the Cases that can happen in the whole Course of a Merchant's Dealing." It is divided into three parts: 1) Proper - "wherein the Merchant trades by and for himself," 2) Factorage - "wherein the Merchant acts as a Factor in Commission, for the one that employs him," and 3) In Company - "wherein two or more Merchants join together in Trade." For each part various cases or transactions are described, and a rule is listed designating the appropriate accounts to debit and credit. It is intended as a handy reference guide for merchants and book-keepers.

Written by Peter McMickle, Paul Jensen, and Mark Turner.

(1)

The JOURNAL.

LONDON, January 1, 1789.

		l.	*s.*	*d.*	*l.*	*s.*	*d.*
	Sundry Accompts Drs. to Stock . . .	10830	14	10½			
1	Cash in ready Money	8000	0	0			
1	Tobacco, for 19 Hhds. qt. 63C. 1qr. 14*lb.* at 4*l.* 14*s.* per C.	297	17	3			
1	Pepper, for 48 Bags, qt. 1026*lb.* at 16*d.* per *lb.*	68	8	0			
2	Canary, for 16 Pipes, at 25*l.* per Pipe, .	400	0	0			
2	Hops, for 30 Bags, qt. 109C. 1qr. 12*lb.* at 2*l.* per C.	218	14	3½			
2	French Wine, for 10 Hhds. at 27*l.* per Hhd.	270	0	0			
2	Holland, for 20 Pieces, qt. 384 Ells, at 3*s.* per Ell	57	12	0			
2	Broad Cloth, for 10 Pieces, qt. 180 Yards, at 10*s.* per Yard	90	0	0			
3	Shalloon, for 7 Pieces, qt. 100 Yards, at 2*s.* 4*d.* per Yard	11	13	4			
3	Drugget, for 5 Pieces, qt. 60 Yards, at 3*s.* 6*d.* per Yard	10	10	0			
3	*Thomas Preston,* Esq; on Demand . . .	100	0	0			
3	*Sir Robert Johnson*	476	0	0			
3	*John Herbert*	250	0	0			
4	Capt. *John Smith* (to pay the 18th Instant)	580	0	0			
					10830	14	10½
1	Stock Dr. to Sundry Accompts . . .	535	13	0			
4	To Capt. *William Andrews* on Demand .	270	0	0			
4	To Sir *Humphrey Parsons* (to pay the 8th Instant)	100	0	0			
4	To *William Baker,* Esq; (to pay the 17th Instant)	150	0	0			
4	To *Watson Warner*	15	13	0			
					535	13	—

Note, The *Inventory* being journalized, as above, you must next turn to your *Ledger,* and therein erect an Account for each of these Particulars, in the following Manner:

(1.) You must begin with *Stock,* and in a good round Text-Hand, on the left Folium of the Book, write *Stock Dr.* and on the right Folium, in the same Hand, write *Per Contra Cr.*

(2.) Because Sundry Accompts are Drs. to *Stock,* you must, in your *Ledger,* make *Stock Cr.* by Sundry Accompts, expressing the whole Value.

(3.) Make every particular Part Dr. to *Stock* for its Quantity (which mention in your inner Columns) and Value respectively.

(4.) Beginning these Particulars with *Cash,* you must, as in *Stock,* make *Cash Dr. per Contra Cr.* and then beneath, in small Hand,

ILLUSTRATION 25. Journal example in 1794 Thomas Dilworth's *The young book-keeper's assistant.* . . .

DILWORTH'S
BOOK-KEEPERS ASSISTANT
IMPROVED:

SHOWING HIM, IN THE MOST PLAIN AND EASY MANNER,

THE *ITALIAN* WAY OF STATING

DEBTOR AND CREDITOR.

WITH

Proper and instructive Notes under every entry made in the Waste-Book, where necessary, by which the method of journalizing is rendered more easy and intelligible; and also the like Notes in the Journal and Ledger, inserted by way of information how to post the Journal, and correct the errors in the Ledger; wherein there is a great variety of Examples, not only in the common and ordinary way of buying and selling, but in that of Trading beyond the Seas, both for a Merchant's self and in company. All which is contained in two sets of books, directing the Learner, not by precepts only, but by Example, how to draw out a new Inventory from the old Books, and insert it in the new ones; and the trade conceived as if it were in the real shop or 'compting-house'.

TO WHICH IS ANNEXED,

A SYNOPSIS OR COMPENDIUM

OF THE

WHOLE ART OF STATING DEBTOR AND CREDITOR,

In all the circumstances of Book-keeping, both in proper Factorage, and Company Accompts, Domestic and Foreign.

THE WHOLE

DESIGNED FOR THE USE OF SCHOOLS,

FOR THE HELP AND ASSISTANCE OF MERCHANTS IN THEIR SEVERAL COMPTING-HOUSES; AND FOR YOUNG GENTLEMEN AT THEIR FIRST ENTRANCE ON THEIR MERCANTILE APPRENTICESHIPS.

THE LIKE, FOR BENEFIT TO THE SCHOLAR, AND EASE TO THE MASTER, NOT EXTANT.

IMPROVED AND CORRECTED FROM THE
LAST LONDON EDITION.

COPY-RIGHT SECURED.

PUBLISHED AND SOLD BY T. B. JANSEN & CO.
Booksellers & Stationers, No. 248 Pearl-Street.
L. NICHOLS, PRINTER, NO. 308 BROADWAY.

1803.

ILLUSTRATION 26. Title page from the 1803 *Dilworth's Book-keepers assistant improved* . . .

Item 8. The Richard Turner Series beginning 1794.

INTRODUCTION TO BOOK KEEEING,
AFTER THE
ITALIAN ME HOD,

DEBTOR AND CREDITOR:
IN WHICH
The THEORY of that Art is not only elucidated, but the PRACTICE made eafy and familiar, by the Addition of a
SET of BOOKS,
Exhibiting the various Incidents which ufually fall in a Courfe of Bufinefs.

THE WHOLE
Laid down in a Manner fo eafy and intelligible as to be underftood in a few Days.

To which is added,
Several FORMS of BILLS, &c.

By the Rev. R. TURNER, LL. D.
Author of a "VIEW of the EARTH"—"A VIEW of the HEAVENS"—"The HEAVENS SURVEYED"—PLAIN TRIGONOMETRY," &c. &c.

The FIRST AMERICAN EDITION,
FROM THE THIRD ENGLISH EDITION.

Deliver all Things in Number and Weight, and put all in Writing that thou givest out, or receivest in.—ECCLES. xlii. 5.

PRINTED at BOSTON,
By I. THOMAS AND E. T. ANDREWS.
FAUST'S STATUE, No. 45, NEWBURY STREET.

1794.

ILLUSTRATION 27. Title page from 1794 Richard Turner's *A new introduction to book keeping* ...

Item 8. 1794. Richard Turner. *A new introduction to book keeping*... First American Edition. Boston: Printed by I. Thomas and E. T. Andrews. 24 [3] [17] [3] pgs. (various pagings) 16 cm. Evans 27824 NUC NT0397210

Other American Printings:

1801. Richard Turner. *A new introduction to book-keeping* ... Salem, Massachusetts: Printed for Cushing & Appleton. 52 pgs. (various pagings). 15 cm. SS 144 NUC NT0397211

1820. Richard Turner. *A new introduction to book-keeping* ... Salem, Massachusetts: Printed for Cushing & Appleton and printed by J. D. Cushing. 81 pgs. (various pagings) 18.5 cm. SS 3499 NUC NT0397212

1824. Richard Turner. *A new introduction to book-keeping* ... Salem, Massachusetts: Cushing & Appleton. 67 pgs. (various pagings) 18 cm. NUC NT0397213

1825. Richard Turner. *A new introduction to book-keeping* ... Salem, Massachusetts: James R. Buffum. 67 pgs. (various pagings) 18 cm. NUC NT0397214

Also contained as a back section in:

1820. Michael Walsh. *A new system of mercantile arithmetic* ... Fourth edition. Salem, Massachusetts: Published by Cushing & Appleton(Proprietors), printed by J. D. Cushing. [11] [1] 265 [54] pgs. (various pagings). 18 cm. NUC NW0053531 (Earlier printings had no bookkeeping)

Other American Printings with book-keeping section:

1822. Michael Walsh. *A new system of mercantile arithmetic* ... Fourth edition. Salem, Massachusetts: Publshed by Cushing & Appleton (Proprietors). [11] [1] 264 [54] pgs. (various pagings). 18 cm. NUC NW0053534

1824. Michael Walsh. *A new system of mercantile arithmetic* ... *Fourth edition.* Salem, Massachusetts: Published by Cushing & Appleton (Proprietors). [11] [1] 264 [67] pgs. (various pagings). 18 cm. NUC NW0053535

1826. Michael Walsh. *The mercantile arithmetic ... a new edition, revised and improved.* Boston: Richardson & Lord. 248 [59] pgs. (Various pagings) 19 cm. NUC NW0053510

1828. Michael Walsh. *A new system of practical book-keeping ...* Boston: Richardson and Lord. NUC NW0053537

1828. Michael Walsh. *The mercantile arithmetic ... a new edition, revised and improved.* Boston: Richardson & Lord. [7] [2] [5] 225 [76] pgs. 19 cm. NUC NW0053511

1831. Michael Walsh. *The mercantile arithmetic ... a new edition, stereotyped, revised and enlarged.* Boston: Richardson and Holbrook. 336 pgs. (Various pagings) NUC NW0053512

1832. Michael Walsh. [Key] *Bookkeeping ... to which is added a key to certain parts of the mercantile arithmetic ...* Boston: Carter, Hendee and Co. [2] 78 pgs. (Not in NUC)

1833. Michael Walsh. *The mercantile arithmetic ... a new edition, stereotyped, revised and enlarged.* Boston: Carter, Hendee, and Co. NUC NW0053513

1835. Michael Walsh. *The mercantile arithmetic ... a new edition, stereotyped, revised and enlarged.* Boston: Carter, Hendee, and Co. [7] [1] 328 pgs. 18.5 cm. NUC NW0053515

1836. Michael Walsh. *The mercantile arithmetic ... a new edition, stereotyped, revised and enlarged.* Boston: C. J. Hendee. [7] [2] 327 pgs. 19.5 cm. NUC NW0053516

1838. Michael Walsh. *The mercantile arithmetic ... a new edition, stereotyped, revised and enlarged.* Boston: C. J. Hendee and G. W. Palmer and Co. [7] [2] 327 pgs. 19.5 cm. NUC NW0053516

Introduction

One of the more popular bookkeeping books during the eighteenth and early nineteenth centuries in America was Richard Turner's *A new introduction to book-keeping.* These books are reprints of Turner's 1761 book published in London. Yet, no reference is made to this book in any British bibliography (Watt, 1824; Allibone, 1900). Even though Turner is credited with writing many books, no major British collection of accounting books contains a copy of Turner's three British editions (British Museum, 1964, 1968, 197a4, 1980; Wright and Purnell, 1968a, 1968b; Purnell, 1953; CAs Eng. & Wales, 1975; CAs Scotland, 1976; Yamey, et. al., 1963). Two copies of the 1761 edition are known to exist (NUC, 1968, V. 605, p. 252) and both copies are in American university libraries.

Understanding why Turner's British editions were overlooked, but his American editions were so popular requires an examination of three factors. First, who was Richard Turner; second, what was in his book; and third, what was happening in British and American accounting.

Richard Turner the man

Richard Turner was born in Great Webley, Worcester, England around 1724. In 1748, at the age of 24, Turner graduated from Magdalen Hall, Oxford University. He became Rector of Camberton in 1752. Two years later, 1754, he became Vicar of Elmley (Foster, 1968). By 1765 he had returned to Worcester as a teacher of Geometry, Astronomy and Philosophy (Watt, 1824). He appears to have continued to live in Worcester until his death on April 13, 1791.

During his later years (1761-1791) Turner wrote several books. These include: *The young gauger's best instructor 1762*; *A view of the earth 1762 (a geography text); Plain trigonometry rendered easy 1765; A view of the earth as far as it was known to the ancients 1779* (classical Geography); *A view of the heavens 1783 (an astronomy text); and Universal history 1787* (Watt, 1824; Alliborn, 1900). Turner was a man of many and wide ranging interests. Like many mathematicians of the period he probably considered bookkeeping a branch of mathematics. Turner's interest in bookkeeping seems to have peaked with the printing of his 1761 edition.

Item 8. The Richard Turner Series beginning 1794.

A Description of *A new introduction to book-keeping*

Turner's books were mainly introductory texts for school children. The title of his 1761 edition reveals that this was also his intention with this book. The full title was: "*A New Introduction to Book-Keeping After the Italian Method by Debtor and Creditor; in Which the Theory of That Art is not only Illucidated (sic) and Clearly Explained, but the Practice Made Easy and Familiar, by the Addition of a Set of Books, Exhibiting the Various Incidents, Which Usually fall in the Course of Business, the Whole Laid Down in a Manner so Easy and Intelligible as to be Understood in a Few Days.*" Today this book would probably be titled "*Principles of Accounting.*"

Several other facts can be gleaned from the title page. Turner describes himself as a "Teacher of Geometry, Astronomy, &C. at Worcester." The printer is also revealed as S. Crowder in Pater-Noster-Row, London. Crowder printed all of Turner's books until 1779 (NUC, 1968) when Crowder went bankrupt. (Plomer et.al., 1982) Unlike the other surviving editions the publication date is in Roman numerals (MDCCLXI) instead of Arabic numerals (1761). Finally the title page includes a quote from the Bible; "Deliver all things in NUMBER and WEIGHT, and put all in WRITING that thou GIVEST OUT OR RECEIVEST IN." ECCLUS. xiii. 5., which is included on the title page of every known edition of Turner's book.

The next page contains the author's preface. It was addressed "To the master's intrusted with the education of youth and to the youth themselves". The preface was signed "The Author." The entire preface was written as a single sentence. After the preface is the main text which can be divided into three sections.

The first section was a description of the three main books of accompt (sic) and how to record common entries. The three main books were the waste-book, journal and leidger (sic). Each book was described in one or two short paragraphs.

After describing the three main books of accompt, the methods for recording several transactions were described. These included entering the inventory, commodities bought in, commodities sold out, bartering, borrowing and lending, bills, accidental losses, accidental profits, foreign trade and household expenses. The inventory was a complete listing of all assets owned by the merchant at their market value and all liabilities owed by the merchant with the difference recorded in the stock (owner's equity) account.

Sales of merchandise were recorded by crediting the appropriate merchandise account such as cider, cheese or sugar. When the books were closed the profit or loss was determined for each commodity and closed to the profit and loss (income summary) account. When barter transactions occurred the new merchandise was recorded at its market value. The old merchandise account was credited for the market value of the merchandise received.

Turner debited certain expenses and credited certain income directly to the profit and loss account. These transactions were accidental losses, household expenses and accidental profits. Accidental losses included gifts to others, spoilage, and gambling losses. Household expenses included all the costs of running the merchants household. Accidental profits included all gifts, inheritances received, and gambling winnings.

The second section consisted of a waste-book, journal and ledger. These contain a series of entries which illustrate those types of transactions covered in the first section. Turner shows several compound entries, and also uses posting references extensively in his examples. The posting references make it simple to track an example from the waste-book to the journal and to the ledger. The book only illustrates entries for a sole-proprietorship type of business. It was the first edition to use dollars and cents exclusively. Also an additional waste-book was added after the 'forms of bills' section. The second waste-book was provided so the reader could have additional practice recording journal entries and ledger postings.

Turner provided good examples and explanations of the necessary transactions. Following are some discussions of his example presentations.

Every occurrence of trade was recorded in the waste-book in

the same order as they actually transpired.

The entries were made in memorandum form on pages ruled with a margin on the left side of the page (where a "J" is placed to indicate that the accompt has been posted to the Journal) and two columns on the right side of the page for "doll cts." (the dollars and cents amounts).

The journal contained the same information found in the waste-book, however, each case was listed more methodically and with specific mention of debtor, creditor and sum of money. It was ruled in the same manner as the waste book with one exception: there were two columns in the left hand margin to indicate the debtor and creditor pages of the posting in the ledger. The date appeared below the transaction.

The ledger was the largest book (it contained the most material). There was a particular accompt for every person dealt with and for every commodity traded. Every entry was "written-double:" the left page showed the debtor and the right page showed the creditor (contra credit). It was ruled with a left hand margin for the day and month, and a column for folio before the doll ct. columns. Note: to aid in finding an accompt in the ledger, there should be an alphabetical listing of all ledger accounts, in the beginning of the book, including the folio where the accompt itself was posted.

In order to use these books properly, Turner suggested one general rule to follow that was said to be able to "carry you through the whole mystery of bookkeeping." This rule follows: whatever comes to you is creditor; and whatever you part with or goes from you is creditor, while the receiving account is the debtor.

The author offered further advice to the bookkeeper: to always post debits first and then credits, to always examine the waste-book before journalizing and the journal before posting, and to remember to always journalize and post in the exact order in which the entries occur.

For the most part this book explained how to keep accounts but with little reference to timing. Dates were important as a means of keeping order, but as for exactly when to balance and close accounts or when to open new sets of books - little was offered. For instance, the ledger was balanced when all journal transactions had been posted. A new account was then formed entitled "Balance Debtor" with the accompanying account entitled "Contra Credit." And, finally, each ledger account was totalled and entered on the corresponding side of the Balance account. This account was considered rightly stated when both sides were equal in amounts. Here again, a potential fallacy, since errors and fraud could be disguised in recording and posting.

In addition to the three books already mentioned there were several other auxiliary books that were necessary for different kinds of businesses. They were as follows: cash book, invoice book, letter book, bill book, house expense book, charges-on-merchandise book, receipt book and till-book. (Examples of these books were included in Turner's book).

There was also a section entitled "Mercantile Precedents" which included examples of different forms, for example, a Foreign Bill of Exchange.

And, finally, Turner wrote about the journal and ledger adapted to single entry bookkeeping. And he gave several illustrations. This approach offered the utmost simplicity and plainness.

With the single entry method the words "dr." are written above the entry when the account is debtor and the work "cr." above an entry to a creditor. Sometimes two entries are necessary.

The 1820 through 1825 editions stated that they were written "on the plan R. Turner, L.L.D." and "revised and improved by a merchant". The revising consisted of forms such as several kinds of receipts, invoices and a settlement statement from a consignment sale. Second, a set of single entry books was added after the 1801 practice waste-book. The single entry books are a curious blend of single and double entry accounting.

Turner's writing dealt with the Italian method of keeping accompts (accounts) which primarily involved the following three books: the waste-book, the journal and the ledger. (Examples of these books and recordings were included in Turner's book).

British and American Accounting in the Late Eighteenth and Early Nineteenth Century

During the latter half of the eighteenth century in Britain two changes were occurring in British accounting and British accounting literature (Brown, 1905; Green, 1930; Murry, 1930). Scottish accountants began to dominate British accounting and accounting literature; also, Edinburgh and London became the primary centers for British accounting and accounting education. Turner, a non-accountant from the hinderlands was probably not taken very seriously by these accountants. Accounting historians, furthermore, generally viewed most of the accounting books, except Jones' *English system* . . . printed between 1750 and 1800 as unimportant (Brown, 1905, p. 181). Any introductory accounting book from this period was likely to be overlooked or downgraded in importance.

After the South Seas Company bankruptcy in 1723, the accounting books on the cutting edge of theory needed chapters on partnership and corporation accounting. Turner's book did not discuss either area. All of these factors combined condemned Turner's book to obscurity in Britain.

In America, however, few books had been printed by 1820 which even mentioned bookkeeping. American businessmen were still predominately small merchants, although medium-sized corporations were beginning to appear. There was a need for a simple explanation of double entry bookkeeping. Turner's book filled this need very well. The same elements in the book which condemned it to obscurity in Britain contributed to its popularity in America.

Conclusion

Richard Turner's book was overlooked in Britain for three main reasons. He was not a professional accountant. He was isolated from the major centers of accounting activity. His book was just one more introduction to bookkeeping among many. His book achieved popularity in America for two reasons. Very few bookkeeping books were available in America at the time and his book described the kinds of transactions encountered by many American merchants of the period. Had Turner taught and written in Boston instead of Worcester, England, he might have achieved popular acclaim during his lifetime instead of after his death.

Written by Greg Nelson, Mark Turner, Peter McMickle and Paul Jensen.

References

Allibone, S. Austin, *Dictionary of English Literature and British and American Authors,* (Vol 3, p. 2480), New York: J. B. Lippincott Company, 1900.

British Museum, *General Catalogue of Printed Books to 1955,* (Vol. 242, p 603), London: Balding & Mansell, 1964.

--------, *General Catalogue of Printed Books Ten-Year Supplement 1956-1965,* (Vol. 46, p 734), London: Balding & Mansell, 1968.

--------, *General Catalogue of Printed Books Five-Year Supplement 1966-1970,* (Vol. 3, p. 886), Chester, Vermont: Readex Microprint Corporation, 1974.

--------, *General Catalogue of Printed Books Five-Year Supplementa 1971-1975,* (Vol. 2, p. 1237) Chester, Vermont: Readex Microprint Corporation, 1974.

Brown, Richard, Editor, *A History of Accounting and Accountants,* London: Frank Cass & Co., 1905; Reprinted, New York: Augustus M. Kelly, Publishers, 1971.

Foster, Joseph, ed., *Alumni Oxonieses 1715-1886 Series 2,* (Vol. 3-4, p. 1450), New York: Kraus Reprint Ltd., 1968.

Green, Wilmer L., *History and Survey of Accountancy,* Brooklyn: Standard Text Press, 1930; Reprinted, Nihon Shoseki, Ltd., 1974.

Herwood & Herwood, CPAs, *The Herwood Library of Accountancy* (pp. 199-200), New York: Herwood & Herwood Certified Public Accountants, 1938.

Institute of Chartered Accounts in England and Wales, *Historical Accounting Literature,* (p. 2351), London: Mansel Information, 1975.

Institute of Chartered Accountants of Scotland, *An Accountant's Book Collection 1494-1930,*. 3rd edition, (p. 52), Edinburgh: Institute of Chartered Accountants of Scotland, 1976.

Murray, David, *Chapters in the History of Bookkeeping Accountancy and Commercial Arithmetic*, Glascow: Jackson, Wylie & Co., 1930.

The Montgomery Library of Accountancy in Columbia University A Checklist of Books, Printed before 1850, in the Montgomery Library of Accountancy at Columbia University, New York: Columbia University Press, 1927.

The National Union Catalogue Pre-1956 Imprints, (Vol. 605, p. 252), London: Mansel Information, 1968.

Plomer, H. R., Bushnell, G.H., and McC. Dix, E.R. *A Dictionary of the Printers and Booksellers.. in England, Scotland and Ireland from 1726 to 1775*, (pp. 6768), London: Oxford University Press, 1932.

Purnell, C. J., ed. *Catalogue of the London Library Third Supplement 1928-1950,* London: London Library, 1953.

Richard Turner, *A new introduction to book keeping...* First American Edition, Boston: Printed by I. Thomas and E. T. Andrews. 1794.

_____. *A new introduction to book-keeping ...* Salem, Massachusetts: Printed for Cushing & Appleton, 1801.

_____. *A new introduction to book-keeping ...* Salem, Massachusetts: Printed for Cushing & Appleton and printed by J. D. Cushing, 1820.

_____. *A new introduction to book-keeping ...* Salem, Massachusetts: Printed for Cushing & Appleton and printed by J. D. Cushing, 1824,1825.

Watt, Robert, *Bibliotheca Britannica or A General Index to British and Foreign Literature,* (Vol. 2, p. 1142), London: Archibald Constable and Company, 1824.

Item 8. The Richard Turner Series beginning 1794.

Wright, C. T. and Purnell, C. J., ed., *Catalogue of the London Library,* (Vol. 2, p. 1142), London: London Library, 1914; Reprinted, New York: Kraus Reprint Ltd., 1968.

_____. *Catalogue of the London Library Supplement 1920-1928,* (p. 942), London: London Library, 1929, Reprinted, New York: Kraus Reprint Ltd., 1968.

Yamey, B. S., Edey, H. C. and Thompson, H.W., *Accounting in England and Scotland: 1543-1800,* London: Sweet & Maxwell, 1963.

A NEW
INTRODUCTION
TO
BOOK-KEEPING,
AFTER THE
ITALIAN METHOD,
BY
DEBTOR AND CREDITOR:

IN WHICH THE THEORY OF THAT ART IS NOT ONLY ELUCIDATED, BUT THE PRACTICE MADE EASY AND FAMILIAR, BY THE ADDITION OF A

SET OF BOOKS,

EXHIBITING THE VARIOUS INCIDENTS WHICH USUALLY FALL IN A COURSE OF BUSINESS.

THE WHOLE LAID DOWN IN A MANNER SO EASY AND INTELLIGIBLE AS TO BE UNDERSTOOD IN A FEW DAYS.

WITH A

WASTE-BOOK

SUBJOINED AS AN EXAMPLE FOR PRACTICE.

AND ALL THE ACCOUNTS ARE REDUCED TO THE FEDERAL CURRENCY.

ON THE PLAN OF R. TURNER, LL. D.

REVISED AND IMPROVED BY A MERCHANT.

Deliver all things in NUMBER and WEIGHT, and put all in WRITING that thou GIVEST OUT or RECEIVEST IN.   ECCLUS. xlii. 8.

SALEM:
PRINTED FOR CUSHING & APPLETON.
J. D. Cushing, Print.
1820.

ILLUSTRATION 28. Title page from 1820 *A new introduction to book-keeping . . . on the plan of R. Turner, LL.D.*

46

Boston, March 1st, 1819.	$.	c.

An Inventory of the Money, Wares and Debts belonging to me, A B, taken this day, as follows, viz.

	dols. cts.		
I have, in money	1009,24½		
6 bags of hops, at 10,00 per bag	60,00		
2 pipes of wine, at 65,50 per pipe	131,00		
5 pieces of broadcloth, at 90,10 per piece	450,50		
Thomas Richards owes me, on demand	25,75		
10 cwt. of Gloucester cheese, at 4,00	40,00		
8 cwt. of Cheshire do. at 3,37½	26,20		
2 hogsheads of tobacco, at 39,60	79,20		
John Jones owes me	97,15		
Andrew Thompson owes me	20,00		
William Cowley owes me	2,45		
1 chest of sugar, weighing 3 cwt. 2 qrs. value	18,32½		
Samuel Taylor owes me	20,71	1980	53

I am Indebted,

	d. c.		
To John Forrest	10,00		
To Richard Payton	17,50		
To James Morgan	40,00	67	50

ILLUSTRATION 29. Waste-book example from 1820 *A new introduction to book-keeping ... on the plan of R. Turner, LL.D.*

		21 Boston, February 16th, 1819.	$.	C.
8		Voyage to New-York Dr. to Sundry Accounts,		
	4	To Cheese, for 2 cwt. 8,75¼		
	1	To Cash paid freight and custom . 2,33¼	11	09
		——— 20th. ———		
3		William Cowley Dr. to Sundry Accounts,		
	8	To Voyage to New-York . . . 11,09		
	7	To Profit and Loss gained by selling cheese 7,23¼	18	32¼
		——— 23d. ———		
3		Sugar Dr. to Sundry Accounts,		
	8	To William Cowley, for one chest, neat weight 3 cwt. 2 quarters . 15.87¼		
	1	To Cash paid freight and custom . 2,45	18	32¼
		——— 25th. ———		
1		Cash Dr. to Profit and Loss,		
	7	For a legacy left me by my uncle . .	20	00
		——— 27th. ———		
7		Profit and Loss Dr. to Cash,		
	1	Paid for supporting the poor	0	87¼
		End of the Journal.		

ILLUSTRATION 30. Journal example from 1820 *A new introduction to book-keeping* ... on the plan of R. Turner, LL.D.

JONES's

ENGLISH SYSTEM

of

Book-Keeping,

BY SINGLE OR DOUBLE ENTRY,

IN WHICH IT IS IMPOSSIBLE FOR AN ERROR OF THE MOST TRIFLING AMOUNT
TO BE PASSED UNNOTICED;

CALCULATED EFFECTUALLY TO PREVENT THE EVILS ATTENDANT ON THE
METHODS SO LONG ESTABLISHED;

ADAPTED TO EVERY SPECIES OF TRADE.

FIRST AMERICAN EDITION.

New-York:
PRINTED BY WILLIAM A. DAVIS,
FOR THOMAS ALLEN, BOOKSELLER AND STATIONER, N° 16, PEARL-STREET.
1796.

ILLUSTRATION 31. Title page from 1796 *Jones's English system of book-keeping, by single or double entry* . . .

Item 9. 1796. [Edward T. Jones., no author listed] *Jones's English system of book-keeping, by single or double entry...* First American edition. New York: Printed by William A. Davis for Thomas Allen. (Various pagings) 26.5 cm. Evans 30644 NUC NJ0148079

Other American Printings:

1797. Edward T. Jones. *Jones's English system of bookkeeping, by single or double entry...* Second American edition. New York: Printed by G. Forman for James Hyer. [56] pgs. (various pagings) 26 cm. Evans 32323 NUC NJ0148080

1816. Edward T. Jones. *Jones's English system of bookkeeping, by single or double entry...* First Western edition. Cincinnati: Published by W. C. Drew. [52] pgs. (various pagings) 27 cm. SS 37965 NUC NJ0148081

It was Jones' intention to introduce a method of bookkeeping that will not allow "evils," such as false statements, errors and obscurity in accounts. Jones was bred in the profession and after spending many years inspecting books with many such evils decided to devise a new system. After five years of work he developed the system introduced in this publication. His system made use of a daybook for original entries as they occur and a ledger with an account for every person with whom he traded. He recognized the fact that a ledger that balanced was not necessarily correct, so, to correct this weakness of the Italian system, he proposed that the day book and the ledger should be used as separate scales. If the totals of these two scales were equal, then the books were considered correctly stated. He criticized the Italian method by saying "Would two pictures being exactly alike, prove that they were a correct copy of the original?" He was referring to the debit and credit columns when he said "two pictures exactly alike and sought to present two different scenes to check the validity of the information.

Jones' system required that the entries in the day-book be posted directly to the ledger. His system does not incorporate a journal. The information was first posted to the ledger according to the month that transpired. Then at the end of the month the total amount of transaction for the month was entered in another column.

Thus, in a small space each transaction was listed separately and a monthly statement was presented for ease in preparing a monthly trial balance if so desired. If this system was adopted, the bookkeeping would post information daily, and it would be easy to determine whether the books were correctly posted, and if not, where the errors occurred. He mentions this error saving and finding concept repeatedly, but it does not appear that the system is as fool-proof as he would have liked.

Jones included an advertisement in his book, and following this ad page was a section which listed 529 names of subscribers. According to the publisher, this list was incomplete. The book contained 56 pages, all of which were devoted to accounting.

There were also two other editions of Jones' book. The only change in the Second American edition was a different publisher. The Third Western edition had a different publisher and included an additional "table of monies."

Written by Mary Helen Ola

CONTENTS.

INTRODUCTION.

	Page
	1
	3
Of the Cash Book	4
———Day Book	
———Bill Book	6

THE FIRST SET OF BOOKS. A.
On Retail Trade

Cash Book	10
Day Book	16
Ledger	68
Remarks	78

THE SECOND SET OF BOOKS. B.
On Domestic & Foreign trade.

Cash Book	80
Day Book	107
Bill Book	142
Ledger	158
Balance Check	204
General Remarks	207

AUXILIARY BOOKS.

Sales Book	213
Progressive Bill Book	226
Account Current Book	237
Invoice Book	241
Bank Book	243

ILLUSTRATION 32. Table of contents page from 1796 William Mitchell's *A new and complete system of book-keeping* . . .

Item 10. 1796. William Mitchell.

A
NEW AND COMPLETE SYSTEM
OF
BOOK-KEEPING,
BY AN IMPROVED METHOD
OF
DOUBLE ENTRY;
ADAPTED TO
RETAIL, DOMESTIC AND FOREIGN TRADE:

EXHIBITING A VARIETY OF TRANSACTIONS
WHICH USUALLY OCCUR IN BUSINESS.

THE WHOLE COMPRISED IN THREE SETS OF BOOKS;

The last Set, being a copy of the Second according to those systems most generally in use, is given in order to exhibit, by a comparative view, the advantages of the system now laid down.

TO WHICH IS ADDED,

A TABLE OF THE DUTIES PAYABLE ON GOODS, WARES AND MERCHANDISE, IMPORTED INTO THE UNITED STATES OF AMERICA.

THE WHOLE IN DOLLARS AND CENTS.

By WILLIAM MITCHELL.

Philadelphia,
PRINTED BY BIOREN & MADAN.
1796.

ILLUSTRATION 33. Title page from 1796 William Mitchell's *A new and complete system of book-keeping* . . .

Item 10. 1796. William Mitchell. *A new and complete system of book-keeping, by an improved method of double entry*... **Philadelphia: Printed by Bioren and Madan.** [8] 454 pgs. 21.5 cm. Evans 30802 NUC NM0654391

Other American Printings: No other known printings.

Introduction

William Mitchell was born in 1763 and died in 1854, but little else is known about his life. Mitchell wrote the book at the age of 32 and, although he lived to be 91, this was the sole edition of his only known publication. [Bywater and Yamey, p. 200]

When published in 1796, Mitchell's book had to compete with imported copies of British works as well as reprints and adaptations of British works published in America. Notable among these was Jones' *English system of bookkeeping* which was published in America in the same year, 1796 [Bywater and Yamey, ibid].

Mitchell's work was not popular enough to merit subsequent editions. This may have been due to its relatively difficult appearance caused by only twenty-eight pages of explanatory text out of four hundred and fifty total pages. The bulk of the work is made up of three sets of model accounts since Mitchell believed the proper method of studying bookkeeping was to concentrate on the accounts, rather than on "elaborate and minute descriptions" [Bywater and Yamey, ibid].

Mitchell particularly criticized Mair's book for being overburdened with rules, problems, and cases, causing the aspiring bookkeeper to become "bewildered and lost" [p. vi]. He termed the use of the classical "Italian method" using waste-book, journal, and ledger as being too difficult to record the transactions of business. His chief objection was the "unwieldy method" of opening separate ledger accounts for each type of merchandise. Instead, he uses a single merchandise account for all merchandise, but goes on to suggest that if a merchant wants to keep a separate account for a particular type of merchandise , "in order to see how it comes out," it could be done by the creation of a separate sales book [p.448].

The main theme of the work is to demonstrate that only one book of original entry is needed for a complete system of double entry bookkeeping. Mitchell was familiar with the writings of Daniel Dowling, William Jackson, John Mair, Thomas Dilworth, and Robert Hamilton. These authors had presented the classical or "Italian Method" of double entry which required that all transactions should first be recorded, in a narrative style, in a small book called a memorandum, waste book, or day book. Information from the day book was later transferred to the more formal journal and at regular intervals the journal was posted to the ledger.

Mitchell recognized that two books of original entry caused an unnecessary duplication of effort. His system divides the day book into a cash book, day book and bill book. The journal is eliminated and posting is made directly to the ledger.

Although Mitchell probably developed these innovations independently, he was not the first author to recognize this weakness in the classical system. As early as 1567, John Weddington had recommended a similar system and several other authors before Mitchell had also developed such "new" systems of bookkeeping. It was not until the late 1800's that the use of one book of original entry (the Journal) became generally accepted.

A Comment on Mitchell's Preface

The author's preface appears to be the beginning of an academic defense of the work undertaken. At the very outset, it is stated that this work ". . .differs from the Systems of Dowling, Mair, and others now in general practice." He commented that the purpose of his change from current practice was that the present systems were too elaborate and just not good for general business. The description of the system to be "laid down" is "A System combining, in a considerable degree, the simplicity of Single, with all the advantages of Double Entry. . . ."

Mitchell considered the current systems of accounting, Mairs especially, as too burdened with rules, problems, etc.. However, Mitchell's was an unusually large book consisting of 454 pages and held for over 50 years the distinction of being the longest American accounting book. In addition to eliminating the journal and attempting to simplify the text material, another advantage discussed in his preface was that it was being done in dollars and cents, which the author felt was superior to currencies. It was the first book to present accounts in dollars and cents. However, Chauncey Lee was the first to use and explain the dollar mark symbols. Mitchell also hoped that Congress would standardize weights and measures the same way it had Federalized currency. This particular preface seemed to be a defense of a treatise presented to one's peers and consumed six pages in its entirety.

Description of *A new and complete system*

Mitchell's book contains 454 pages, of which 28 pages were devoted for the explanatory text and the rest devoted to the presentation of three sets of model accounts. Mitchell avoided giving larger descriptions or remarks on the numerous books because he believed that more real knowledge of book-keeping would be obtained from paying attention to the actual statements of accounts than from the most elaborate and minute description. It might be interesting to note that this method of extensive examples and little explanation was popular at this time. In addition, it follows the hallowed method of teaching by lecture. Books were relatively expensive items, thus the student had an example and it was up to the tutor to fill in the individual explanation.

He divides the books used in his system into two groups: 1) The requisite books consisting of the cash book, the day book, the bill book, and the ledger; and, 2) The auxiliary books which consist of the sales book, progressive bill book, account current book, invoice book, bank book, letter book, insurance book, receipt book, petty charges book, postage book, and memorandum book.

Mitchell provides examples using three sets of books. The first example is the set of books of a retail business. The second set is adapted for the domestic and foreign merchant, and the third set is a copy of the second, according to the systems of Dowling, Jackson, Mair, Dilworth, Hamilton, and others. He also adds a table of duties payable on goods, wares, and merchandise, imported into the United States of America.

Mitchell explains the requisite books in detail, then he illustrates the cash book, the day book, and the ledger for the retail or country storekeeper without explanation; being upon a plain, simple, and easy method readily understood by any one who has never been accustomed to accounts. He recommends strongly, "the entering the first day book all the articles purchased as a matter of convenience in having at all time for inspection of an account of all the purchased goods."

The second set of books is for the domestic and foreign merchant, exhibiting transactions in business in the cash book, the day book, the bill book, and the ledger. This particular example began on page 79 and concluded on page 204. Mitchell recommends that the Ledger should be posted from the cash, bill and day books at the end of each month. The principal advantages of his system of bookkeeping are the arrangement of entries into the three primary books, the postings of the same at once into the ledger, and the readiness with which any account in the ledger may be investigated. Besides the four principle books, he also explains and illustrates the Auxiliary or Subsidiary Books: Sales Book, Progressive Bill Book, Invoice Book, and Bank Book. He explains the Balance Check which completely detects any errors and omissions.

This extraordinary explanation of error removal in this new system is given on page 204. It is used for checking all transactions, plus both sides of the ledger. His section entitled Balance and Checks to Second Set of Books, though short, gives an interesting insight for simplifying error detection. In the form of a formula it looks like this:

Cash Dr. + Cash Cr. + Merchandise Dr. + Merchandise Cr. + Bills Dr. + Bills Cr. + Sundries Dr. = Ledger Dr. OR Ledger Cr.

It is a rather neat method of error detection. In addition, it can help lead one to the account which may be in error (or omitted). Keep in mind that this particular system is a hybrid single/double entry. For verification, the example in the text was analyzed. It works!

The third set of books was intended to compare his system with those of Dowling, Jackson, Mair, Dilworth, and others which usually used three books: waste book, journal, and ledger. It is an example of what perhaps was considered to be "generally accepted" at the writing of this text. Mitchell shows that his system requires much less labor and time than the others' systems. The entries used were the same as put forth in the second set discussed above, but were to illustrate the complexity of this 'generally accepted' method. This set consisted of the Waste book, journal, index, and ledger. It approximates what would be called the 'Italian method'. This particular recopy of transactions from the second set above entailed the use of pages 250 to 447, more than 70 pages longer than the premise put forth by the author in the second set. Every transaction of others' systems requires at least four distinct entries; first into the waste book; second, into the journal; third to the Dr.; and, fourth to the Cr. of the respective accounts in the ledger. Mitchell's method reduces the repetition of entries. He complains that using Journals would tend only to consume the bookkeeper's time unnecessarily and occasionally cause errors and omissions, often arising from copying, which might otherwise be avoided.

Written by Ray Williams, Ron Allen, and Peter McMickle

References:

Green, Wilmer L. *History and Survey of Accountancy*. Brooklyn, New York: Standard Text Press, 1930; Reprinted., Osaka: Nihon Shoseki, 1974.

Bywater, M. F. and Yamey, B. S. *Historic Accounting Literature: a Companion Guide*. London: Scholar Press, 1982.

PREFACE.

IT is with some diffidence I offer to the public a method of Book-Keeping essentially different from those now generally in practice. The length of time which the Systems of Dowling, Mair and others, commonly called the Italian method, have been in general use, and the celebrity they have acquired, must, no doubt, operate against any thing new offered on this subject.—Convinced, however, from experience, that those Systems are too diffuse, elaborate, and on the whole not well calculated for general and extensive business; I have hazarded the one now laid down: A System combining, in a considerable degree, the simplicity of Single, with all the advantages of Double Entry; being much more concise and better adapted for real business in any line; not requiring more than one half the time or trouble, whilst it affords a more decisive check upon all the transactions, than any of the others.—Indeed the method of keeping books according to those Systems is, by several merchants, getting into disuse.

ILLUSTRATION 34. First page of Preface in 1796 William Mitchell's *A new and complete system of book-keeping . . .*

PREFACE.

Some, perhaps, will object to my having thrown aside the use of the Journal; to this objection I would answer, that by the method here laid down, there is no occasion for it; and even according to those other Systems, the utility of such a Book appears to many, somewhat doubtful.

I have avoided giving larger descriptions, or remarks, on the different Books, than what I considered really necessary; being convinced that more real knowledge of Book-Keeping will be obtained, from paying attention to the actual Statements of accounts, than from the most elaborate and minute description, that could possibly be given.—It appears to me that this is the general fault of those other Systems, particularly that of *Mairs*, which is so overburthened with rules, problems, sections, cases, &c. that the young Book-Keeper, instead of deriving a benefit from them, gets bewildered and lost.

I have given the currency in Dollars & Cents, in preference to that of any particular State, as having been adopted by all the Banks and Public Offices under Government,—coming daily into use among the Merchants, and, in the course of a few years, must become general throughout the United States.—This decimal mode of reckoning, for facility in calculation and accounts, is, perhaps, superior to any other that possibly could be devised; and it is to be hoped that Congress will also adopt some thing similar in respect to weights and measures.

ILLUSTRATION 35. Final page of Preface in 1796 William Mitchell's *A new and complete system of book-keeping* . . .

Item 11. 1797. Chauncey Lee.

American Accomptant;

BEING A

PLAIN, PRACTICAL AND SYSTEMATIC

COMPENDIUM

OF

FEDERAL ARITHMETIC;

IN THREE PARTS:

DESIGNED FOR THE USE OF SCHOOLS,

AND SPECIALLY CALCULATED FOR THE

COMMERCIAL MERIDIAN

OF

THE UNITED STATES OF AMERICA.

BY *CHAUNCEY LEE*, A. M.

LANSINGBURGH:

PRINTED BY WILLIAM W. WANDS.

M,DCC,XCVII.

[*Published according to Act of Congress.*]

ILLUSTRATION 36. Title page from 1797 Chauncey Lee's *The American accomptant...*

Item 11. 1797. Chauncey Lee. *The American accomptant...*
Lansingburgh, New York: Printed by William W. Wands.
[8] 254 [15] pgs. 17.5 cm. Evans 32366 NUC NL0196251

Other American Printings: No other known printings.

Introduction

Chauncey Lee was born in Conventry, Connecticut in 1763. Lee was the son of the Rev. Jonathan Lee, the first minister of Salisburg. He graduated from Yale, A.B., in 1748 and A.M. in 1787. After practicing law a short time, he studied theology and was pastor of Congregational churches at Sunderland and Rutland, Vermont between 1790 to 1797; of Colebrook, New York, in 1800 to 1827; and of Marlborough, Conn. in 1827 to 1835. He was skilled in music, a poet, a classical scholar, a mathematician and a man of learning. He received the honorary degree of D.D. from Columbia College in 1823. He died at Hartwick, N.Y., 1842.

Lee published numerous books including *A compendiumn of federal arithmetic, designed for the use of schools, and especially calculated for the meridian of the United States* (1797); *Poetical version of the book of job* (1807); *Sermons for revivals* (1824); and, *Letters from aristarchus to philemon* (1833).

Bentley (p.iv) states that Lee's book is the "first arithmetic by an American author to contain a treatise on double entry bookkeeping." This 310 page arithmetic book includes 44 pages of bookkeeping. The bookkeeping portion is comprised of two sections. The second section entitled "A Compendious Treatise of Book-keeping; or, Accomptantship Reduced to Practice" has 42 pages devoted entirely to double entry. The final section entitled "Farmer's Book-keeping" is a 2 page description of single entry.

Lee comments in his preface that the knowledge of bookkeeping "will also greatly tend to prevent some of the betterest evils in life, such as vexatious lawsuits, confused and quarrelsome arbitrations, loss of property - loss of friendship and good neighborhood." (p. xxxiii) The primary bookkeeping section begins with a five page narrative that is segregated into Books of Accompt; the waste-book; the journal; the ledger; general rules 108; balancing; direction; and, general observation. The remaining portion of this section includes waste book, journal, and ledger examples. The Farmers' Book-Keeping section is approximately one page of narrative and one page of single entry examples.

Description of *The American accomptant*

The book is divided into three parts: Arithmetic, Computation, and a Companious Treatise or Book-keeping, or Accomptantship reduced to practice. The book begins with a section of Recommendations including four recommendations. The first is signed by three judges of the Superior Court of Vermont, who recommend it for learning arithmetic, calling it extensively useful to men of business. The second is from the President of Williams College who states it will promote arithmetic in the youth of schools and will be useful to business men. A third recommendation is from Rev. Job Swift, the County Surveyor of Connecticut. He recommends it as a math work and for the decimal scale it defends. These recommendations are one evidence of the success of this book. Another evidence of its success is that the subscription list for the book was for 1,146 copies, when it was the usual custom for arithmetic books to be printed in 1,000 lots or less. One unique feature is that the subscription list is printed at the end of the book and all 1,146 names are broken down by state.

The Recommendations section is followed by a very long Introduction section of 35 pages in which Lee gives a synopsis of each part of the book. He states his purpose is to "simplify the system of commercial arithmetic to make rules more easy and concise - an easy guide to the young student and useful to a man of business. Students are made to learn rules like a parrot without knowing their reason or application. The elementary parts of arithmetic should be explained. Foundations must be laid before building on them. The student must proceed from Notation (writing figures), to Addition, to Subtraction, to Multiplication, and to Division." Lee believed that dollar units should be expressed in decimals and not fractions. Federal money should be established on a decimal scale, and he believed that Congress would have to effect this.

Lee thought bookkeeping should be done in the Italian mode agreeable to Gordon's system. He was referring to William Gordon's *The universal accountant and complete merchant* published in 1763 in Edinburgh, England, and in wide use in the Colonies until 1800. Lee says "the art of accomptantship is usually learned only in apprenticeship but should be taught in schools." He repeatedly calls bookkeeping an "art." Bookkeeping "enables a man to readily, at any time, ascertain the exact state of his affairs. "

The first part of the book is Arithmetic which he defines as "an art of computing by numbers, either whole or in fraction." This part contains thirty lessons. It is in this section on page 56 that Lee presents his famous Table of Federal Money. This table expresses dollars and cents by symbols that he calls "characteristics." He set forth a system of "characteristics" by which one vertical stroke designated the mill; two the cent; these two parallel lines crossed by an S shaped the dime; and, the two parallel lines crossed by two S's shaped the dollar. His book is sited as the first text to use the American dollars expressed with the dollar sign. Karpinski (1940 p. 118) mentions that Lee's 1797 book is the "first book to use the dollar symbol in print."

The second part of Lee's book is entitled "Commutation" which is defined as "the changing of numbers or quantities of one denomination into others of different denominations." There are numerous rules for changing money of one state or country into money of another state or country. The Decimal Practice is in Part III. Lee states that fractions are unnecessary and he does not present a section on fractions. He simplifies the system of commercial arithmetic. To "render many of its rules more easy and concise", he has omitted several rules contained in former treatises "that are more puzzling than to profit the common school student, or at least are inapplicable or unnecessary to trade and business."

The bookkeeping section

In the section "A Compendious Treatise on Book-keeping," which begins on page 248, Lee mentions the importance of accomptantship to the businessman. He believes that the Italian method of book-keeping is so perfect a system that the mercantile would have generally adopted it in the management of accompts. The purpose of this "compendium is to give a concise specimen of book-keeping, in the method of double-entry." He states that "three books are indispensably necessary for every man in mercantile business: the waste-Book, journal, and ledger; in addition many subsidiary books, according to the variety and extent of his business, are suggested."

The waste-book contains the subject matter from which the two other books are formed. In this book every transaction relating to a merchant's business, ought to be explicitly entered.

The journal is a book preparatory to the ledger, into which every entry from the waste-book, ought to be fairly transcribed. This book is considered necessary because of the difficulty of posting from the waste-book together with the mistakes arising from the inaccuracy and negligence of clerks.

The ledger is the grand book of accompt, made up from the journal, wherein the several articles composing the different accompts are arranged to exhibit a true statement of a merchant's affairs which is the sole end and design of Accomptantship.

The invoice and letter books are the subsidiary books used by most men in business. Whereas, the use of the bill-book, book of commissions, etc., depends on the ingenuity and discretion of merchants.

Lee gives the general rules for journalizing and for posting into the ledger. Profit and loss was invented to supply the defect of a debtor or creditor, when no other accompt could be debited or credited, for any things received in, or paid out. Merchants are induced to balance their books once a year, or more often to show the true state of their affairs and to determine whether their accompts have been kept with accuracy.

Following these narratives are examples of the three types of books. These books are for a "Peter Lovetrade." There are 8 pages of a waste book, 9 pages of the journal and 19 pages of the alphabet index to the ledger and the ledger.

The single entry section follows these examples. Lee calls this section "a new method or Farmer's Book-keeping" which is single entry for farmers and business men. It uses only one book, the ledger, and is suggested for "Farmers, Mechanics, many country merchants, and to all whose business are not very extensive." The ledger is the only book of account to be used in single entry. There is a final section on Clerkmanship, and the book ends with the list of subscribers.

Written by Tom Clevenger, L. C. Middleton, Peter McMickle, and Paul Jensen.

56   NOTATION.

Of Federal Money.
                              Characteristics.
10 Mills (/) make 1 Cent.   //
10 Cents - - - 1 Dime.   ⚹
10 Dimes - - - 1 Dollar. $
10 Dollars - - 1 Eagle.*   E.

Q. *What are the names of the several foreign and federal gold, silver and copper coins, circulating in the United States, and their value in Federal Money?*

A.   Gold Coins.

         ⎧ A Double Johannes is 16.00 0
         ⎪ A Single ditto, - -   8.00 0
         ⎪ An English Guinea, -   4.66 7
         ⎪ A Half ditto, - -   2.33 3
Foreign. ⎨ A French Guinea, -   4.59 8
         ⎪ A half ditto, - - - 2.29 9
         ⎪ 4 Pistoles, - - -   14.45 2
         ⎪ 2 Pistoles, - - -   7.22 6
         ⎪ 1 Pistole, - - -   3.61 3
         ⎩ A Moidore, - - -   6.05 8
Federal. ⎧ An Eagle, - - - - 10.00 0
         ⎨ A Half ditto, - -   5.00 0
         ⎩ A Quarter ditto, -   2.50 0

          Silver Coins.

         A French Crown is   1.10
         A Half ditto, - - 0.55
         A Pistareen, - -   0.20
         A Half ditto, - - 0.10
         Spanish & Federal Dol. 1.00
         Its parts are in proportion.

* *The Eagle is the largest Gold Coin of the United States. Dimes are annexed to Cents, and only the*

ILLUSTRATION 37. Description of dollar mark $ characteristics in 1797 Chauncey Lee's *The American accomptant* . . .

A COMPENDIOUS TREATISE ON
BOOK-KEEPING;
OR,
ACCOMPTANTSHIP REDUCED TO PRACTICE.

THE importance of Accomptantship is so generally known, and its utility so universally acknowledged, that any commendation will be unnecessary, further than to observe, that a thorough knowledge of the art is essential to the character of a Man of Business. The *Italian* method of Book-Keeping is so perfect a system of its kind, that the mercantile world have generally adopted it in the management of accompts. Its principles are founded in reason, since it is evident, that no transaction can be made, that is not accountable to another. It is my object, therefore, to give a concise specimen of Book-Keeping, in the method of double-entry.

Of BOOKS *of* ACCOMPT.

Three books are indispensably necessary for every man in mercantile business, viz. the WASTE-BOOK, JOURNAL, and LEDGER; besides a number of subsidiary books, according to the variety and extent of his business.

1. *The* WASTE-BOOK.

The *Waste-Book* contains the subject matter from which the two other books are formed. It opens with an Inventory of the several articles composing a merchant's stock, together with the debts incumbering it; after which follow the daily occurrences of trade, such as buying, selling, &c. In this book, every transaction relating to a merchant's business, ought to be explicitly entered, without paying that particular attention to method and style which ought to be observed in the Journal, where the several Debits and Credits are clearly ascertained.

ILLUSTRATION 38. First page of book-keeping section in 1797 Chauncey Lee's *The American accomptant* ...

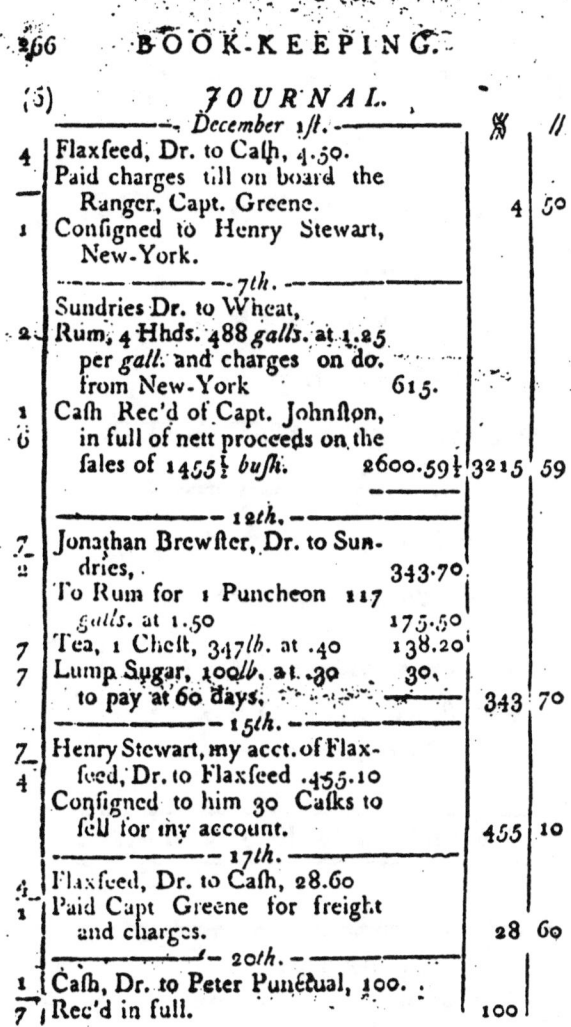

ILLUSTRATION 39. Journal entries from 1797 Chauncey Lee's *The American accomptant* ...

A TREATISE

OF

PRACTICAL ARITHMETIC,

AND

BOOK KEEPING,

CONTAINING

ALL THE RULES OF ARITHMETIC,

Which are generally useful in transacting Business

where Arithmetic is required.

FOR THE USE OF STUDENTS.

By F. NICHOLS.

Published according to Act of Congress.

BOSTON:
Printed by Manning & Loring,
For *DAVID WEST*, No. 56, Cornhill.

JULY, 1797.

ILLUSTRATION 40. Title page from 1797 Francis Nichol's *A treatise of practical arithmetic and bookkeeping* ...

Item 12. 1797. F. [Francis] Nichols. *A treatise of practical arithmetic and bookkeeping*... **Boston: Printed by Manning & Loring for David West.** [5] 108 pgs. 17.2 cm. Evans 32583 NUC NN0244931

Other American Printings: No other known printings.

This 103 page book is primarily devoted to arithmetic, however, the last 24 pages include a section entitled "Bookkeeping by the Method of Single Entry." In the preface, Nichols comments "That the learner may be furnished with every part of Arithmetic, which is generally useful in the common affairs of life, a short system of Book Keeping is subjoined, exhibiting a specimen of a shop book kept by the method of Single Entry. This specimen is of the simplest and most convenient form, and is fully adequate to the purpose, except perhaps in large concerns, where a form a little different in some respects may be preferable". It may be that Nichols is referring to double entry when he mentions a different method for large concerns.

Some confusion has existed in regards to Nichol's publications. Francis Nichols was a bookseller in the Boston and Philadephia areas. In 1808 a book entitled *Book-keeping by the method of single entry for the use of young persons* was printed for F. Nichols. Although the title page of the 1808 book does not give an author, the preface is signed by O.E. Bentley's *Bibliography* lists the author as O.E. The Shaw *Bibliography* and *The National Union Catalog* mistakenly lists the author as O.D. Bentley acknowledges that the author is probably Francis Nichols. The 1808 publication, which is totally devoted to accounting, is based upon the 1797 book. Perhaps Nichols included in his 1797 arithmetic book a bookkeeping section which was written by O.E. and then in 1808 used it for a separate text with O.E. writing the preface. Although this sounds plausible, the bookkeeping section in the 1797 book included Francis Nichols as one of the ledger accounts. The conclusion appears to be that both bookkeeping selections are probably authored by Francis Nichols.

The bookkeeping section of Nichol's 1797 book is twenty-three pages long providing examples of a Day Book and Ledger. Accounts are shown in U.S. dollars and cents. There is a table of Federal Money showing that 10 mills make 1 cent, 10 cents make 1 dime, 10 dimes make 1 dollar and ten dollars make an eagle. This table is similar to the one in Lee's *The American accomptant*, but it gives symbols of c, d, dol and E for cents, dimes, dollars and eagles. Nichols illustrates how the accounts can be balanced and transferred to a new ledger at the end of each year.

The day book begins on page 80. The debits have the 'To' and the credits have the 'By'. There are two vertical columns for the amount and they are headed 'dol' and 'c' (dollars and cents). The ledger - alphabet where each person's account is listed, is presented after the day book. The ledger accounts are shown with debits on one page and credits on the opposite. The considerably short narrative, beginning on page 102, is as follows: "At the end of every year tradesmen take an account of stock and balance their accounts, in order to know the state of their trade. In this case they transfer their book debts to a new ledger, or to new pages of the same ledger, and draw out a balance account at the end of the old ledger, as is done below." This is the only narrative in this bookkeeping section. There follows a listing of accounts with an outstanding balance, the amount and then a total. A new ledger index is shown with these outstanding accounts only.

The entries in these books appear to be those of an owner of a store selling general merchandise such as liquor, foodstuffs, cloth, chairs, glasses, silverware, china, truck locks, silk stocking, wood, charcoal, scissors, razors, and shoes. The account of Mr. Peter Vinal seems to be that of a school teacher since he buys copy books, ink stands, Pike's *Arithmetic*, and quills.

Written by L. C. Middleton

BOOK KEEPING. 85

					dol	c
1796	Mr. Thomas Marriot Dr.					
				dol c		
July 10	To 3450 *lb* of cotton	at	25		862	50
	10 firkins of butter		18 per *lb*		100	80
	12 *lb* of nutmegs		75 per *oz*		144	
	13 *hhd* of rum		1 25 per *gal*		1023	75
					2131	5
	Mr. Frederic Tudor Dr.					
17	To 18 *cwt* of tobacco	at	20 per *lb*		403	20
	20 hops		75 per *lb*		1680	
	22 tons of hay		4 25 per *cwt*		1870	
	99¼ bushels of oats		1 25		124	37¼
					4077	57¼
	Mrs. Jane Mason Dr.					
28	To 543 yards of linen	at	75		407	25
	12 *cwt* of sugar		15 per *lb*		201	60
	5 rice		6 per *lb*		33	60
	234 *lb* of tea		1 80		421	20
					1063	65
	Mr. Benjamin Thompson Dr.					
Aug. 1	To 24 Russel's History of Modern Europe	at	2		48	
	12 Paley's Philosophy		1 87½		22	50
	36 Paley's Evidences of Christianity		1		36	
	6 Nicholson's Chemical Dictionary		8 30		49	80
					156	30
	Mr. James White Dr.					
9	To 18 Blair's Sermons	at	3 50		63	
	12 Porteus's do		3		36	
	24 Watson's Theological Tracts		10 50		252	
	60 Watson's Apology		50		30	
					381	

H 2   Mr.

ILLUSTRATION 41. Day book example from 1797 Francis Nichol's *A treatise of practical arithmetic and bookkeeping* ...

120 Item 12. 1797. Francis Nichols.

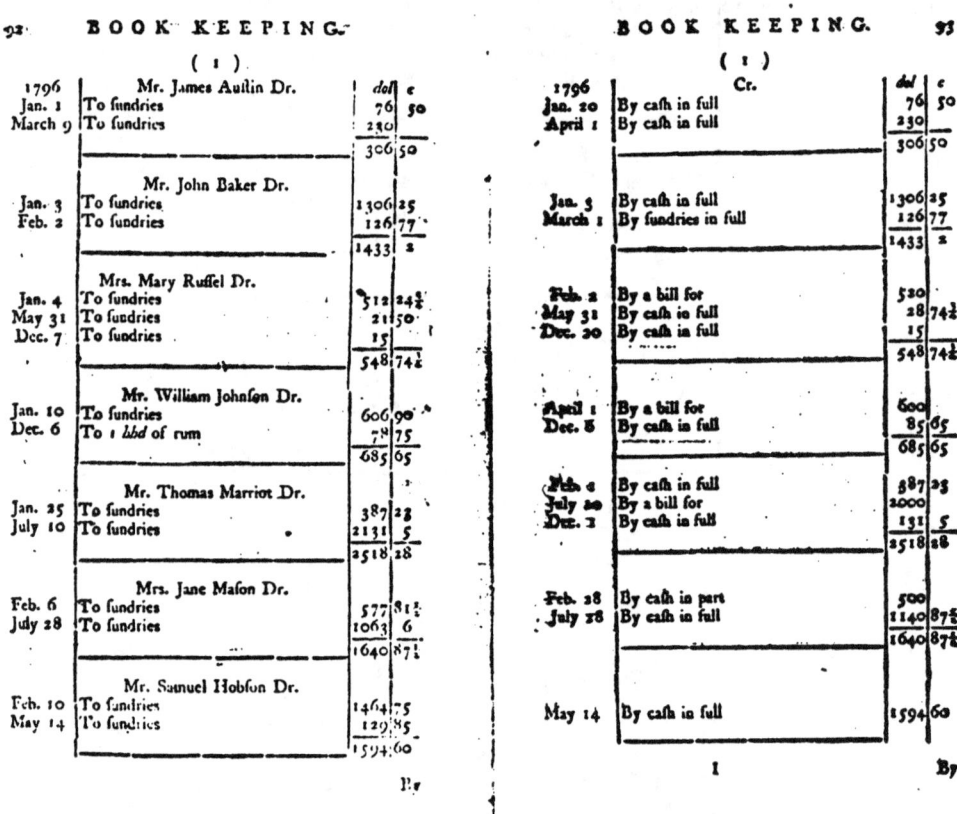

ILLUSTRATION 42. Ledger example from 1797 Francis Nichol's *A treatise of practical arithmetic and bookkeeping* ...

102   *A ·TREATISE* of

At the end of every year tradesmen take an account of stock and balance their accounts, in order to know the state of their trade. In this case they transfer their book debts to a new ledger, or to new pages of the same ledger, and draw out a balance account at the end of the old ledger, as is done below.

Balance Dr.

1796		dol	c
	Mr. Thomas Edwards	984	50
	Mr. Arthur Young	124	86
	Mr. Robert Davis	94	
	Mr. Job Orton	282	90
	Mrs. Susan Gray	74	
	Mr. Christ. Anderson	390	..
	Mr. Thomas Lawson	130	
		2080	26

A C. Anderson	B	C	D R. Davis
E T. Edwards	F	G S. Gray	H
I	K	L T. Lawson	M
N	O J. Orton	P	Q
R	S	T	V
W	X	Y A. Young	Z

Mt.

ILLUSTRATION 43. Balancing entry example from 1797 Francis Nichol's *A treatise of practical arithmetic and bookkeeping*.

A

CONCISE

INTRODUCTION

TO

Practical Arithmetic;

IN WHICH,

All the Rules that occur in common Business
are applied to the

𝕱𝖊𝖉𝖊𝖗𝖆𝖑 𝕮𝖚𝖗𝖗𝖊𝖓𝖈𝖞.

Designed for the Use of Schools in the United States.

By SAMUEL TEMPLE, A. M.

Second Edition.

BOSTON:
Printed and sold by SAMUEL HALL, No. 53, Cornhill.
1798.
[WITH THE PRIVILEGE OF COPY-RIGHT.]

ILLUSTRATION 44. Title page from 1798 Samuel Temple's *A concise introduction to practical arithmetic*...

Item 13. 1798. Samuel Temple. *A concise introduction to practical arithmetic; in which all the rules that occur in common business are applied to the federal currency...* Second edition. Boston: Printed and sold by Samuel Hall. 118 pgs. 18 cm. (Not in Evans) NUC NT0089286 (1796 first edition had no bookkeeping.)

Other American Printings:

1802. Samuel Temple. *A concise introduction to practical arithmetic; in which all the rules that occur in common business are applied to the federal currency...* Third edition. Boston: Printed by Munroe & Francis. 118 pgs. 18 cm. SS 3147 (Not in NUC)

1803. Samuel Temple. *A concise introduction to practical arithmetic; in which all the rules that occur in common business are applied to the federal currency...* Fourth edition. Boston: Printed by Munroe & Francis for Hall and Hiller. 118 pgs. 18 cm. SS 5147 NUC NT0089287

1804. Samuel Temple. *A concise introduction to practical arithmetic; in which all the rules that occur in common business are applied to the federal currency...* Fourth edition. Boston: Printed by Munroe & Francis for Hall and Hiller. 118 pgs. 18 cm. (Not in SS) (Not in NUC)

1805. Samuel Temple. *A concise introduction to practical arithmetic; in which all the rules that occur in common business are applied to the federal currency...* Fourth edition. Boston: Printed by Munroe & Francis for Hall and Hiller. 118 pgs. 18 cm. (Not in SS) (Not in NUC)

1805. Samuel Temple. *A concise introduction to practical arithmetic; in which all the rules that occur in common business are applied to the federal currency...* Fifth edition. Boston: Samuel Hall for Hall and Hiller. 118 pgs. 18 cm. SS 9460 NUC NT0089288

1808. Samuel Temple. *A concise introduction to practical arithmetic; in which all the rules that occur in common business are applied to the federal currency...* Fifth edition. Boston: Samuel Hall for Hall and Hiller. 108 pgs. 18 cm. (Not in SS)

1808. Samuel Temple. *A concise introduction to practical arithmetic; in which all the rules that occur in common business are applied to the federal currency* . . . Sixth edition. Boston: Printed by Lincoln & Edmands. 108 pgs. 18 cm. SS 16293 NUC NT0089289

1813. Samuel Temple. *A concise introduction to practical arithmetic; in which all the rules that occur in common business are applied to the federal currency* . . . Seventh edition. Boston: Printed and published by Lincoln & Edmands. 108 pgs. 18 cm. SS 29926 NUC NT0089290

1818. Samuel Temple. *A concise introduction to practical arithmetic; in which all the rules that occur in common business are applied to the federal currency* . . . Seventh edition. Boston: Printed by Lincoln & Edmands. (Not in SS) NUC NT0089291

1818. Samuel Temple. *Concise introduction to practical arithmetic; in which all the rules that occur in common business are applied to the federal currency* . . . Eighth edition. Boston: Printed by Lincoln & Edmands. 108 pgs. 18.5 cm. SS 45848 NUC NT0089292

1825. Samuel Temple. *Temple's arithmetick. A concise introduction to practical arithmetic; in which all the rules that occur in common business are applied to the federal currency* . . . Ninth edition, improved. Boston: Printed by Lincoln & Edmands. 107 [1] pgs. 18 cm. NUC NT0089293

1825. Samuel Temple. *Temple's arithmetick. A concise introduction to practical arithmetic; in which all the rules that occur in common business are applied to the federal currency* . . . Ninth edition, improved. Boston: Printed by Lincoln & Edmands. 107 pgs. NUC NT0089294

1827. Samuel Temple. *Temple's arithmetick. A concise introduction to practical arithmetic; in which all the rules that occur in common business are applied to the federal currency* . . . Tenth edition. Boston: Printed by Lincoln & Edmands. 107 [1] pgs. NUC NT0089295

This text originally appeared in 1796 and went through 10 editions. There was virtually little, if any, difference observed between the editions other than errors or print changes.

Little attention was paid to accounting as the entire bookkeeping section consisted of only two pages. However, the accounts are interesting in that they reflect the nature of debits and credits in exchange transactions employing cash and sundry items.

The accounts shown in the accompanying illustrations reveal a trade transaction between Soloman Thornton of Randolph and Walter Underwood. The books apparently belong to Walter Underwood and the accounts show the debits 'To' Solomon Thornton given 'By' Walter Underwood. Walter Underwood gave Solomon Thornton such items as wheat, beef, 4 days' work and oxen, 2 days' work at hoeing, pork, etc. Thornton agreed to pay Underwood such items as salt, flour, linen, Sherry wine, brass kettle, etc., with the remaining debt to be paid in cash.

An interesting item in this account example consists of the signatures of both Thornton and Underwood as verification that the account was closed. This appears to be a formal auditing of the closing of accounts including the signature validation.

Written by Phil Siegel

Book-Keeping.

Solomon Thornton of Randolph, Dr.

1798.		dols. cts.
Feb. 3.	To 8 bushels wheat, at 1,66 cts.	13, 28
9.	To 29 lb. beef, at 6½ cts.	1, 88½
17.	To 3 bushels rye, at 1,50 cts.	4, 50
20.	To 5 bushels potatoes, at 25 cts.	1, 25
25.	To 10 pair of shoes, at 1,75 cts.	17, 50
March 3.	To 75 lb. cheese, at 10 cts.	7, 50
12.	To 3 thousand of clear boards, at 13 dols. a thousand.	39, 00
16.	To 7 cords oak wood, at 3 dols.	21, 00
25.	To 4 days' work done by myself and 1 yoke of oxen, at 1,40 cts.	5, 60
May 7.	To 28 yds. tow-cloth, at 22 cts.	6, 16
15.	To 19 lb. butter, at 20 cts.	3, 80
June 5.	To 2 days' work at hoeing, done by myself, at 83 cts. a day.	1, 66
29.	To 7 lb. pork, at 18½ cts.	1, 29½
Sept. 25.	To 9 barrels of cider, at 1,33 cts.	11, 97
		136, 40

Settled October 15, 1798.

FORMS OF NOTES.

$100.   Boston, July 4, 1808.

For value received, I promise to pay Peregrine Pickle, or order, one hundred dollars, on demand, with interest.

        WITNESS,   Jonathan Trusty.
Thomas Tinker.
Robinson Crusoe.

$.95,06   Boston, July 4, 1808.

For value received of Peter Industry, I promise to pay him, or order, in ninety days from date, ninety five dollars, six cents, with interest after.

        Attest,   Harry Recompense.
Dick Remember.
John Steady.

ILLUSTRATION 45. Account for goods and services provided to Samuel Thornton from Walter Underwood in 1798 Temple.

Book-Keeping.

to Walter Underwood, Cr.

1798.		dolls. cts.
March 8.	By 4 bush. salt, at 75 cts.	3, 00
12.	By 1¾ cwt. flour, at 6 dols. per cwt.	10, 50
19.	By 3 gal. W. I. rum, at 1,50 cts.	4, 50
28.	By 18 yds. of linen, at 40 cts.	7, 20
April 2.	By 10 lb. sugar at 15 cts.	1, 50
9.	By 2 pieces nankeen, at 1,25 cts.	2, 50
15.	By a side of soal-leather, weighing 28lb. at 20 cents.	5, 60
23.	By 12 yds. broadcloth at 4,50 cts.	54, 00
29.	By 3 qts. Sherry wine, at 35 cts.	1, 05
May 5.	By 4 doz. waistcoat buttons, at 67 cts. a dozen.	2, 68
23.	By ½ cwt. of rice, at 3,34 cts.	1, 67
July 5:	By a brass kettle, weighing 25lb. at 50 cts. per pound.	12, 50
Oct. 15.	By cash to balance.	29, 70
		136, 40

October 15, 1798. Settled all books accounts heretofore contracted between us.
Walter Underwood.
Solomon Thornton.

ORDER.

Boston, July 4, 1808.

Mr. Richard Bountiful,
 Sir, Please to pay Ned Needy, *nine dollars, forty-six cents,* and place the same to my account.
$.9,46
                         Constant Charitable.

RECEIPTS.

Boston, July 4, 1808.
Received of William Pitt *twenty dollars on account.*
$.20.
                         Charles Fox.

$.100.   Boston, July 4, 1808.
Received of Christopher Columbus *one hundred dollars, in full of all demands.*
                         Americus Vespacius.

ILLUSTRATION 46. Account for goods and services received by Walter Underwood from Samuel Thornton in 1798 Temple.

Item 14. 1799. William Cobb.

THE
COUNTRY TRADER's ASSISTANT
OR
YOUNG CLERK's DIRECTORY
IN THE ART OF
BOOK-KEEPING,
ON A NEW AND APPROVED PLAN.
TO WHICH IS ADDED,
A Record of TRADE, a Record of NOTES and BILLS.
ALSO,
A few Forms of Notes, Orders, Receipts, Bills, &c.

By WILLIAM COBB, Jun.

BROOKFIELD,
PRINTED for the AUTHOR.
1799.

ILLUSTRATION 47. Title page from 1799 William Cobb *The country trader's assistant* ...

Item 14. 1799. William Cobb. *The country trader's assistant.* **.. Brookfield, Massachusetts: Printed for the author. 46 pgs. Evans 35315 NUC NC0501740**

Other American Printings: No other known printings.

History tells very little about William Cobb, Jr. *The country trader's assistant. . .* was printed for the author, which suggests that Cobb was either a bookdealer or possibly a country teacher. Because so little is known about him, (no other publications are known to be authored by Cobb and only one printing was made of this book) one presumes that this book was his only effort and that it had only local influence.

According to the author, the Italian method was found to be "wanting and of little use to country traders." To meet their needs, he offered his book as a "plain and concise introduction to the art of bookkeeping." Even in his simplified form, he felt some would not be "equal to the task." He correctly recognized that bookkeeping requires some modicum of discipline, a fact that still escapes a considerable number of small merchants even today. For those who would put forth the effort, there is the satisfaction of seeing the "true state of one's trade."

The Simplified method consists of four record books: the blotter, day book, ledger, and record of trade.

The blotter is a memorandum of every event (transaction) concerning sales on account. Any mistake is blotted out and rectified, hence, the name blotter. Transactions are recorded in one of three columns: credits for (sales) by book (account) or notes; produce received in payment for goods; and, cash or produce received in discharge of accounts or notes.

The day book is a record of the charges and discharges from the blotter. The record is to be posted at periodic intervals (usually a week or so).

The ledger is a record of the day book entries in account form. The ledger contains no other transactions, therefore, it is, in essence, simply a record of account and note receivable balances.

The record of trade, as the name implies, is the record of sales. It has four columns: the inventory of all goods available for

Item 14. 1799. William Cobb.

sale; all sales whether for cash, goods or on account; sales on account or notes only; and, collections on account or notes. The blotter is the source for all entries in the record of trade.

There are examples of how each record is to be kept. The last part of the book also provides examples of the form and wording of promissory notes, receipts, and bills (invoices).

The author's primary goal is to provide a method for keeping track of account and note receivable balances, inventory and sales. Unlike many of the authors of his day, he uses double instead of single entry for his simplified method. Double entry was usually limited to the larger, more sophisticated business enterprise.

Written by Stan Tonge

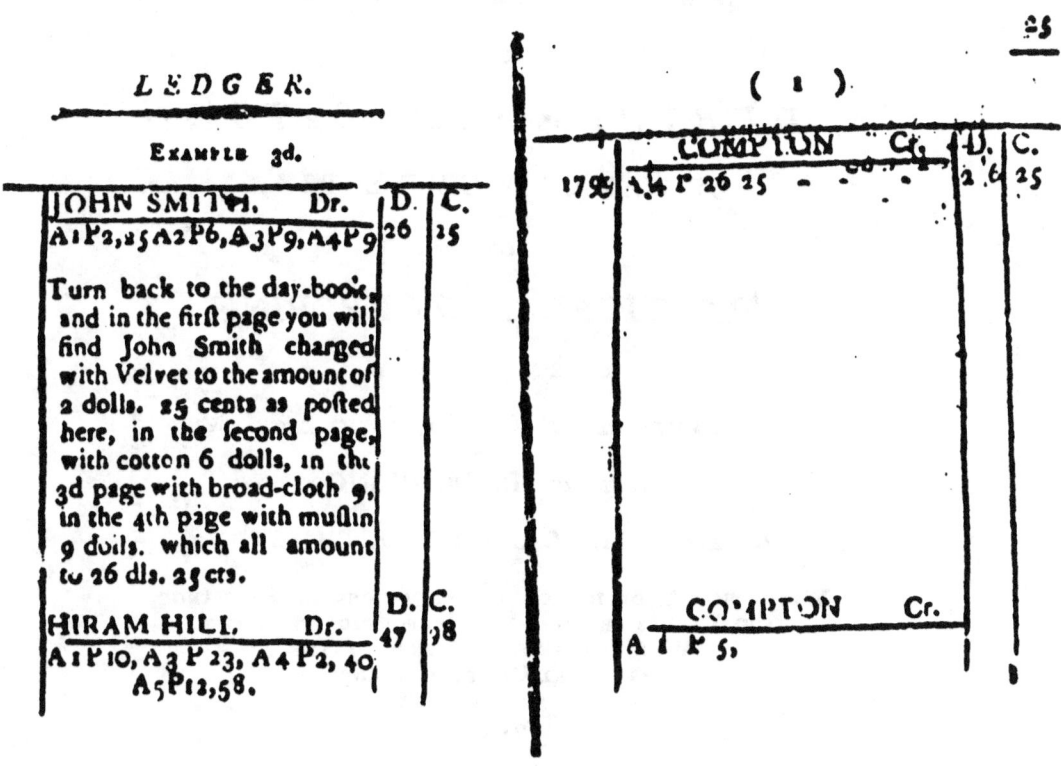

ILLUSTRATION 48. Ledger example from 1799 William Cobb *The country trader's assistant* ...

BOOK-KEEPING

IN THE

TRUE ITALIAN FORM

OF

DEBTOR AND CREDITOR

BY WAY OF DOUBLE ENTRY;

OR,

PRACTICAL BOOK-KEEPING

EXEMPLIFIED

FROM THE PRECEPTS OF THE LATE

INGENIOUS D. DOWLING,

AUTHOR OF MERCANTILE ARITHMETIC.

WITH THE ADDITION OF COMPUTATIONS IN EXCHANGE, AND TABLES SHEWING THE PROPORTION THAT THE WEIGHTS AND MEASURES OF THE PRINCIPAL CITIES IN EUROPE BEAR TO EACH OTHER.

By WILLIAM JACKSON, ACCOUNTANT.

PHILADELPHIA:

PRINTED BY JOHN BIOREN, CHESNUT STREET, FOR H. & P. RICE, NO. 16 SOUTH SECOND STREET. AND JAMES RICE, BALTIMORE.
1801.

ILLUSTRATION 49. Title page from 1801 William Jackson *Book-keeping, in the true Italian form* . . .

Item 15. 1801. William Jackson. *Book-keeping in the true Italian form...* Philadelphia: Printed by John Bioren. [8] 296 pgs. 22 cm. SS 706 NUC NJ0008040

Other American Printings: See also Item 33, 1820, James Bennet, *The American system of practical book-keeping.* . . . One printing of the first edition of this work contains a section entitled *Jackson's book-keeping adapted to the coin and commerce of the United States.* . . . The section is separately dated 1821.

1804. William Jackson. *Book-keeping in the true Italian form...* New York: C. Brown. [8] 288 pgs. 22 cm. SS 6545 NUC NJ0008041

1804. William Jackson. *Book-keeping in the true Italian form...* New York: Printed by Sage and Clough for T. B. Jansen & Co. [8] 288 pgs. 22 cm. SS 50446 NUC NJ0008041

1804. William Jackson. *Book-keeping in the true Italian form...* New York: Printed by Sage and Clough for M'Dermit & Thompson. [8] 288 pgs. 22 cm. SS 50447 NUC NJ0008041

1811. William Jackson. *Book-keeping in the true Italian form...* New York: E. Duyckinck. [8] 233 pgs. 22 cm. (Not in SS) NUC NJ0008042

1811. William Jackson. *Book-keeping in the true Italian form...* New York: E. Duyckinck. [8] 288 pgs. 22 cm. (Not in SS) NUC NJ0008043

1811. William Jackson. *Book-keeping in the true Italian form...* New York: Printed by George Long. [8] 288 pgs. 22 cm. SS 23104 NUC NJ0008044

1815. William Jackson. *Book-keeping in the true Italian form...* New York: Printed and published by George Long. [8] 288 pgs. 22 cm. (Not in SS) NUC NJ0008046

1816. William Jackson. *Book-keeping in the true Italian form...* New York: Evert Duyckinck. [8] 288 pgs. 21 cm. (Not in SS) NUC NJ0008048

1816. William Jackson. *Book-keeping in the true Italian form...* New York: George Long. [8] 288 pgs. 21 cm. (SS 37944) (Not in NUC)

1823. William Jackson. *Book-keeping in the true Italian form...* New York: Printed and published by George Long. [8] 288 pgs. 22 cm. NUC NJ0008049

Introduction

This book is a revision of an earlier work, *Mercantile arithmetic*, written by D. Dowling of Dublin, Ireland. Jackson takes other writers to task for "deviating too much from natural simplicity and introducing sundry needless accounts tending rather to perplex than elucidate . . . ."

The author states that "In conducting of business, Order and Method contribute very much to lighten the care, facilitate the dispatch, and ensure the success there of." Among the Hollanders, it is taken for a maxim, "that he who fails in business, or becomes a bankrupt, must have been ignorant of this important branch of knowledge."

In the accounting system described by Jackson, the three main books are the waste book, journal, and ledger. He calls the ledger the chief or grand book of accounts and all other books are subservient to it. The author explains in detail how an article is to be worded, or expressed in the Journal and Ledger. The method of recording the transaction by its proper Drs and Crs is emphasized and there is a discussion on the closing procedure.

The last section is entitled "Computation in Exchange" and includes exchange with Ireland, America, Holland, Austria, the Netherlands, Hamburg, France, Spain, Portugal, Genoa, Leghorn, and Venice.

Jackson explains in great detail how the different books are kept, and supports his explanations with copious examples. According to the author, there are three things of which a merchant is to keep accounts: "His effects, his debts active and passive, and his gains and losses." He further distinguishes three types of accounts which are real, personal, and imaginary. Real accounts are accounts relating to a person's property and personal accounts are the accounts of the persons dealt with. Finally, imaginary accounts are fictitious titles invented to represent the merchant himself and used to record such gains and losses as cannot be ascribed to any real or personal account.

The author lists several pages of rules and maxims for the use of debit and credit. A careful examination of these so-called rules indicates that debit and credit actually mean the same today as it did in Jackson's time. After the rules of debit and credit, there are several pages of discussion on the closing procedure. Accounts that would not be closed in a modern system are closed to an account called balance, and Jackson's profit and loss account is somewhat analogous to what we would call income summary.

This book contains an unusual feature for the period: questions and answers on pages 230 to 254. Apparently, the author intended for his book to be used as a text. The modern reader will find it difficult to labor through some of the examples, but for the most part it is easy to understand.

Written by Ray Williams and Mein-Ein Wong

Item 15. 1801. William Jackson.

WASTE-BOOK No. II.   (11)   89

		£	s.	d.
DUBLIN, 26th. October 1797.				
Sold to *Thomas Bell*, viz.	*l. s. d.*			
1 Puncheon *James Pearson's* Rum qt. 110 Gallons at 4s. per	22 00 00			
Received from him in payment				
Said *Bell's* Bill of 250 Livres *Tourn.* on *Samuel Spence* of *Nantz*, at 12d. per; remitted *Abel Archer* for the balance of my Acct. with him	*l. s. d.* 13 00 05			
Cash, for balance — —	8 19 7	22		
———— 28th. ————				
Received from *Loftus* and Company, *Paris*, my account two Bills, viz.	*l. s. d.*			
Their Bill of the 28th. Currt. *N. S.* on *Digby* and Co. *Dublin* at Usance, value 2024 Livres *Tou.* (the balance of my account with Do.) at 12½d. per, which said *Digby* has accepted	105 8 4			
A Bill on *Digby* and Co. *London*, pay. 1 Dec. O. S. for 200l. *Eng.* with orders to get it discounted for their Acct. Exc. at 10 per C. and Disct. at 6 per Cent per An. which bill, on said terms, I keep for my own Acct. and is	218 15 5	324	3	9
———— 31st. ————				
Received from Sundries this Month, per Cash-Book		370	12	4
Paid Sundries this Month, per Cash-Book		320	5	—
———— November 3d ————				
Received advice from *Eben. Pike*, *Cork*, that he has, according to my orders, shipped in the *Success* of said place *John Rover* master for *Nantz*, 150 Barrels Beef, for the account and risk of *Abel Archer* there; and that, for the Cost, (amounting to 110l. 5s.) he has drawn on *Lewis Lestock*, *London*, for my Acct. a bill of 100l. *Eng.* (being the value) at 10½ per cent.		110	5	—

N

ILLUSTRATION 50. Waste-book example in 1801 Jackson's *Book-keeping, in the true Italian form*...

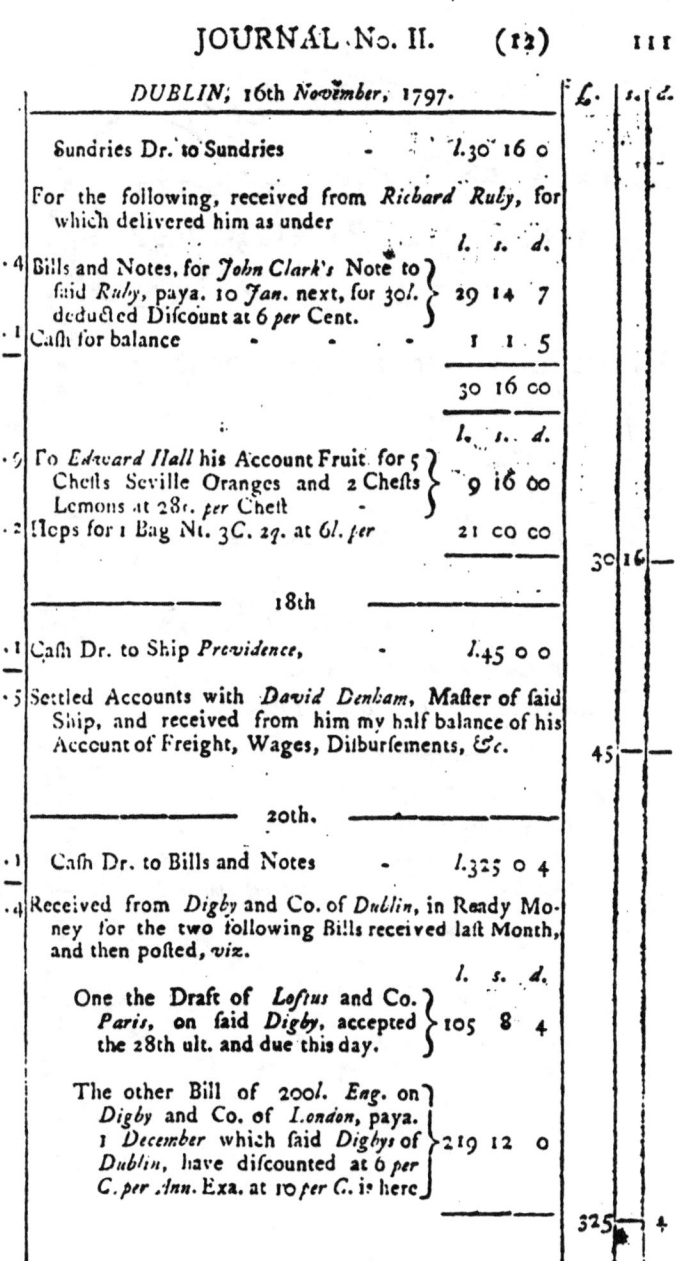

ILLUSTRATION 51. A journal example in 1801 Jackson's *Book-keeping, in the true Italian form* ...

THE ELEMENTS OF

BOOK-KEEPING;

COMPRISING

A System of Merchants Accounts,

FOUNDED ON

REAL BUSINESS,

AND

ADAPTED TO MODERN PRACTICE:

WITH

AN APPENDIX ON EXCHANGES,

Including the Recent Alterations in

FRANCE, HOLLAND and ITALY.

BY P. KELLY,

MASTER OF FINSBURY-SQUARE ACADEMY, LONDON.

From the Second London Edition, Augmented and Improved.

Philadelphia:

PRINTED AND SOLD BY JAMES HUMPHREYS,
At the N.W. Corner of Walnut and Dock-streets.

1803.

ILLUSTRATION 52. Title page from 1803 Patrick Kelly's *The elements of book-keeping* . . .

Item 16. 1803. Patrick Kelly. *The elements of book-keeping. .* **Philadelphia: Printed by James Humphreys. [14] [1] 203 pgs. SS 4470 NUC NK0084487**

Other American Printings: No other known printings.

Dr. Patrick Kelly was born in 1756. He was a noted mathematician and became the astronomer and examiner at the Trinity House. His *The elements of book-keeping. . .* comprised a system of merchants' accounts founded on real business, arranged according to modern practice and adapted to the use of schools.

Kelly comments that single entry is chiefly used in retail business, while double entry is adopted in wholesale affairs. He also emphasizes that one should constantly check all entries in the books. He says that "even intentional mis-statements may be prevented by a check ledger, that is by having the ledgers kept by different persons. The general practice is to examine the books every day or week by which mistakes are most readily corrected. This is done by one person reading the journal while another inspects the ledger and a like examination should also take place between the waste book and journal."

He further explains that the "system of book-keeping founded on real business. . . the waste book, is divided into a certain number of subsidiary books, each adapted to a particular kind of business, which are the cash book, bill book, invoice book and sales book." He then continues by stating that the "waste book contains the particulars of such occurrences as cannot be brought under any of the foregoing heads and also gives a general account of every transaction with a reference to the subsidiary book where the particulars are to be found." Kelly provides an example of a trial balance and states that it "never appears in the books of a merchant, it is here inserted for assistance of the learner." He gives an example of an "account current" and comments on an interest account.

Reference

Eldridge, H. J., *The Evolution of the Science of Book-keeping*, London: Gee & Company (Publishers) Limited, 27-28 Basinghall Street, 1954.

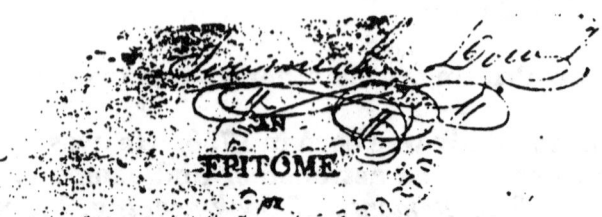

AN
EPITOME
OF
BOOK-KEEPING BY DOUBLE ENTRY;

Delineated on a Scale suited to the Faculties and Comprehension of
SENIOR SCHOOL BOYS AND YOUTH,
DESIGNED FOR THE MERCANTILE LINE.

Comprising Systematic and Unerring Rules for the forming
MONTHLY STATEMENTS OF BOOKS,
As well as those for OPENING, CONDUCTING, ADJUSTING and CLOSING
them;—with
Explanations of THEORY, and Exhibitions of PRACTICE,
Rendered easy to the smallest capacity;
And calculated to initiate them in the true PRINCIPLES, and to make
them perfect in the RULES, by a little practice.

TO WHICH ARE ADDED,
RULES FOR KEEPING RETAIL BOOKS BY DOUBLE ENTRY,
Without altering the process of SINGLE ENTRY in the DAY-BOOK or
JOURNAL, for all sales of Merchandize; by which one half the writing is saved, and the LEDGER exonerated from items, and rendered
a prompt and sure proof of MONTHLY BALANCES AND ANNUAL
PROFITS.

ALSO,
The most Easy, Concise, and Safe way of
CALCULATING ANY RATE PER CENT.
And especially that of INTEREST at SIX per CENT. per Annum.

By THOMAS TURNER,
Professor and Teacher of Book-Keeping, at Portland.

Portland:
Printed by JAMES & SHIRLEY,
For THOMAS CLARK (Proprietor) and for sale at his Bookstore,
Fish Street, and by the principal Booksellers in the United States.
1804.

ILLUSTRATION 53. Title page from 1804 Thomas Turner's *An epitome of book-keeping by double entry . . .*

Item 17. 1804. Thomas Turner. *An epitome of book-keeping by double entry...* **Portland, Maine: Printed by Jenks & Shirley for Thomas Clark. 148 pgs. 17.5 cm. SS 7396 NUC NT0397559**

Other American Printings: No other known printings.

1801. Listed in Shaw Shoemaker as (1446) is actually a ghost of the 1804 edition arising from a poorly printed illustration in Karpinski.

Introduction

Book-keeping by double entry was published in 1804 by Jenks and Shirley for Thomas Clark (proprietor) in Portland, Maine. There was only one printing, suggesting that it was not particularly popular among "senior school boys and youth." It contains 144 pages, of which 129 are on book-keeping. Thomas Turner is a "professor and teacher of Book-keeping, at Portland." Nothing else seems to be known about him.

Description of *Bookkeeping by double entry*

A major portion of the book consists of illustrations and examples. In the preface, Turner alludes to his purpose for the book saying it was written because of the "increase of the commerce of this country, and the unabounded field open to it for speculation and commercial prospects ... in this view, it is an object of the first consequence to that part of the rising generation designed for mercantile pursuits, to become early acquainted with the principles of book-keeping; and the most judicius rules that can be devised to obviate error in the process, and embarrassment in the adjustment and closure of books."

The introductory chapter begins by defining book-keeping by double entry as "a system of charge and discharge." He further states, "a charge is single entry, exhibiting the debtor side only, and does not form a complete account without the discharge. A charge and discharge exhibits a complete account of debtor and creditor, with the balance due on either side." If the total of the debits and credits are not equal, then there must be an error. "The principle of double entry determines profit and loss, by the simple ascertainment of the difference between the charge and discharge, in every account of your property, merchandise, and concerns of business."

The books to be used for recording the various transactions are identified as the wastebook, journal, ledger, and cash book. Other subsidiary books are optional. The instructions that follow the brief description of the primary books are essentially a list of rules identifying appropriate journal entries for particular transactions. They are then illustrated by a sample journal and ledger. The cash book is a ledger for all cash transactions.

At monthly and quarterly intervals, a trial balance is prepared to prove the books. Turner comments, "it is for want of this precautious process, that so much difficulty and embarrassment frequently occurs in the closure of books; and more time is often wasted in examining the books throughout, in order to find out where an error exists, than is required in the forming ten years monthly statements." Specific directions for preparing the trial balance are then outlined for both a monthly and a quarterly basis.

The next section in *Book-keeping by double entry* is patterned after the first, but is directed at partnerships, and the dual nature of each partner's stock account.

Retail books are discussed in a separate section. The major item of interest in keeping retail books by double entry, is to do so "without altering the process of single entry, for all daily sales of merchandise." This is suggested primarily to reduce the amount of writing and essentially describes the sales journal.

The final section of the book, entitled "Calculations", is a short treatise on arithmetic. It includes teachings on decimals, fractions, interest, and exchange of British for U.S. money.

Written by Mark Turner

22   ADJUSTMENT AND CLOSURE OF BOOKS.

concerns, including expence accounts, that stand Dr. on the monthly statement trial balance (after a full discharge is given to the old account for the value of property on hand, and a charge made thereof to new account) is loss.

All accounts of property, merchandize and concerns of your own, that in same manner stand Cr. is gain.

All the remaining accounts, nominal and personal, on the trial balance, are to be closed by a transfer of their balances to new account.

Five journal entries are required for the closure of all books. viz.

P. L. 1st.—Profit and Loss closes all accounts of expences, property, merchandize and concerns, of your own, that exhibit a balance in manner before mentioned, on the Dr. side.

P. L. 2. 2d Entry.—Profit and Loss closes all accounts of your own property, merchandize and concerns, that in same manner exhibit a balance on the Cr. side.

S. 3. 3d Entry.—Stock closes profit and loss, and the balance of the latter is carried to the former account, in conformity to the statement required.

B. 4. 4th Entry.—All remaining accounts, personal and nominal, exhibiting a balance on the Dr. side of trial balance, are to be closed by a charge thereof to Dr. of new account.

B. 5. 5th Entry.—All remaining accounts, nominal and personal, exhibiting a balance on the Cr. side of trial balance, are to be closed by a credit given to the new account.

ILLUSTRATION 54.   Steps for closing the books explained in the 1804 Turner's *An epitome of book-keeping . . .*

62 QUARTERLY STATEMENT—LEDGER FIRST.

Fo.	Heads.	Jan. Feb. March. Dr.		Cr.		April, May, June. Dr.		Cr.	
1	Stock,	12	50	41	75			29	25
1	Cash,	112	50	96	35	16 81	15 3	96	12
2	John P. B. Storer,	3				3		3	
2	Peter Paywell,	14	50	12		2 30	50	32	50
2	Samuel Neverpay,	3	75			3	75	3	38
2	George Tucker,			5		5		5	
2	John Dean,			3				3	
3	Thomas Cotton,			4	50			4	50
3	Notes Payable,	25		75		50		50	
3	Bank,	50		30		20 58		20	
4	Expence Account,	18	85			18 1	85 30		
4	Adven. to Havanna,	27				27		46	25
5	Charges on Merchandize,	2	50	2	25	4	25 95		
5	Commission Account,				60				60
5	John Trader,			11	15	11	15	11	15
6	Notes Receivable,	12				12 60		72	
6	Nankins,	281	60	281	60	20		30	
6	Interest Account,						30		6
7	Sugar,					64	58	26	
7	India Cottons,					36		30	
						522	81	522	81

ILLUSTRATION 55. First half of quarterly statement and trial balance in 1804 Turner *An epitome of book-keeping . . .*

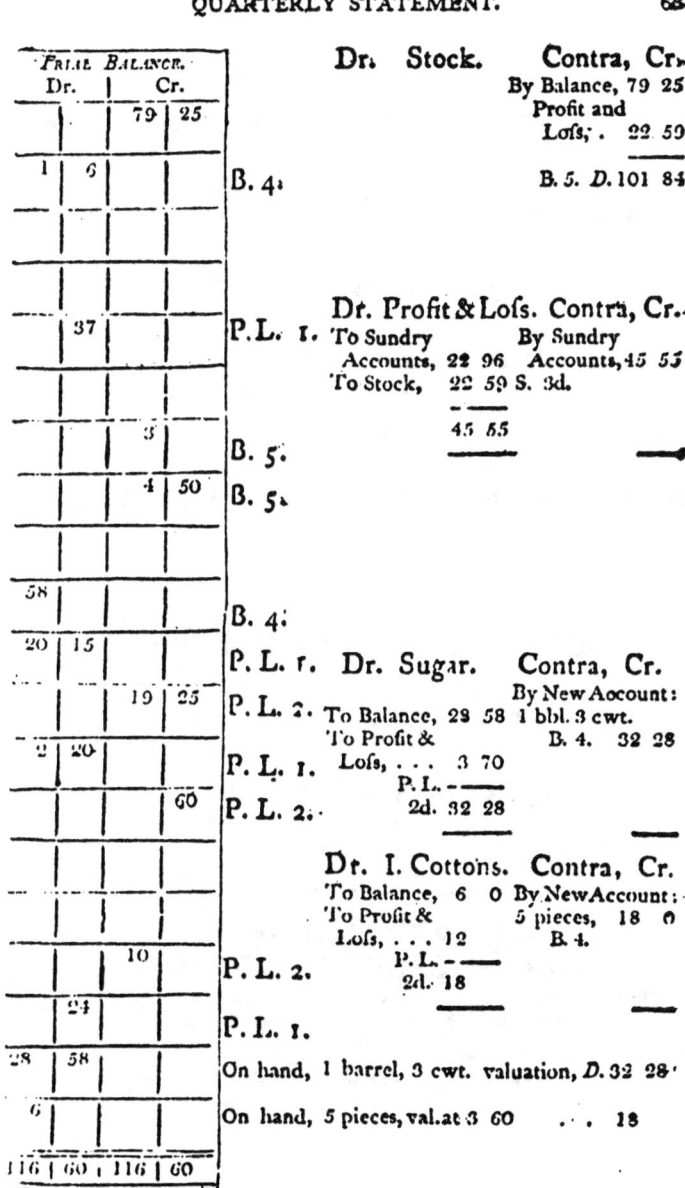

ILLUSTRATION 56. Second half of quarterly statement and trial balance in 1804 Turner *An epitome of book-keeping . . .*

Item 18. 1807. William Kinne.

A

SHORT SYSTEM OF

PRACTICAL ARITHMETIC,

COMPILED

FROM THE BEST AUTHORITIES;

WITH

DEMONSTRATIONS OF THE RULES.

TO WHICH IS ANNEXED

A SHORT PLAN OF BOOKKEEPING.

THE-WHOLE DESIGNED

FOR THE USE OF SCHOOLS.

HALLOWELL, MAINE,
PUBLISHED BY EZEKIEL GOODALE,
Sold by him at the HALLOWELL BOOKSTORE, sign of the BIBLE,
and by most of the BOOKSELLERS in the State.
Dec. 1807.
NATHANIEL CHEEVER, PRINTER.

ILLUSTRATION 57. Title page from 1807 William Kinne's *A short system of practical arithmetic*...

Item 18. 1807. [William Kinne, no author's name on first edition]. *A short system of practical arithmetic, compiled from the best authorities, with demonstrations of the rules, to which is annexed a short plan of book-keeping* ... Hallowell, Maine: Published and sold by Ezekiel Goodale. Printed by: N. Cheever. 173 pgs. 17.2 cm. SS 12869 NUC NK0152979.

Other American Printings:

1809. William Kinne. *A short system of practical arithmetic, compiled from the best authorities, with demonstrations of the rules, to which is annexed a short plan of book-keeping* ... Second edition. Hallowell, Maine: Published and sold by Ezekiel Goodale. Printed by N. Cheever. 177 pgs. 18 cm. [Kinne's name was on this and later editions.] SS 17873 NUC NK0152980.

1816. William Kinne. *A short system of practical arithmetic, compiled from the best authorities, with demonstrations of the rules, to which is annexed a short plan of book-keeping* ... Third edition. Hallowell, Maine: Printed and Published by Ezekiel Goodale. 139 pgs. 18.5 cm. SS 38014 NUC NK0152981.

1822. William Kinne. *A short system of practical arithmetic, compiled from the best authorities, with demonstrations of the rules, to which is annexed a short plan of book-keeping* ... (Improved edition with question). Fourth edition. Hallowell, Maine: Printed and published by Goodale, Glazier & Co. 240 pgs.

1823. William Kinne. *A short system of practical arithmetic, compiled from the best authorities, with demonstrations of the rules, to which is annexed a short plan of book-keeping* ... (Improved edition with question). Fourth edition. Hallowell, Maine: Printed and published by Goodale, Glazier & Co. NUC NK0152982.

1825. William Kinne. *A short system of practical arithmetic, compiled from the best authorities, with demonstrations of the rules, to which is annexed a short plan of book-keeping* ... (Improved edition with question). Fifth edition. Hallowell, Maine: Glazier & Co. NUC NK0152983.

1827. William Kinne. *A short system of practical arithmetic, compiled from the best authorities, with demonstrations of the rules, to which is annexed a short plan of book-keeping . . .* (Improved edition with questions). Sixth edition. Hallowell, Maine: Glazier & Co. [8] 240 pgs. 17.5 cm. NUC NK0152984.

1829. William Kinne. *A short system of practical arithmetic, compiled from the best authorities, with demonstrations of the rules, to which is annexed a short plan of book-keeping . . .* (Improved edition with questions). Seventh edition. Hallowell, Maine: Glazier, Masters & Co. [8] 240 pgs. 17.5 cm. NUC NK0152985.

1831. William Kinne. *A short system of practical arithmetic, compiled from the best authorities, with demonstrations of the rules, to which is annexed a short plan of book-keeping . . .* (Improved edition with questions). Eighth edition. Hallowell, Maine: Glazier, Masters & Co. [8] 240 pgs. 18 cm. NUC NK0152986.

1833. William Kinne. *A short system of practical arithmetic, compiled from the best authorities, with demonstrations of the rules, to which is annexed a short plan of book-keeping . . .* (Improved edition with questions). Ninth edition. Hallowell, Maine: Glazier, Masters & Co. [8] 240 pgs. 18 cm. NUC NK0152987.

1836. William Kinne. *A short system of practical arithmetic, compiled from the best authorities, with demonstrations of the rules, to which is annexed a short plan of book-keeping . . .* (Improved edition with questions). Tenth edition. Hallowell, Maine: Glazier, Masters & Smith. [8] 240 pgs. 18 cm. NUC NK0152986.

About the author

Very little is known about William Kinne. It is interesting to note that the title page does not acknowledge Kinne as the author. By contrast, the *American Antiquarian Society* copy contains the author's signature on the title page. Whether the signature is authentic is unknown, but most biographical works credit Kinne for this text on arithmetic and bookkeeping.

Description of *A short system of practical arithmetic*

Primarily an arithmetic textbook, this treatise contains 34 pages on bookkeeping. The book proved so popular, it was continued for a period spanning 29 years. It is unknown whether its popularity was due to the larger arithmetic section, the smaller bookkeeping section, or both. Another possible explanation for the book's success was Mr. Goodale's marketing acumen. The book contains advertising for not only this book but Mr. Goodale's bookstore, as well. Additionally, Mr. Goodale included numerous recommendations for the book immediately following the title page.

The author considered bookkeeping to be that "branch of science which teaches one to record mercantile transactions in a regular and systematic way." He purported to describe single entry, the principle method used by traders in retail business, farmers, and mechanics.

His simplified method consists of two books: the Day Book and Ledger.

The day book is a chronological record of all "occurrences of trade", meaning the buying and selling of only merchandise. Buying and selling activities involve both debits and credits, which are recorded one on top of the other with a notation as to which it is. The bookkeeper is instructed to make complete notations in the day book, for "if a dispute were to arise . . . it would be the chief support" as to the exact nature of the transaction. An unusual posting reference style in the form of an = was suggested.

In addition to trade, the day book also contains an inventory of the merchant's estate as the first entry for each year. Evidently, this entry is done only as a way of reducing the inventory to writing at least once a year, since the inventory is not posted to the ledger. The ledger is used to gather together the dispersed transactions of each person from the day book. Debits are posted on the left hand page and credits on the opposite (right hand side) page of the same folio. All accounts are prefaced with an index.

Item 18. 1807. William Kinne.

By nature of the transactions, the ledger is basically a record of accounts receivable and payable transactions.

To further assist the bookkeeper, the author includes examples of the form and wording of promissory notes, bills of exchange (both foreign and domestic), receipts, invoices and account current. It is interesting to note that errors are accepted in the Account Current. Also included are discussions and illustrations of barter, loss and gains, simple and compound interest, commission, insurance and discount.

Beginning with the fourth edition (1823), the text was greatly enlarged by Daniel Robinson, who became the text editor beginning with the 5th edition. As part of the enlargement, a comprehensive section on "taxmaking" was added. At the time of this review, the fourth and later editions were not available. Accordingly, the nature of the revisions is unknown. Additionally, no information on Daniel Robinson is known, except that no other bookkeeping books by him could be found.

Written by Stan Tonge

BOOK KEEPING. 139

When two or more persons or things are included in the same account, they are expressed by the term *sundries*.

EXAMPLE.

Suppose David Davis owes me 450 dollars for the balance of an account with him, April 1st, 1807 ; the next day April 2d, I buy of him 200 bushels of wheat at 1 dollar 50 cents per bushel, and 100 bushels of corn at 75 cents per bushel ; the next day April 3d, I sell Jonathan Worth 150 bushels of wheat at 1 dollar 75 cents per bushel ; April 4th, Jonathan Worth pays me 200 dollars in cash, and David Davis pays me 50 dollars in cash ; required the Day Book and Ledger of the transaction.

DAY BOOK, No. 1.

Hallowell, April 1, 1807.

			Dolls.	cts.
=	*David Davis*	Dr.		
	To balance due on old account, . . .		450	00
	———April 2.———			
	David Davis	Cr.		
=	By 200 bushels wheat, ... at $1,50		300	00
	100 do. corn, ... 75		75	00
			375	00
	———April 3.———			
	Jonathan Worth	Dr.		
=	To 150 bushels wheat, ... at $1,75		262	50
	———April 4.———			
	Jonathan Worth	Cr.		
=	By cash in part for wheat, ...		200	00
	David Davis	Cr.		
=	By cash fifty dollars, ...		50	00

To post the above accounts, open an account for David Davis, debit him for 450 dollars ; and for the second days transaction credit him for 375 dollars, for the third open an account for Jonathan Worth, debiting him 262 dollars 50 cents ; and for the fourth day credit him for 200 dollars and credit David Davis for 50 dollars.

ILLUSTRATION 58. Example problem in 1807 William Kinne's *A short system of practical arithmetic* . . .

152 *Item 19. 1808. O. E.*

BOOK-KEEPING,

BY THE

METHOD

OF

SINGLE ENTRY.

———

FOR THE USE OF YOUNG PERSONS.

═══════

PHILADELPHIA,

PRINTED FOR F. NICHOLS,

BY T. & G. PALMER, HIGH STREET.

1808.

ILLUSTRATION 59. Title page from O. E.'s 1808 *Book-keeping by the method of single entry. for the use of young persons.*

Item 19. 1808. O. E. *Book-keeping by the method of single entry. for the use of young persons.* **Philadelphia: Printed for F. Nichols by T. & G. Palmer.** [38] pgs. 24 cm. (Shaw-Shoemaker misclassifies the author as O. D. see SS 14817) (Not in NUC)

Other American Printings: No other known printings.

About the Author "O. E."

The identity of O.E. is unknown. It is presumed the author was a he, however, one possibility is that O.E. was in fact a she and obscured her identity. It has also been suggested that O.E. and F. Nichols were one in the same, with the full name being Francis Nichols. In 1797 a book entitled *A treatise of practical arithmetic and bookkeeping* was authored by Francis Nichols. This 1808 book entitled *Book-keeping by the method of single entry for the use of young persons* was printed for F. Nichols. Although the title page of this 1808 book does not give an author, the preface is signed by O.E. Bentley's *Bibliography* lists the author as O.E. The Shaw *Bibliography* and *The National Union Catalog* mistakenly list the author as O.D. Bentley acknowledges that the author is probably Francis Nichols. The 1808 publication, which is totally devoted to accounting, appears to be based upon the 1797 book. Perhaps Nichols included in his 1797 arithmetic book a bookkeeping section which was written by O.E. and then in 1808 used it for a separate text with O.E. writing the preface. Although this sounds plausible, the bookkeeping section in the 1797 book included Francis Nichols as one of the ledger accounts. The conclusion appears to be that both bookkeeping selections are probably authored by Francis Nichols.

Discussion of *Book-keeping by the method of single entry*

The author represents his book as "a treatise on a single entry Shop Book." This was considered the simplest and most convenient form for a boy of fourteen or fifteen years of age. For double entry, he recommends Kelly's, which was, "generally considered to be the best on the subject printed in the U.S." Presumably, he meant Patrick Kelly's 1803 *The elements of bookkeeping: comprising a system of merchant's accounts founded on real business.*

Item 19. 1808. O. E.

His records consist of two books: day book and the ledger. The day book is a chronological listing of all sales transactions. The record is arranged in four columns: date; description of item sold; unit prices; and total sales amount.

The bookkeeper is instructed to leave sufficient space between the entries for each customer so subsequent transactions for regular customers can be recorded together.

The ledger is simply a record of all the accounts with each customer arranged in account form. The day book is the source of those transactions. To facilitate posting and follow up, the ledger contains an alphabetical index of the locations of each customer's account.

The method for keeping each book is illustrated. Also illustrated is the form and wording for Bills of Parcels (invoices) and a Statement of Accounts (called Book Debt).

A very unusual feature for one of these books is the illustration of a Balance Sheet in account form. It is recommended that an account of all property be taken at each year end before opening a new ledger. The source of the debits and credits not involving sales and accounts, not discussed, is apparently derived from physical inventories and other documents in the possession of the shop-keeper.

Written by Stan Tonge

PREFACE.

A CONCISE treatise of book-keeping, in which the prices of the articles are expressed in federal money, is much wanted in places of education, and would be very useful to young persons who are intended for wholesale or retail stores. Though accounts are, I believe, generally kept in federal money, yet all our treatises of arithmetic and book-keeping, which I have seen, exhibit numerical calculations in the various currencies of the different states. For the sake of uniformity and ease of calculation, it would be far more commodious to express monies generally according to the decimal or federal notation and division.

The following system exhibits a specimen of a shop-book kept by the method of single entry. It is of the simplest and most convenient form, and may be learned, in a short time, by a boy or girl of fourteen or fifteen years of age.

To persons who desire to learn book-keeping by the method of double entry I recommend Kelly's Book-keeping, which has been reprinted in this country, and is generally considered the best extant.

O. E.

Philadelphia, June, 1808.

ILLUSTRATION 60. Preface from 1808 O. E. *Book-keeping by the method of single entry. for the use of young persons* .

Item 20. 1810. Oliver Steele

THE

MERCANTILE MANUAL,

OR,

ACCOUNTANT'S GUIDE;

EXHIBITING

A CLEAR AND COMPREHENSIVE VIEW

OF THE SCIENCE OF

BOOK-KEEPING:

ADAPTED TO THE COUNTING-ROOM,

AND

Schools where Book-Keeping is scientifically taught.

PRINCIPALLY EXTRACTED FROM THE ENCYCLOPEDIA.

NEW-HAVEN,
PRINTED BY OLIVER STEELE AND CO.
1810.

ILLUSTRATION 61. Title page from 1810 *The mercantile manual, or, accountant's guide* ...

Item 20. 1810. [No author given]. *The mercantile manual, or, accountant's guide* ... **New Haven: Printed by Oliver Steele and Co. (Only a 15 page fragment of a much larger book survives.) 24 cm. (Not in NUC)**

Other American Printings: No other known printings.

Only 15 pages of this much larger book survives. The author is not identified in *The mercantile manual, or; accountant's guide* . Steele is the printer and states on the title page that the book was "principally extracted from the *Encyclopedia*." The particular *Encyclopedia* from which this text was extracted is not provide; however, it may have been the *Edinburgh Encyclopedia* acknowledged by Bennett in his 1820 book (see Item 33).

The mercantile manual, or; accountant's guide presents the "Italian Method" or double entry bookkeeping. The author states that the "Italian Method" is "generally preferred . . . and the accountant who understands it, will find little difficulty in following, or even in inventing other methods, that are better accommodated to any particular purpose." He includes the three generally accepted principal books which are the Waste-Book, Journal, and Ledger.

The first section is a discussion of the waste-book, or "day book", and is defined as "containing an exact register of all occurrences in business in the same order as they take place. It begins with an inventory of every thing belonging to the owner, a list of the debts due to him, and of the debts he owes to others." The author continues by stating that "the accountant's first care should be to have nothing ambiguous; his second, to have nothing superfluous." The procedures for using the waste-book is discussed in some detail. Steele emphasizes that "this book must be kept with the greater care, as it contains the materials from which the other books are composed; and any error or defect in this will occasion a like one in the others."

The second section is a description of the ledger where "articles of the same kind are collected together; and for that purpose, it is divided into many accounts, under which the different branches of business are arranged." This section contains a rather lengthy discussion of the use of the ledger. He sums the section up by stating that "the same sum is entered on the Dr. of one account and on the Cr. of the other; and it follows from this that if all the accounts in the ledger be added, the amount of the sums of the Dr. will be equal to those of the Cr."

The third section is a discussion of the journal. The journal is described as "a fair record of all the transactions compiled from the waste book, in the same order as they stand there; but expressed in a technical style, that it may be transferred to the leger with more ease."

Examples are provided on the next seven pages. The fourth section describes the posting and balancing of the ledger. Only a remnant of this section remains. The remainder of this much larger book is lost.

Written by Paul Jensen and Peter McMickle

12   A TREATISE

Ex. 2.] Sold William Draper,
  25 pieces of cloth, at $ 40 per piece, $ 1000
  130 Stones wool, at $ 1 per stone,   130
                                             ———1130

If the two articles sold to William Draper, were entered separately in the waste-book, and transferred to the Journal by Rule I. they would stand thus:

William Draper Dr. to Cloth, sold him 25 pieces, $ 40,   1000
William Draper Dr. to Wool, sold him 130 Stone,
  at $ 1 30,   130

And if these were posted to the leger, there would be two articles placed to the Dr. of William Draper, one to the Cr. of Cloth, and one to the Cr. of Wool.

But the sales may be entered in the form of one complex journal-post, as follows:

William Draper Dr. to Sundries.
To Cloth, for 25 pieces at $ 40, $ 1000
To Wool, for 130 Stone, at 1,   130
                                            ———1130

And then there is only one article on the Dr. of William Draper in the leger.

Ex. 2.] Sold 10 pieces cloth to W. Draper, at $ 40, - 400
        do. 12 do.   to J. Mercer, at 40,   480
                                                  ———880
        22

This example also falls under Rule I. But whereas there was one Dr. and two Crs. in the former example, there are two Drs. and one Cr. in this: William Draper and John Mercer, the purchasers, are Drs. for their respective quantities; and cloth, which is the only thing delivered, is Cr. for the whole quantity. The Journal post is,

Sundries Drs. to Cloth.
W. Draper, for 10 pieces at $ 40,   400
J. Mercer, for 12 do.   at 40,   480
                                            ———880

Ex. 3] Bought from H. Hood, 5 puncheons rum,
  at $ 150,   750
    do.   do.   do. 3 hds. claret, at $ 120 - 360
    do.   do.   do. 2 pipes Madeira, 200   400
                                            ———1510

This example falls under Rule II. The articles received, rum, claret, and Madeira, are Drs. and the person from whom they are received is the only Cr.

Sundries Drs. to Henry Hood.
Rum, for 5 puncheons, at $ 150, $ 750
Claret, for 3 hds. at 120,   360
Madeira, for 2 pipes, at 200,   400
                                            ———1510

Ex. 4.] Bought 50 quarters Wheat from J. Talcott, at $ 7,   350
    do.   12 do. do. from S. Ellis, at $ 7, 84
                                            ———434

ILLUSTRATION 62. Bookkeeping discussion from 1810 *The mercantile manual, or, accountant's guide* . . .

THE
PRIVATE INSTRUCTOR,

AND

YOUNG GENTLEMAN'S

POCKET COMPANION,

COMPRISING EVERY THING NECESSARY IN ARITHMETIC, MENSURATION, GUAGING, BOOK-KEEPING, AND CONVEYANCING, TO FORM AND COMPLETE THE MAN OF BUSINESS.

ALSO,

Tables shewing the value, in dollars and cents, of any number of pounds, shillings, and pence, from one penny to a thousand pounds, New Jersey, or the like currency; tables of interest and bank discount; tables of board measure, guaging, &c. &c.

The whole upon a new and improved plan, and adapted wholly to private instruction.

By JOHN BLAKE,

Arithmetician, and Teacher of Youth, Burlington county, New-Jersey

TRENTON. N. J.
PUBLISHED BY D. FENTON.
1815.

ILLUSTRATION 63. Title page from 1815 John Blake *The private instructor* . . .

Item 21. 1815. John Blake. *The private instructor* **... Trenton, New Jersey: Published by D. Fenton. [7] [1] [4] 232 pgs. 18.5 cm. SS 34144 NUC NB0532002**

Other American Printings: No other known printings.

About the author

There is no biographical data on John Blake. The title page refers to him as an "arithmetician, and teacher of youth, Burlington County, N.J." He notes in the preface that the book is being printed far from his residence. The preface ends with the notation "Black Horse, October 21, 1815" under his name. A location with the name Black Horse could not be found, but it could be presumed that it was located in Burlington County, New Jersey, where he taught. Evidence indicates that he is probably not John Lauris Blake, a well known contemporary author.

Preface and a reference to *The young man's companion*

The author refers to *The young man's companion* "as of little use to the man of business, and still less for that of schools." In order that "the young gentleman might be able to acquire, in as short a time, and with as little expense as possible, a competent knowledge of the different branches of which he treats, the author has given only what deemed necessary to qualify him for business." The book was originally intended for private instruction, but it may be used as a "School Book."

Description of the book-keeping section

Only 15 pages of 244 pages are devoted for the Book-keeping section which begins on page 166. Blake describes book-keeping "the method commonly called single entry; a method which every person in, or intended for business, should learn and understand completely." The rest of the book is devoted to penmanship, letter writing, arithmetic, mensuration, gauging, miscellaneous questions, mercantile forms and conveyancing.

The principal books of accounts are the day book and the ledger. The day book contains entries of several articles "in the successive order of their dates; making each person Dr. to what he becomes accountable for, or Cr. by what is received of him on account."

Item 21. 1815. John Blake.

This is followed by explanations of the day-book, the ledger, and posting. Instructions for the day-book are as follows: 1) Each person is made "Dr. to what he becomes accountable for, or Cr. by what is received of him on account;" 2) Dates are placed in the middle of the page; and, 3) The left margin is used to indicate the ledger folio number to which the entry is posted.

The ledger "is the grand book of accounts, wherein all the several debts (sic) and credits of each particular person's account, which lie scattered in different parts of the day-book, are collected into spaces allotted for them, placed in such a manner as to show the whole state of the account at once."

Under "Posting" are the following instructions: 1) Take the first entry in the day-book and open an account in the ledger writing the account name in the center and "Dr" and "Cr" at the top of the appropriate money columns; 2) Enter the year in the margin opposite the name and enter the month and day in the margin opposite the entry; 3) Write the entry starting with "To" and "By" for debit and credit entries, respectively; 4) If there is more than one article, make the entry "To" or "By" Sundries; 5) Write the ledger folio number in the day-book margin; 6) Insert the ledger name and folio in the alphabet; 7) Leave enough room after the entry to insert more entries; 8) Start the next account below the previous on the same page unless that page is filled; 9) Entries can be marked paid in the margin of the day-book, in which case they are not posted to the ledger; 10) When ledger A is filled, transfer all unsettled accounts to ledger B.

Sample entries in a day-book in single entry form begin on page 168. On page 177, there is an alphabet (alphabetized index) of the ledger. Because ledger accounts are started in the order in which they occur in the day-book, it is necessary to have this index to indicate on which folio the particular account is to be found. Pages 177 to 180 are sample ledgers which have been posted from the day-book on pages 168 - 176. Columns are available for the date, an explanation, the debit amount, and the credit amount in dollars. This ledger form is unusual in that both the debit and credit columns are located on the same ledger page side by side so that both debit and credit entries can be made chronologically one below the other.

On page 181, under the title "Balancing" we are told to open an account of "Stock", either at the end of the ledger, or on a separate piece of paper. Account balances are then "closed" to this account. The "Balance" account is then totaled, a net credit balance being the "Balance due me". Ledger B is then provided on page 181. One unsettled account is shown here, having been transferred from ledger A.

The authors note here that other books are used by merchants but are not shown. These could include an expense book, a cash book, and invoice book, and others.

Written by Jerry Jeakle and Wanpen Wasinarom

PREFACE.

THE author has had the subsequent work in contemplation for above these three years past; and most parts of it have been written and altered several times since he began the compilation, as improvements suggested themselves. Under the conviction that a work of this kind is much wanted, he has ventured to give it to the public in its present form: the utility of which must be obvious to every one who considers that most of the treatises on Arithmetic, Mensuration, &c. are not altogether calculated to give that instruction, in a short time and with little expense, which a young man intended for business ought to receive. The *Young Man's Companion*, now extant, is but of little use to the man of business, and still less for that of schools. That the young gentleman might be able to acquire, in as short a time, and with as little expense as possible, a competent knowledge of the different branches of which he treats, the author has given only what he deemed necessary to qualify him for business. In Penmanship, Letter Writing, Arithmetic, Mensuration, Guaging, Book Keeping and Conveyancing, he will find every thing necessary and useful: all irrevelant and unnecessary matter being excluded.— The work, though originally intended for private instruction, yet, nevertheless, it may be used as a School Book, especially by such who are to receive but a small proportion of schooling. As most of the questions are so wrought or stated, that a person who has the least knowledge of figures, may very readily understand them,

ILLUSTRATION 64. Preface from 1815 John Blake *The private instructor* . . .

BOOK-KEEPING.

BY Book Keeping here meant, is that method commonly called single-entry; a method which every person in, or intended for business, should learn and understand completely. The principal books of accounts are the Day Book and the Ledger: the forms and ruling of which may be sufficiently known by inspecting the following specimen.

THE DAY-BOOK,

Contains entries of the several articles in the successive order of their dates; making each person *Dr* to what he becomes accountable for, or *Cr.* by what is received of him on account. The dates are in the middle of the page, and in the margin are written the numbers of the Ledger folios, to which the respective articles are posted.

THE LEDGER

Is the grand book of accounts, wherein all the several debts and credits of each particular person's account, which lie scattered in different parts of the Day-Book, are collected into spaces allotted for them, placed in such a manner as to shew the whole state of the account at once.

POSTING.

In posting or transferring the debts and credits, from the Day-Book into the Ledger, always begin thus: open an account in the Ledger for the first person who stands *Dr.* or *Cr.* in the Day-Book, that is, write his name and the contraction *Dr.* and *Cr.* in the respective columns assigned them, as in the following specimen; then, if the person be *Dr.* post the article, beginning the entry with *To*, entering the *year* in the margin, opposite the name, and, the *month* and *day* in the same line with the article, placing the amount in the *Dr.* columns: But, if he be *Cr.* enter it in like manner, beginning the entry with *By*, and placing the amount in the *Cr.* columns, observing

ILLUSTRATION 65. First page of bookkeeping section in 1815 John Blake *The private instructor* . . .

Item 22. 1815. Briant Sheys.

THE AMERICAN BOOK-KEEPER;

PART THE FIRST.

COMPRISING

A SYSTEM OF BOOK-KEEPING

BY

SINGLE AND DOUBLE ENTRY:

ADAPTED TO THE

MERCHANT, FARMER, AND MECHANIC,

WITH THE

PRINCIPAL AUXILIARY BOOKS ANNEXED.

TOGETHER WITH

A NEW METHOD

OF

POSTING AND PROVING THE BOOKS,

NEVER BEFORE PUBLISHED.

DESIGNED FOR THE USE OF SCHOOLS AND PRIVATE PERSONS

IN THE UNITED STATES.

By B. SHEYS, Accountant.

NEW-YORK:
PRINTED BY ———— 194 GREENWICH-STREET,
CORNER OF VESEY.
1815.

ILLUSTRATION 66. Title page from 1815 Briant Sheys *The American book-keeper; part the first*...

Item 22. 1815. B. [Briant] Sheys. *The American book-keeper; part the first. comprising a system of book-keeping by single and double entry*... New York: Printed by N. Van Riper. [7] 153 pgs. 21 cm. SS 35925 NUC NS0504501

Other American Printings: See Item 29, which is a another book (over 95% different) by the same author.

1822. B. [Briant] Sheys. *The American book-keeper: part the firs. comprising a system of book-keeping by single and double entry.* New York: D. D. Smith [7] 153 pgs. 21 cm. NUC NS0504503.

This is the first of two books on accounting written by Briant Sheys. The book gives a very extensive coverage of book-keeping by single entry with only a brief explanation of double entry. Sheys' second book, printed in 1818, covers only double entry book-keeping.

The author's definition of book-keeping is "the art of recording the business of a merchant in such a form as to exhibit a distinct view of the state of his affairs; and of the debts due to and by him." Sheys says that single entry book-keeping is simple, short, and generally only used by storekeepers and mechanics, etc. whose dealings are neither extensive nor involve foreign trade.

In the single entry method all accounts are closed to a balance account. The balances are then carried forward to the new ledger when it is opened. The author mentioned that it was common not to take inventories, but he recommended the practice.

Sheys explained the use of the post journal. Debits and credits pertaining to each person are summarized monthly and their total listed in the monthly post journal. He says: "This is a most excellent plan for detecting errors, and a summary way of preventing the increase of the ledger, for the space therein is always precious."

Sheys gives numerous examples to support his explanations. He also demonstrates how to account for goods on consignment. The merchant receiving the goods treats it as an account payable and the merchant who sent the goods out on consignment treats it like an account receivable.

Even though financial statements as such did not exist at this time, the author does provide a method for calculating "neat stock". According to Sheys, one should "take the state of all debts due to and by you, to which add the inventory on hand and ready money, your neat stock will be known; and this compared to your neat stock last found shows the gain or loss during the year."

Written by Karen Costley and Lynn Rockwell

15

The manner of correcting Errors in the Day-Book and Ledger.

1. If an entry has been omitted, enter it in the next vacant space, with a reference in the margin pointing out where it ought to have been.
2. If a misnomer or wrong name is entered, either erase or cross it lightly with two lines intersecting each other, and put the true one at the top.
3. If an article has been miscalculated, it is easy to alter it and put it right with a light hand and a good penknife.

Errors in the Ledger are corrected in a similar manner, except where a debtor is entered on the credit side, prefix (if it cannot be handsomely erased) the word *error* before it in the margin, and bring it to the Dr. side, where it must be entered twice, once for right, secondly to balance the error on the credit side, the same rule is to be observed with respect to the Dr. side.

But if you enter an article on the Dr. or Cr. side of any account to which it does not belong, the error is corrected by placing the same once on the opposite side.

Errors are discovered by pointing or pricking the books thus: begin with the first entry in the Day-Book, examine whether it is truly posted or transferred to its proper account in the Ledger, if you find it right it is well, if not correct it there and in the Ledger, prefix a dot (.) to the reference figure in the margin of the Day-Book, which denotes that the entry has been examined and is now right, proceed in the same manner with all the succeeding entries and posts until the whole is finished. And then if you

ILLUSTRATION 67. Error correcting discussed in 1815 Briant Sheys *The American book-keeper; part the first* . . .

Item 23. 1817. Edmund Gale.

AN EPITOME

OF

BOOK-KEEPING BY SINGLE ENTRY;

PARTICULARLY CALCULATED FOR

MECHANICS AND RETAIL DEALERS.

TO WHICH ARE ADDED,

FORMS OF THE MOST IMPORTANT WRITINGS USED

IN BUSINESS.

BY EDMUND GALE.

COPY RIGHT SECURED.

NANTUCKET:
PRINTED BY A. G. TANNATT.
1817.

ILLUSTRATION 68. Title page from 1817 Edmund Gale's *An epitome of book-keeping by single entry* . . .

Item 23. 1817. Edmund Gale. *An epitome of book-keeping by single entry...* **Nantucket: A. G. Tannatt. 40 pgs. 17.5 cm. SS 40883 NUC NG0015875**

Other American Printings: No other known printings.

Introduction

The purpose of this book, according to the author, is to meet the "need of a treatise on this subject suited to the capacities of scholars, and adapted to the business of mechanicks and retail dealers." He claims that existing books are "too intricate for the understanding of scholars in general; and too complex for the business of the mechanic and retailer." Single entry bookkeeping is the most suitable for the above purpose.

The author contends that the popular belief that bookkeeping can only be learned through actual experience in business, is a result of a need for a practical guide.

Accounts related to liquors are avoided to protect youth from thinking that they are proper for trade.

The bookkeeping section

The first twenty-seven pages are devoted to single entry bookkeeping and the remaining pages are devoted to forms. In the section of "Book-Keeping by Single Entry" Gale provides explanations of the daybook and ledger, rules for daybook entries, procedures for the correction of errors, and procedures for partnership.

Pages 5 to 15 are sample daybook entries in single entry form. In the daybook, "accounts are entered promiscuously according to the order of time." The viewpoint is that of a merchant with numerous sales on account. Also included are sales for cash or merchandise. There are examples of orders (to pay) on other merchants and consignments. There is also an example of an account where the merchant takes in supplies from a customer, finishes the product, and receives cash for 2/3 of the profit. Explanatory notes are found throughout the daybook to indicate proper procedure.

Procedures for the ledger and for the correction of errors are on page 16. In the ledger, "the items of each person's partic-

Item 23. 1817. Edmund Gale.

ular account, are brought together, the debts on one side and the credits directly opposite on the other." On the bottom of page 16 is a note on closing: "Accounts ought to be closed, at least once in a year, and the balance carried to its proper side immediately below if there is room, as is here practised. If the space allotted for the account is filled up, it must be opened at another folio; the manner of doing which is shown elsewhere."

Page 17 contains the alphabetized index of the accounts. The alphabet contains the alphabetized index of the accounts. Because ledger accounts are started in the order in which they occur in the daybook, it is necessary to have this index to indicate on which folio the particular account is to found.

Pages 18 to 27 are illustrations of the ledger. The examples are posted from the daybook illustrated earlier. Ledger errors are corrected as follows: 1st) If entered on the wrong side--first debit or credit the account "To" or "By" Error to correct; 2nd) If there is an error in amount--if too little, make an additional entry stating the reason; if too much, debit or credit "To" or "By" Error to correct; and, 3rd) If not entered at the proper time--make the entry at a convenient place and refer to this entry in the margin at the proper place.

The remaining section of the book is composed of merchant forms entitled "Forms of Some of the Most Important Writing Used in Business which includes Bills of Exchange, Forms of Inland Bills of Exchange, Forms of Foreign Bills of Exchange, Promissory Notes, Receipts, Bills of Parcels, Account Current, Invoices, Form of a Bill of Lading, Account of Sales, Form of a Charter Party, Form of a Bill of Sale, Deeds, and Form of a Will."

Written by Jerry Jeakle

PREFACE.

The author of the following system of Book-keeping has, for a considerable time felt the need of a treatise on this subject suited to the capacities of scholars, and adapted to the business of mechanicks and retail dealers. It must be obvious to every one, who has attentively considered the subject, that the treatises on Book-keeping commonly used, are by far too intricate for the understandings of scholars in general ; and too complex for the business of the mechanic and retailer.

Book keeping by Double-entry, though excellent on many occasions, is not well calculated for either of the kinds of business before mentioned ; for these single entry seems most suitable.

Scholars in general, on leaving school, are very deficient in the knowledge of this important part of education : so much so, that the belief has become very prevalent, that it can be learnt only in actual business. Indeed Book keeping seems hardly to be considered a part of an ordinary school education ; and it must be confessed, that where some attention is paid to it at school very little progress is often made. This seems to be on account of the want of some plain and familiar guide. The little work here presented will, it is thought, in some measure answer this description.

Particular care has been taken, to avoid the introduction of accounts relating to spirituous liquors. It is matter of astonishment, that these baneful articles, are so much brought to view in our school-books, as proper for trade : certainly every reflecting mind will shudder, at the probable consequences of familiarizing children and Youth to this view of them.

ILLUSTRATION 69. Preface from 1817 Edmund Gale's *An epitome of book-keeping by single entry* . . .

174 *Item 24. 1817. Charles Gerisher.*

MODERN

BOOK-KEEPING,

BY DOUBLE ENTRY,

ADAPTED TO

COMMISSION BUSINESS,

AS IT IS CONDUCTED IN THE

UNITED STATES OF AMERICA,

DESIGNED FOR

𝔐𝔢𝔯𝔠𝔞𝔫𝔱𝔦𝔩𝔢 𝔜𝔬𝔲𝔫𝔤 𝔐𝔢𝔫.

BY CHARLES GERISHER.

NEW-YORK:

PRINTED BY E. CONRAD,

FRANKFORT-STREET.

1817.

ILLUSTRATION 70. Title page from 1817 Charles Gerisher's *Modern book-keeping, by double entry* . . .

Item 24. 1817. Charles Gerisher. *Modern book-keeping, by double entry*... **New York: Printed by E. Conrad. 158 pgs. (Various pagings) 23.5 cm. SS 40908 NUC NG0146264**

Other American Printings: No other known printings.

The Preface

Charles Gerisher was a bookkeeper by trade. In his younger years he plied his trade in several of the "first houses" of Europe. Having for some time been employed in the same capacity in "one of the more respectable commercial establishments" in New York, he was repeatedly called upon to instruct young "Gentlemen" on the art of bookkeeping as it applied to the commission business. Because he was so busy with his other avocations, the author prepared this treatise to assist in this calling. Gerisher believed that, "young men, even of moderate abilities, who are tolerable proficients in the science of arithmetic, may, by careful perusal of the rules, here laid down, by their own industry, and without the aid of a teacher, be qualified to take their station in any countinghouse in such manner as will be respectable to themselves and beneficial to those who may employ them." He found the book entirely suitable for the intended purpose.

He had not intended the treatise to be published, but at the urging of several "intelligent and respectable merchants" he submitted it to the public" not as the work of a "mere theorist" but that of a skilled practitioner. The book was primarily designed for the commission business, for which the Italian method by double entry "is unquestionably the best." For the "accountant who perfectly understands that system," the book could readily be adapted to other types of businesses by selectively omitting certain records and/or inventing other methods.

"Modern Bookkeeping"

The books required to carry on the commission business are divided into primary and subsidiary categories. The primary books are: waste, or day book; sales book; journal; and ledger. The subsidiary books consist of: memorandum; expense; invoice, inward; postage; invoice, outward; month; account current; warehouse; cash; receipt; check; letter book; and, bill.

The waste book is a chronological listing of all transactions, beginning each period with the inventory of the merchant's estate, ie. what he possesses and what he owes. Each page is headed with the place of residence together with the month, date and year.

The sales book is the record of consigned and are entered on the left hand side and sales on the right hand side. When all goods are sold, the commission is computed, with the excess of the sales over costs and commissions being the consignor's profit. The profit is not remitted to the consignor until the proceeds for sales on credit are collected.

The journal is used to properly arrange all transactions from the waste book into debitors and creditors. Unlike present day journals, there are no debit and credit columns. Accordingly, "to form a Journal entry correctly, it is required that the terms Debtor and Creditor be well understood, which knowledge may be acquired by the following rules, on which, in fact, the whole art of the Italian mode of book-keeping depends: Anything that you receive is a Debtor to the thing or person from whom you receive it; and anything that you give out or deliver, is a Creditor by the thing for which it is given or person to whom it is delivered."

The ledger is the chief book in which all journal transactions are entered in account form. Debits are on the left hand and credits on the right hand side of the same page, rather than facing pages so common to the Italian method. To the ledger is appended an alphabetical index to all the accounts.

It is recommended that transactions from the journal be entered at the end of every business week - (Saturday) after a careful examination of the waste book and journal so any error might be corrected. The accounts are all to be closed to profit and loss at the end of each year.

The memorandum is used to record events before they are properly recorded in the waste book. For example, notice of a consignment before the paperwork is executed would be recorded in the memorandum.

The account current book is not really a book, but a periodic statement of account for each correspondent. The statement is drawn up once or twice a year, or any time the correspondent desires. The account includes all transactions, interest and allocation of common expenses incurred at the time of the rendering.

The cash book contains a summary record of all sums received and paid out of those amounts deposited in a bank. The check book is used by those merchants that have large and frequent dealings with banks, therefore requiring more detailed records. Entries in the check book bypass the waste book and are entered directly to the ledger.

The bill book is a detailed record of all amounts owed to the merchant. The month book is a detailed record of the amounts owed by the merchant. The month book is laid out with columns for each month so the merchant can see at a glance when and to whom amounts are owed.

The expense book is used to accumulate all small charges. At least once a week these charges are summarized and transfered to the waste book.

The postage book is a detailed record of all postage paid, both inward and outward, including the account for which the postage was incurred. If incurred for the merchant, the postage is charged to expense. Postage for the accounts of correspondents is carried to the waste book and charged to each. The balance of the other books is generally self-explanatory.

The treatise also includes a short section on domestic trade or wholesale and retail business. The primary difference is the elimination of sales, memorandum, invoice inward, invoice outward, postage, month book, and warehouse books. Commission is also eliminated and merchandise is added to the accounts.

Written by Stan Tonge

Item 24. 1817. Charles Gerisher.

(1)
Cash

Dr.					Cr.
1816 Jan.	1	To Stock petty Cash in Till.	90	1816 Jan. 3 By Thomas Sutton Sales paid Freight for 10 Tierces blue Vitriol,	15 —
	22	—Amos Stilwell, received from R. Dunscomb, for my Draft on former,	3060 29	—Daniel Thompson, paid Lang & Turner for Subscription,	5 —
	27	—Check from Union Bank	50 —	5 Daniel Thompson Sales, paid Freight for 40 Chests Tea, . . .	10 —
	31	—Geo. Harrison received from R. Turnbull for my Draft on former,	517 94	—Savage & M'Clure Sales paid Ditto, for 50 Kegs Borax, ...	12 25
				8 —Thomas Seymour Sales paid Ditto, for 50 Ceroons Bark, . . .	15 —
				13 —Primrose, Moore & Co. Sales, paid Ditto, 4 Cases Prussian Blue,	14 72
				23 —Union Bank deposited,	3060 29
				27 —House No. 101 Cheapside Street paid Insur.	19 —
				31 —Union Bank deposited,	517 94
				31 —Expense Account, for Expenses this month. as pr. Ex. Book, $41 34	
				—Postages, as pr. Postage Book, 5 1½	46 35½
				—Personal Exp. Acct. for personal Expenses this month, as pr. Ex. Book.	— 75
				—Balance N. Acc. 1st Feb.	1 92½
			4613 23		4613 23
Feb.	1	To Balance from O Account,	1 92½	Feb. 3 By Union Bank deposited,	800 —
	3	—Samuel Turner, received of him for Bill of Borax,	834 67	7 — Ditto. Ditto.	300 —
	7	—Behhan & Welling rec'd. on account of Brig Fly,	300 —	9 —Owners Brig Sarastro, paid Pilotage	19 50
	21	—Wm. Wilkes, rec'd. for Bill of Gin, ...	4195 97	21 —Union Bank deposited,	7000 73
		—John Birdsall rec'd. for Do.	2804 76	22 —Unger & Rothenholf Sales paid guaging Gin,	31 25
	22	—Check from Union Bank,	50 —	23 —Union Bank deposited, .	900 —
	23	—Arthur M'Pherson, for my draft on Ephm. Langdon, ...	922 74	29 —Exp. Acct. for Expenses this month, as pr. Exp. Book. . . . $15 61 Postages, Do. 3 38	18 97
				—Personal Exp. Acct. for personal Expenses this month, as pr. Exp. Book.	8 —
				—Balance N. Acct. 1st Mar.	31 61¼
			$9110 6¼		$9110 6¼

ILLUSTRATION 71. Cash book example from 1817 Charles Gerisher's *Modern book-keeping, by double entry* . . .

PROFIT & LOSS SHEET.

Dr.   *Profit & Loss.*   *Cr.*

To Expense Account,	$ 133|80½	By Commission Account,	$ 4074|46
–Personal Expense Account,	86|75	–Storage Account,	27|7
–House 101 Cheapside st.	54|50	–Interest Account,	8|77
–Stock Nett Gain,	6835|24½	House 101 Cheapside street,	3000|—
	$ 7110|30		$ 7110|30

BALANCE SHEET.

Dr.   *Balance Account.*   *Cr.*

To Cash,	7559|37½	By Notes Payable,	10351|8
–Notes Receivable,	35036|58	–Bonds Payable,	1187|30
–Store & Office Furniture,	220|—	–Henry Minugh,	2000|—
–Household Ditto,	150|25	–Daniel Russell,	500|—
–House 101 Cheapside street,	3000|—	–Edward Pierce,	500|—
–Amos Stilwell,	1|12	–Thomas Sutton,	612|17
–Thomas Greenwood,	2|62	–Thomas Seymour,	616|45
–George Harrison,	|13	–Daniel Thompson,	2895|74
–Ephraim Langdon,	177|3	–Owners of Brig Fly,	819|37
–Newcomb & Allison,	11|34	–Savage & M'Clure,	700|83
–Wm. Osborn,	13|—	–Primrose Moore & Co.	1166|38
			–Stock the Nett of my Estate	13835|27½
	$ 46171|44½		$ 46171|11½

ILLUSTRATION 72. Financial "sheets" from 1817 Charles Gerisher's *Modern book-keeping, by double entry* ...

Item 25. 1817. James Maginness.

THE
FAMILY CLERK
AND
STUDENTS' ASSISTANT,

CONTAINING A NEAT, CONCISE, AND PLAIN METHOD OF

BOOK-KEEPING,

BY SINGLE ENTRY;

AND

A VARIETY OF

USEFUL FORMS

OF

Bills, Acc'ts Current, Deeds of Conveyance, Method of obtaining
Administration Acts, Petitions, patents for land,
Receipts, Orders, Letters on business, How to apply for warrants
Notes, Bonds, Short & easy method of Forms of application,
Leases, & Releases, calculating interest, Manner of proceeding
Powers of Attorney, Discount & Bank interest, at the land office, &c.

AND

DIRECTIONS TO A YOUNG SCHOLAR,

WHAT COURSES ARE NECESSARY TO PURSUE IN ORDER TO ACQUIRE

A USEFUL ENGLISH EDUCATION, &c.

BY JAMES MAGINNESS.

HARRISBURG:
PRINTED BY WM. GREER, FOR THE AUTHOR.
1817.

ILLUSTRATION 73. Title page from 1817 James Maginness'
The family clerk and student's assistant ...

Item 25. 1817. James Maginness. *The family clerk and student's assistant*... **Harrisburg, PA: Printed by Wm. Greer. [4] 190 [2] pgs. 21.5 cm. SS 41330 NUC NM0112634**

Other American Printings: No other known printings.

The book is written principally for the "use of boys going to school, in order to afford them useful exercises in writing." About one third of the book is devoted to bookkeeping. The text focuses on some rudiments of bookkeeping and definitions. The book describes bookkeeping as "the art of keeping accounts in a proper manner."

The first section includes lists and descriptions of the various types of books to be kept. The day book is the first one mentioned and a detailed description of how it is properly prepared is given.

The leger is discussed in the next section and the relationship between the leger and the day book is explained. The book describes how entries in the day book are posted to the leger. Leger accounts are not closed in a formal sense but are balanced. This balancing will determine whether the entity is better or worse off.

The memorandum book contains "everything you wish to remember, viz. your engagements, purchases, sales, etc." In addition, the expense book "should be kept; which may be done in manner as exemplified immediately after the form of a memorandum. A man, by so doing, can better see where and in what he can contract, or whether he can enlarge his expenses."

Directions are given to a boy learning bookkeeping. The book then provides examples entered into a day book and posted into the leger. This is followed by examples of a memorandum book and an expense book.

Toward the end of the book, there is a discussion and a presentation of a sales and purchases journal. This presentation summarizes the firm's sales, purchases, inventory, and certain expenses. It also shows the cost of goods sold and calculates profit. It was the only attempt made to discuss income.

The book also discusses estate accounting. An account form for executors and administrators is illustrated. The remaining pages are devoted to various topics such as computing interest, writing, officers of government, warrants, wills, advertisements, receipts, etc.

Written by Phil Siegel and Wanpen Wasinarom

1

Harrisburg, January 1st, 1816.

		D.	C.
Benjamin Bradley, *Dr.*			
L. 1. To 4½ yds. sup'fine b'd cloth, at 10 00		45	
3 do linen,	75	1	25
2 doz. gilt buttons,	1 00	2	
2 skeans silk,	12½		25
		18	50
Cornelius Cummins,			
L. 1. To 5 galls. 4th proof brandy, at 3 00		15	
15 lbs. lump sugar,	20	3	
		18	00
David Denny, esq.			
L. 1. To 1 box 8 by 10 glass, at 15 00		15	
12 lbs. Spanish whiting,	6		72
2 q'ts lintseed oil,	25		50
		16	22
—3d.—			
Edward Evans,			
L. 1. To 4 gall's sug. house molasses 1 00		4	
Frederick Foust,			
L. 1. To 1 qr. Cwt. best green coffee, at 30		8	40
1 do. best brown sugar,	20	5	60
1 lump do. wt. 9 lbs.	25	2	25
		16	25

ILLUSTRATION 74. Day book example from 1817 James Maginness' *The family clerk and student's assistant . . .*

1806	Benjamin Bradley, *Dr.*		D.	C.		1816	Contra,	*Cr.*		D.	C.
Jan'y 1	To sundries	1	48	50		Feb 25	By sundries		9	21	
Ap'l 21	do do	1	38	20		June 30	do balance due me	B	55	70	
			86	70					86	70	
1816	Cornelius Cummins,					1816	Contra,				
Jan'y 1	To sundries	1	18			Feb 10	By sundries	8	13	30	
June 30	do balance due him	A	5	30		Ap'l 27	do cash	14	10		
			23	10					23	30	
1816	David Denny, Esq.					1816	Contra,				
Jan'y 1	To sundries	1	16	22		Feb 16	By cash	8	16	22	
Feb. 13	do do	8	34	50		Ap'l 30	do do	15	20		
			50	72		June 30	do balance due me	B	14	50	
									50	72	
1816	Edward Evans,										
Jan'y 3	To 4 gallons molasses	1	4			1816	Contra,				
Mar. 6	do James Jenkins' order on him	10	30			Feb 12	By cash	8	10		
31	do sundries	12	15	50		June 30	do balance due me	B	83		
May	do do	15	43	50					93		
			93								
1816	Frederick Faust,					1816	Contra,				
Jan'y 3	To sundries	1	16	25			By cash	8	15		
May	do do	1	76	50			do balance due me	B	77	75	
			92	75					92	75	

ILLUSTRATION 75. Leger example from 1817 James Maginness' *The family clerk and student's assistant* ...

Item 26. 1818. Thomas H. Goddard. *The trial balance, or the book keeper's directory; showing a complete system of book keeping, commenced, carried on, and closed, and new books opened, upon a clear and experimental plan.* New York: Printed by J. Seymour. 1 page broadside 73 x 49.5 cm. (Not in SS) (Not in NUC)

Other American Printings: No other known printings.

This broadside is a concise presentation of a complete system of bookkeeping. It has never before been recognized as a complete accounting work. Bentley discusses this work, but did not realize that it was a broadside and warranted separate treatment as an accounting work. Goddard, in 1821, published *The merchant; or practical accountant,* and in describing this work, Bentley suggested that *The trial balance* was possibly a preliminary part of *The merchant; or practical accountant.* Bentley mentions another work, *The partnership; or, a system of book-keeping commenced in partnership*, which he also suggests may be a preliminary part of *The merchant; or practical accountant.* However, it seems plausible that *The partnership; or, a system of book-keeping commenced in partnership* is also a broadside similar to *The trial balance.*

The trial balance consists of a waste book, journal, ledger, cash book, check book, and journal No. 2. Numerous account are presented in the ledger section. In addition, subsidiary ledgers for bills payable and bills receivable are provided. A balance sheet is also presented that was "taken before closing the books."

Goddard's *The trial balance* is indeed a "complete system of book-keeping" and warrants separate attention as an accounting work. *The trial balance,* as a broadside actually contains more accounting than some of the previous texts discussed.

Written by Peter McMickle and Paul Jensen

186 *Item 26. 1818. Thomas H. Goddard.*

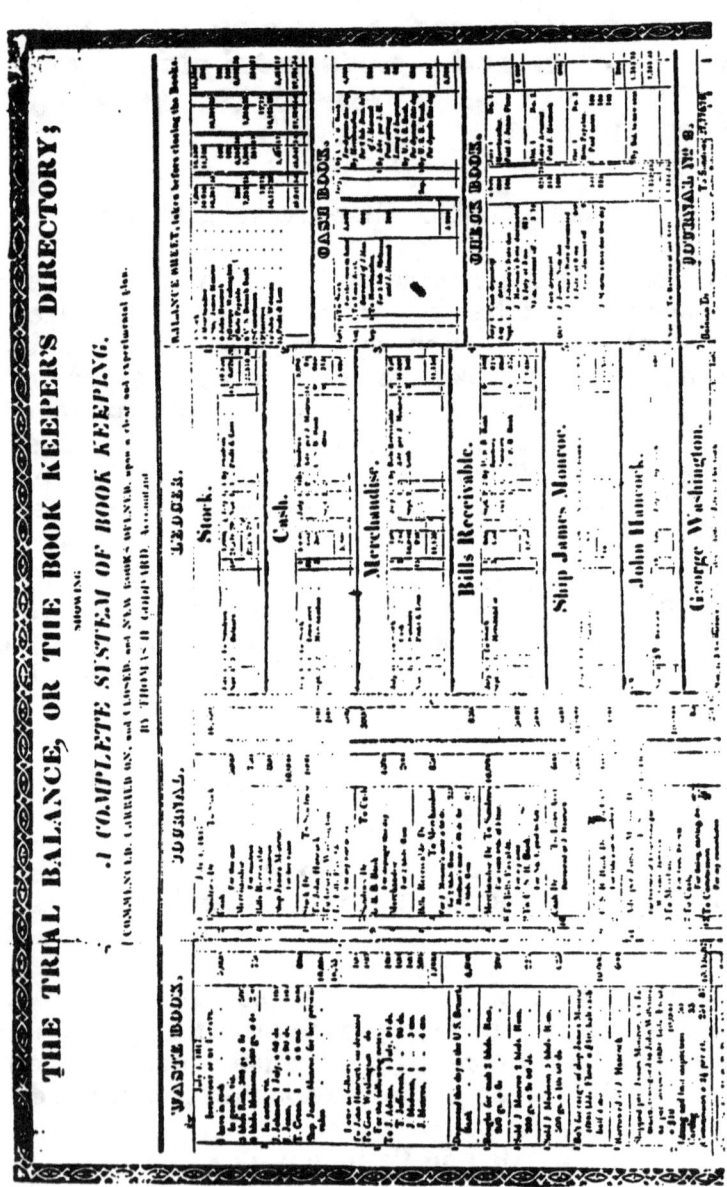

ILLUSTRATION 76. Top of Thomas H. Goddard's 1818 broadside entitled *The trial balance . . .* (greatly reduced).

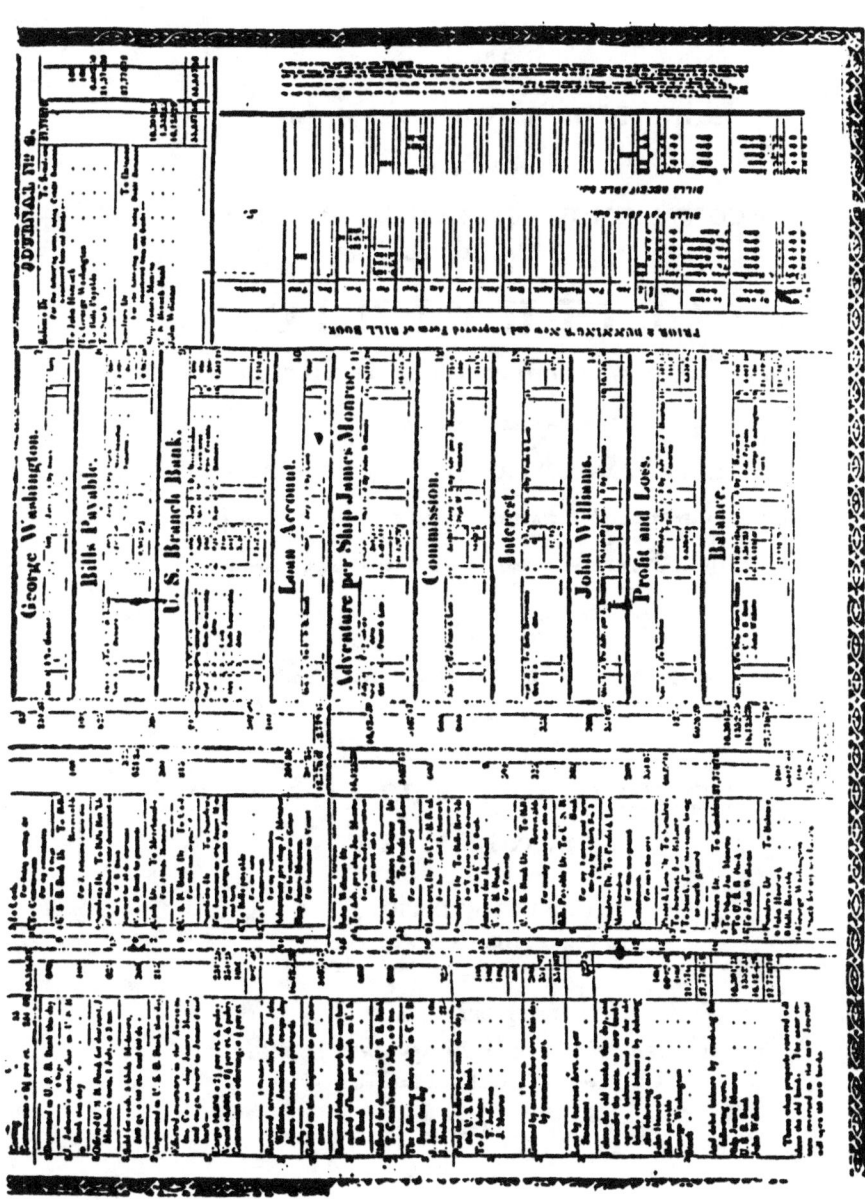

ILLUSTRATION 77. Bottom of Thomas H. Goddard's 1818 broadside entitled *The trial balance* . . . (greatly reduced).

THE

American Tutor's Assistant,

IMPROVED: OR,

A COMPENDIOUS SYSTEM OF DECIMAL,
PRACTICAL

ARITHMETIC,

COMPRISING THE USUAL METHODS OF CALCULATION,

WITH THE ADDITION OF

FEDERAL MONEY, AND OTHER DECIMALS,

Dispersed through the several rules of that useful science.

Adapted for the easy and regular instruction of Youth
in the United States.

COMPILED BY ZACHARIAH JESS.

CONTAINING ALSO,

COURSE OF BOOK KEEPING,

BY SINGLE ENTRY.

TWELFTH EDITION,
WITH CORRECTIONS AND ADDITIONS.

PHILADELPHIA:
PUBLISHED AND SOLD BY M'CARTY & DAVIS.
S. E. corner of Ninth and Race streets.
1819.

ILLUSTRATION 78. Title page from 1819 Zachariah Jess *The American tutor's assistant, improved* ...

Item 27. 1819. Zachariah Jess. *The American tutor's assistant, improved*... **twelfth edition. (Copyright 1818.) Philadelphia: Published and sold by McCarty and Davis. 188 [2] [23] pgs. 17 cm. SS 48375 NUC NJ0090410 (Earlier printings had no bookkeeping.)**

Other American Printings (with bookkeeping):

1821. Zachariah Jess. *The American tutor's assistant*... Philadelphia: Published and sold by McCarty and Davis. 188 [2] [23] pgs. 17 cm. NUC NJ0090411

1827. Zachariah Jess. *The American tutor's assistant*... Baltimore: Cushing. NUC NJ0090418

1828. Zachariah Jess. *The American tutor's assistant*... Pittsburgh: L. Loomis & Co. 188 [11] [10] 16 pgs. (Various pagings) 17 cm. NUC NJ0090420

[No Date]. Zachariah Jess. *The American tutor's assistant, improved*... (Copyright 1818.) (Stereotyped by D. & G. Bruce, New York) Philadelphia: Published by M. Polock. 188 [11] [10] 16 pgs. (Various pagings) 17 cm. SS 1818 (Not in NUC)

Introduction

This series attributed to Jess borrowed extensively from Hutton's single entry work. However, Jess made major alterations to Hutton's work and deserves separate treatment from the Hutton series.

The *National Union Catalogue* lists Jess's 1818 *The American tutor's assistant* as the edition in which bookkeeping begins. However, the 1819 edition is actually the first edition to contain any bookkeeping. The source of this error is a book in the Jess series that contains a copyright date of 1818, but the title page does not provide a publication date. It was apparently assumed that because the text examples were dated 1818 and the copyright was 1818, that the book must be an 1818 publication. However, upon close inspection, the title page states that the book is "stereotyped by D. & G. Bruce, New York." Stereotyping was not available for use until approximately the 1930's. Consequently, this book picked up by the *National Union Catalogue*, and others, as an 1818 edition containing bookkeeping, is actually a much later reprint.

Item 27. 1818. Zachariah Jess.

The bookkeeping section

The twelfth edition of *The American tutor's assistant* contains 216 pages in all, out of which 28 pages are devoted to bookkeeping. The section on bookkeeping carries the title "A Course of Bookkeeping by Single Entry." The title is followed by a page and a half of an introductory note which comprises the entire textual material of the bookkeeping section. This section stresses the need for all businessmen to be familiar with bookkeeping procedures. It has also been pointed out that the single entry calculations are easy and can be utilized without much difficulty in daily business. The rest of the introduction contains step by step instructions for day book entries and posting to the ledger.

The procedure for making day book entries has been explained as follows: "After preparing your day book with proper lines, you will notice that you must insert every person's name therein as follows, viz. Dr. for the articles and money that you obtain from any person."

The relationship between the day book and the ledger has been discussed in the following manner: "For all persons with whom the Day Book records any dealing the Ledger is thus made use of. The goods or money for which you are indebted are entered on the righthand or Cr. side, and those for which others are indebted to you are placed on the lefthand or Dr. side."

Posting to the ledger from the day book has been explained thus: "At the stated and proper periods, say at the end of each month's account, transfer your accounts from the Day Book to the Ledger, which is called posting. Thus divide the page into three equal parts beginning with the names of persons as they occur, writing them as you see by reviewing any page of the Ledger."

The day book does not have separate debit and credit columns. There is a single column showing sections for dollars and cents (dollar signs were not in use yet). Debit or credit is indicated by writing Dr or Cr at the right corner of the column for explanations. An alphabetical index has been used to locate the ledger page on which a particular account appears. In case of numerous transactions an account could appear on two or more separate pages of the ledger, and was so indicated on the alphabetical index. Posting references have been provided by writing in the day book or ledger folio on the margin.

The ledger has a date column, debit and credit columns, and money columns on each side. The corresponding debit or credit column in the ledger accounts is used to record the settlement of that account by way of receipt or payment of cash, or to transfer the account to another ledger folio. In effect the system represents accounting for accounts receivables and payables. There is no mention of assets, liabilities, expenses, and revenues.

Written by Peter McMickle, Khursheed Omer, and Paul Jensen

A

COURSE OF BOOK KEEPING,

BY

SINGLE ENTRY.

It would be superfluous to state, that every person of business ought to be acquainted with Book Keeping; the consequences of ignorance in so necessary a part of education too many have experienced, in the course of their commercial transactions. It is hoped the following treatise will be found to contain all the essential examples pertaining to Book Keeping by Single Entry. The calculations are easy, various, and such as generally occur in business. After preparing your Day Book with proper lines, you will notice that you must insert every person's name therein, as follows, viz. *Dr.* to the articles he or she receives on credit, and *Cr.* for the articles or money which you may obtain from any person. For all persons with whom the Day Book records any dealings, the Ledger is thus made use of. The goods or money, for which you are indebted, are entered on the right hand or *Cr.* side, and those for which others stand indebted to you are placed on the left or *Dr.* side. At stated and proper periods, say at the end of each month's account, transfer your accounts from the Day Book to the Ledger, which is called *Posting*. Thus: divide the page into three equal parts, beginning with the names of persons as they occur, writing them as you see by reviewing any page of the Ledger, and then entering them in the alphabet with each sirname under its proper letter, with the page in which it stands in the Ledger; remembering to insert in the small column to the left of that for dollars and cents marked D. B. or Day Book page, the page said account stands on in the Day Book; likewise noting in the margin of the latter, the page it is posted on in the Ledger, writing also the date of

ILLUSTRATION 79. First page of book keeping section in 1819 Zachariah Jess *The American tutor's assistant, improved* . . .

(1)

DAY BOOK.

	January 1, 1818.				D.	C.
1	*William Davis*,		*Dr.*			
	To 25 gallons rum,	. . .	at 1 25			
	16 lbs. candles,	. . .	0 20			
	11 soap,	. . .	0 14		35	99
1	*James McCorkle*,		*Dr.*			
	To 12 reams fine paper,	. . .	at 4 00			
	6 do. wrapping do.	. . .	1 50		66	00
	5th.					
1	*Peter Calhoun*,		*Dr.*			
	To 20 yards carpeting,	. . .	at 1 75			
	16 pieces hanging paper,	. .	0 62½		45	00
2	*Young & Davis*,		*Dr.*			
	To 4¾ yds. super cloth, at 9 00	. .	42 75			
	6¼ silk, 2 12½	. .	12 75		55	50
	6th.					
	Barton Smith,		*Dr.*			
	To 1C. 2qr. 14lb. coffee, at ,25	. .	45 50			
	2 16 sugar, ,13½	. .	9 36			
	17 indigo, 3 00	. .	51 00			
	2½ tea, 1 40	. .	3 50		109	36
	7th.					
2	*William Andrews*,		*Dr.*			
	To 3 M. quills at 7 50,	. .	22 50			
	4 doz. spelling books, at 2 25	. .	9 00		31	50
	9th.					
3	*Shadrach Mercer*,		*Dr.*			
	To 26 bushels Virginia coal, at .31	.	3 06			
	1 bbl. superfine flour,	. .	10 50		13	56

ILLUSTRATION 80. Day book example in 1819 Zachariah Jess *The American tutor's assistant, improved . . .*

Item 28. 1818. D. C. Roscoe

A NEW AND COMPENDIOUS SYSTEM OF BOOK-KEEPING;

BY

𝕯𝖔𝖚𝖇𝖑𝖊 𝕰𝖓𝖙𝖗𝖞:

ADAPTED TO THE COMMERCE OF THE UNITED STATES,

AND

CALCULATED, AS WELL TO EXONERATE THE ACCOUNTANT FROM THE TEDIOUS, COMPLEX AND LABORIOUS OPERATIONS OF THE ITALIAN SYSTEM, NOW IN USE, AS TO ENABLE THE MERCHANT EASILY TO ASCERTAIN THE TRUE STATE OF HIS AFFAIRS.

BY D. C. ROSCOE.

HAGERS-TOWN:
PRINTED BY WILLIAM D. BELL.
1818.

ILLUSTRATION 81. Title page from 1818 D. C. Roscoe's *A new and compendious system of book-keeping; by double entry* . . .

Item 28. 1818. D. C. Roscoe. *A new and compendious system of book-keeping; by double entry* . . . Hagers-Town, MD: Printed by William D. Bell. [4] [7] [9] [18] [16] pgs. 20 cm. SS 45579 NUC NR0420035

Other American Printings: No other known printings.

Introduction

The purpose of this book, as stated by the author, is "to lessen the labors of the accountant, render him less liable to err, and to present every necessary transaction in the most plain and simple form." The author also mentions that "very few persons acquire a complete knowledge of this art without practice; and as the Italian system, with most others founded upon it, in their explanatory matter, are very diffuse, and crowded with many complicated divisions, subdivisions, and intricate illustrations, the student toils through this heterogeneous mass, and after all his labour, is often compelled to abandon the study, with little better knowledge of the subject, than when he first began."

Description of the bookkeeping sections

The first major section of the book is entitled "Of Bookkeeping." According to the definition, book-keeping is "the history of public or private property, and shows, numerically, its increase or dimunition." This bookkeeping section is segregated into several parts.

The first part in this section is "Of the Journal." A journal of eight columns is put forth and several examples are provided. It is suggested that every transaction must be entered in its two parts for posting. These two parts are Debit and Credit with the Debit being the first part of every entry. In this part, the author explained numerous account entries. He stated that "Stock" may consist of cash, merchandise, and debts due to the merchant while "Cash" received is the debtor and paid away is the creditor. The "Stock and Cash Total" is a double-check system done page-by-page with no carry over of this total for a running balance for a period. An index of the accounts opened, as they occur, should be kept and no blank pages were to be allowed. This also was a method to ease finding entries and also a check against used pages in the pre-bound books of that time.

The second part in this section is "Of the Ledger." The

headings for the ledger were to be, in order: Date, Day, Explanation, Reference, Debit, and Credit. The reference column referred to the journal and an index of the ledger was also kept with no blank pages. The reference column could also be for the closing period and if it represented the "Balance" then it was to be so marked.

The third part is "Of the Different Accounts." Standard account titles were given, the first being "Stock" to which the value of all merchandise was debited. Next was "Cash" to which that at the commencement of business and all received or paid thereafter was debited or credited respectively. "Bills Payable" was debited for the cost while a Credit showed the consideration passed. On the other hand, "Bills Receivable" was debited for the consideration received and credited for what is paid thereon. An account for goods "at risk" (on adventure) or consigned was called "Suspense" and were kept separate from those items of unknown conclusion. The "Personal" account was to be such that "the debit shows the Merchant's charge against the person; and the credit shows his charge against the person; and the credit shows his charge against the merchant." The final account is the "Balance". The only purpose of this account was in the closing process such as may be said of the current use of "Income Summary". The debit in this account shows what is the worth and from the description from the other accounts of what it consists.

The fourth part is "Of Closing the Accounts." A separate page is used to add up all of the ledger accounts, and if they are equal, closing can be accomplished without added entry; however, if the debit is less, the closing consists of Debit To Balance while if the credit is less, the entry is Debit By Balance.

The fifth part is "Of the New Set of Books." After the first set of books is closed, a new set should be started from the old. Every unsettled account should be transferred to the new.

The last part is "Of Partnership." Each partnership entered will be kept separate. The profit or loss in the partnership will be figured using the "Stock".

The rest of this book contains 9 pages of examples of journal, 18 pages of ledger, and 16 pages of appendix. The items included in the appendix were bills of exchange, inland bill or draft, orders, checks, promissory notes, receipts, endorsement on a note, bill of purchase, exchange rates, interest, commissions, and discounting. These were given as simple examples for "copy work" as one may need or to use for adaptation.

Written by Thomas Clevenger and Ming-Ein Wang

JOURNAL.

L.	Vergennes, Jan. 1st, 1817.	STOCK.	CASH.
7	Stock Dr. to Samuel Strong,		
	For Cash 2000		
	For 26 Yds. Blk. Cloth, at 10$ 260		
	For 30 Yds. Blue Cassimere, at 2$ 60		
	For 50 Pieces Gurrahs, at 3$ 150		
	For 41 Cwt. Brown Sugar, at 10$ 410		
	For 6000lb. Green Coffee, at 15c. 900		
	For 12 Chests Imperial Tea, at 25$ 300		
	For Lewis Dean's Note, at 2 mo 494		
	For Reuben Brush's Note, at 20 d. 150		
	4734 00	. . .	. . .
	1.		
0	Cash Dr. to Stock,		
	For 2000$, in Stock	2000 00	2000 00
	1.		
8	Bill Receivable Dr. to Stock,		
	For Lewis Dean's Note, at 2 mo	494 00	. . .
	1.		
8	Bills Receivable Dr. to Stock,		
	For Reuben Brush's Note, at 20 d	150 00	. . .
	2.		
0	Stock Dr. to Cash,		
	For Repairing Store Room .	17 50	17 50
	2.		
0	Stock Dr. to Cash,		
	For Sundries, purchased of Richard Roe, per Bill	975 50	975 50
	2.		
9	Suspense Dr. to Stock,		
	For 2 Tons Madder, at 300$, shipped in the Dromes of Vergennes, James Farrar master, and consigned to Arza Crane, of Burlington, to sell for me . .	600 00	. . .
	Stock and Cash . . .		

ILLUSTRATION 82. Journal example from 1818 D. C. Roscoe's *A new and compendious system of book-keeping; by double entry*.

LEGER. 5

		STOCK.		Dr.	Cr.
1817.					
January	2	For the amounts frō Journal	3	5747 00	3214 00
	6	For do.	4	608 00	1469 00
	18	For do.	5	400 00	1540 69
	26	For do.	6	194 00	3927 8
	29	For do.	7	10 94	37 09
	30	For do.	8	. . .	755 40
	31	For do.	9	85 43	348 67
February	1	To Balance	L 18	664 59	. . .
				7966 96	7966 96

NOTE.—The debit of this account, showing, as before mentioned, the cost of all merchandise, with every expense and loss; and the credit, the produce by sales:—it is plain, that the gain is $664.59, which is placed to the credit of Balance in page 18. The gain will be cash, debts due to the Merchant, or both.

ILLUSTRATION 83. Leger example from 1818 D. C. Roscoe's *A new and compendious system of book-keeping; by double entry* ...

Item 29. 1818. Briant Sheys.

THE

AMERICAN

BOOK-KEEPER;

COMPRISING

A COMPLETE

SYSTEM OF BOOK-KEEPING;

IN THE

True Italian Form,

OR

BY DOUBLE ENTRY:

BOTH BY THEORY AND PRACTICE.

WITH THE

PRINCIPAL AUXILIARY BOOKS ANNEXED.

TOGETHER WITH

A NEW METHOD OF POSTING AND PROVING THE BOOKS.

DESIGNED FOR THE USE OF SCHOOLS, ACADEMIES AND COUNTING HOUSES, IN THE UNITED-STATES.

BY B. SHEYS, ACCOUNTANT.

New-York:
PRINTED AND SOLD BY COLLINS AND CO. 189, PEARL-STREET.

1818.

ILLUSTRATION 84. Title page from 1818 Sheys *The American book-keeper; comprising a complete system of book-keeping* ...

Item 29. 1818. B. [Briant] Sheys. *The American book-keeper; comprising a complete system of book-keeping...* **New York: Printed and sold by Collins and Co. [8] 333 [1] pgs. 22 cm. SS 45709 NUC NS0504502**

Other American Printings: No other known printings. See Item 21, which is another book (over 95% different) by the same author.

Introduction

This is the second book on accounting written by Briant Sheys and describes only double entry bookkeeping. His first book, printed in 1815, primarily covered single entry bookkeeping, although it did have a short section on double entry accounting.

In his preface, Sheys states that "bookkeeping is an art of daily use in life, and of the greatest importance in all commercial transactions, both foreign and domestic. To be well acquainted with it, both in theory and practice, is a necessary qualification to every man of business, in which all persons are more or less concerned." He continues his defense of bookkeeping by saying that "ignorance and inattention in this department, are rocks upon which thousands have split, and made shipwreck, not only of fortune, but of honesty and good conscience. It will greatly contribute to prevent some of the severest evils in life, such as vexatious lawsuits, perplexed arbitrations, loss of property, loss of friendships and good fellowship." Sheys also identifies the four principal difficulties in bookkeeping as "Journalizing; Proving the books; Detecting errors; and, Closing accounts by all the various ways that occur in practice."

In his introductory section, Sheys' states that "the whole of the work, interspersed with explanatory notes and instructions, formed on the most simple plan, is designed for the use of Schools, Academies and Counting-Houses in the United States."

A concise view of the contents

The first section of Sheys' book is entitled "An Introduction to Book-keeping" and is presented from pages 1 through 190. It provides "two sets of books on the theory of the art, in which the whole mystery of Journalizing, a principal difficulty, is explained in the completest manner." Numerous instructive notes are provided including the method of posting the books, closing the ledger, and opening the new books from the former balance account.

The next section, entitled the "third Set of Books" begins on page 191 and continues through page 270. This section includes descriptions and examples of the invoice book, sales book, cash book, expense book, check book and bank account book. A ledger is annexed to the set and includes all the various ways of closing the accounts "which often occur in practice." Also, the day-book, the manner of proving the books, and detecting errors by means of the proof journal, are fully explained.

The following section is called the "Manner of keeping the books in Banks" and comprises an explanation of bank bookkeeping. This section continues from page 271 to page 300. Sheys states that "as Banks have become numerous in all the States ... the author has subjoined, in miniature, the manner of keeping Bank books, with their several uses in practice."

His final section, pages 301 to 333, consists of an explanation of partnership bookkeeping and is entitled "Of Partnership in Separate Books." The section is made up entirely of account examples with the narrative portions actually contained within the account entries as "notes". The last two pages of this section "exhibit the manner of closing the books, when each Partner's Dividend is added to the former Stock, in order to increase their Capital."

The last few pages of the text contain advertisements for several books including Murray's *English Reader*.

Written by Paul Jensen

.37

    Cash Dr. to Sundries, received of A. B. principal and dividend,   5000.
    To A. B. my acct. in Co. for capital withdrawn   4000.
    To Profit and Loss, for interest, or dividend received,   1000.
    1. Debit Cash, to Sundries, received of A. B. Stock and Gain,   5000.
    2. Credit A. B. my acct. in Co. By Cash for capital withdrawn   4000.
    3. Credit Profit and Loss, By Cash, received of A. B. dividend,   1000.

Correcting Errors in the Waste Book and Journal.

Which are of six kinds, and may be corrected as follows:

    1. A whole post or entry may be omitted, which is corrected by writing it in a different place, with a reference to its proper place.
    2. Some words may be omitted, which can be supplied by interlining them, or writing them in the margin.
    3. A whole entry may be repeated, which can be corrected by cancelling, or crossing the superfluous part.
    4. If a word or sentence is repeated, cancel what is superfluous.
    5. If a Misnomer, or wrong name, is entered, either erase or cross it with two lines intersecting each other, and put the true one at the top.
    6. If the sum in any addition is wrong, or short extended, cancel the false sum, and mark it right.

To correct Errors in the Ledger.

    1. When an article is quite omitted, it is to be corrected by writing it on the proper side of the account, but not to crowd it in between two articles, where it should have stood; write it after the last article. And though it stands out of its place, as the date will shew, that will plainly appear to have been an omission.

ILLUSTRATION 85. Error correcting discussed in 1818 Sheys *The American book-keeper; comprising a complete system ...*

STANIFORD'S
PRACTICAL ARITHMETIC,

IN WHICH

THE RULES ARE RENDERED SIMPLE IN THE OPERATION, AND ILLUSTRATED BY A VARIETY OF

USEFUL QUESTIONS,

CALCULATED TO GIVE THE PUPIL A FULL KNOWLEDGE OF

FIGURES,

IN THEIR APPLICATION TO TRADE AND BUSINESS;

ADAPTED PRINCIPALLY TO

FEDERAL CURRENCY;

DESIGNED AS AN ASSISTANT TO THE PRECEPTOR IN COMMUNICATING, AND TO THE PUPIL IN ACQUIRING THE

SCIENCE OF ARITHMETIC;

TO WHICH IS ADDED,

A NEW AND CONCISE SYSTEM OF

BOOK-KEEPING,

BOTH BY

SINGLE AND DOUBLE ENTRY;

THE FORMER

CALCULATED FOR THE USE OF TRADERS IN RETAIL BUSINESS, FARMERS AND MECHANICS;

AND THE LATTER

FOR WHOLESALE DOMESTIC AND FOREIGN TRADE, AS CONDUCTED IN THE

UNITED STATES.

The whole designed for the use of Schools and Academies.

BY DANIEL STANIFORD, A. M.
Author of the Art of Reading and the Elements of English Grammar.

Tantum scimus, quantum memoria tenemus.

BOSTON:
PRINTED BY J. H. A. FROST, FOR WEST, RICHARDSON & LORD.
No. 75, Cornhill.
1818.

ILLUSTRATION 86. Title page from 1818 Daniel Staniford's *Staniford's practical arithmetic* . . .

Item 30. 1818. Daniel Staniford. *Staniford's practical arithmetic* **...** **Boston: Printed by J. H. A. Frost for West, Richardson & Lord.** **[7] 324 pgs. 19 cm. SS 45789 NUC NS0860884**

Other American Printings:

1820. Daniel Staniford. *Staniford's practical arithmetic* ... Second edition. Boston: Printed by J. H. A. Frost for West, Richardson & Lord. [7] 324 pgs. 19 cm. SS 3307 NUC NS0860885

Introduction

Daniel Staniford (1766-1820) authored four textbooks. His *The art of reading* went through twelve editions from 1800 through 1817. Two grammar books, *The elements of English grammar* and *A short but comprehensive grammar*, were published in 1813 (second edition in 1815) and 1794 (fourth edition not dated) respectively. Staniford's *Practical arithmetic* was published in 1818. A second edition was published in 1820, the year Staniford died.

The purpose of Staniford's *Practical arithmetic* was to illustrate the general rules of arithmetic with easy practical questions and to "prepare the scholar for business." His treatment of arithmetic is fairly standard for the time. The book is noteworthy, however, in that a full forty percent of the total number of pages is devoted to bookkeeping. Staniford writes in his preface that the neglect of the study of bookkeeping is a "material defect in the present system of education." Nearly seventy-five percent of Staniford's treatment of bookkeeping is in the form of examples such as journal and waste book entries and ledger accounts.

Practical arithmetic is divided into three sections consisting of practical arithmetic, bookkeeping by single entry, and bookkeeping by double entry. The book, including preliminary matter, is 324 pages long. The preliminary information consists of a title page, an attestation by the Clerk of the District of Massachusetts of authorship, a preface, errata, two recommendations, an explanation of characters used, and the contents. Three of the eight pages of introductory material are numbered. The section on practical arithmetic is 188 pages long, one unnumbered page and pages 10-196. The first bookkeeping section, single entry bookkeeping, consists of a title page, one unnumbered page, pages 199-233, and a blank page. The total number of pages in this section is 38. The section on double entry bookkeeping also has its own title page, three unnumbered pages, and pages 237-315. The total number of pages in this section is 83. An appendix to this bookkeeping section has one unnumbered page and pages 319-324 for a total of seven pages.

Single entry bookkeeping

In the section on single entry bookkeeping, Staniford described the form and use of the waste book and ledger. The textual material on single entry bookkeeping is rather brief (four pages). Most of the section consists of journal entries and ledger accounts. According to Staniford, single entry bookkeeping is more "concise and simple" than double entry bookkeeping. The former is primarily for the use of retailers, mechanics, and farmers. Staniford provides the somewhat curious acronym "Idoc" which stands for "In Dr. Out Cr." as an aid to jog the scholar's memory. Another interesting matter is Staniford's description of the balancing of the accounts.

> When all the transactions are correctly posted into the Ledger, each account is balanced by subtracting the less side from the greater, entering the balance on the less side, by which both sides will be made equal. The balances being added to the cash on hand and the value of the goods unsold, the sum is the net of the estate, which compared with the stock at commencing business exhibits the profit and loss.

Staniford states that single entry bookkeeping is "essentially defective in its not giving the merchant a correct knowledge of the state of his affairs, without the laborious task of 'taking account of stock', which is very subject to error." On the other hand, the double entry method is valuable to merchants and traders because it does give knowledge of the state of affairs. The so-called Italian method is the more "complicated and perfect" method of bookkeeping. With double entry bookkeeping, "things, as well as persons are made Drs. and Crs."

Double entry bookkeeping

In the section on double entry bookkeeping, Staniford briefly describes the journal. He says that the experienced bookkeeper can eliminate either the waste book or the journal. Staniford lists 45 rules for distinguishing the title Dr. and Cr. These rules are accompanied by a few sentences of explanations and notes. References are made to the examples of waste book and journal entries which he provides. In addition to giving directions for writing in the journal and posting the journal, Staniford gives a more comprehensive treatment of the ledger in this section. He lists eighteen rules with explanations for debiting, crediting, and balancing accounts in the ledger. The trial balance and closing of ledger accounts are also discussed. In addition to the waste book and journal entries, Staniford provides an example of a ledger index and ledger accounts.

Examples of mercantile forms which were often illustrated in arithmetic books are given in the appendix. Staniford also describes twelve auxiliary books commonly used by merchants. These books include the cash book, bill book, invoice book, sales book, account current book, commission book, book of ship's account, expense account book, letter book, postage book, receipt book, and check book.

Written by Debra Wright

A

SHORT AND PLAIN

SYSTEM

OF

BOOK-KEEPING,

BY

SINGLE ENTRY;

CALCULATED FOR THE USE OF

RETAILERS, MECHANICS AND FARMERS.

BOSTON, SEPTEMBER, 1818.

ILLUSTRATION 87. First page of single entry book-keeping section in 1818 *Staniford's practical arithmetic* . . .

The Birth of American Accountancy

```
202                  JOURNAL.

              Boston, January 1, 1817.
A. F.                                                    $   C
      Inventory of ready money, goods, and debts
        due to Aaron Richardson, merchant, Boston.
       Money on hand              .    .    .   $740
    3  John Grant owes me         .    .    .    140
    2  Thomas Moore               .    .    .    175
    4  William Young              .    .    .    224
       75 yards broadcloth a 3$   .    .    .    225
       121¾ yards of linen a ,75  .    .    .     91,31
       20 cwt. sugar a $10,75     .    .    .    215
       800 lb. coffee a ,20       .    .    .    160
                                                          1970 31
                        ————————
      List of debts owed by the said Aaron Rich-
        ardson.
    2 To Thomas Andrews, as per account    .    $320
    3    Amos Penniman            .    .    .     78
    2    James Trask              .    .    .    132
                                                           530
                        ———— 5 ————
    1 David Eaton, Dr.
      To 5 yards broadcloth       .    .    .  a $4,25
         6 do. linen              .    .    .  a   ,80
         20 lb. coffee            .    .    .  a   ,29
                                                            31 85
                        ———— 12 ————
    1 James Munson, Dr.
      To 8 yards broadcloth       .    .    .  a $4,25
         2 cwt. sugar             .    .    .  a  12,75
         30 lb. coffee            .    .    .  a    ,29
                                                            68 20
                        ———— 15 ————
    2 Thomas Andrews. Dr.
      To Cash, paid him in part   .    .    .    140
                        ———— 22 ————
    3 Rufus Perkins, Cr.
      By 3 chests hyson tea containing 230lb. net, a $1,20
         3 do. bohea tea containing 270lb. net a ,75
                                                           478 50

      N.B. By single entry goods bought are entered either in an in-
      voice book, kept for that purpose, or posted immediately into the
      Ledger, from the invoices or bills of parcels. This mode, howev-
      er, is not adopted here, but credited the seller at the time, and
      afterwards transferred to his account in the Ledger.
```

ILLUSTRATION 88. Single entry journal example from 1818 *Staniford's practical arithmetic*...

A

NEW AND CONCISE

SYSTEM

OF

BOOK-KEEPING,

BY

DOUBLE ENTRY;

CALCULATED FOR THE USE OF

WHOLESALE, DOMESTIC AND FOREIGN

TRADE,

AS CONDUCTED IN THE

UNITED STATES.

The whole designed for the use of Schools and Academies.

BY D. STANIFORD, A.M.

ILLUSTRATION 89. First page of double entry book-keeping section in 1818 *Staniford's practical arithmetic* ...

278 — JOURNAL.

Boston, January 1, 1817.

Dr. L.F.	Cr. L.F.		$	C.
	1	**Sundries Dr. to Stock** $22527,50		
1		Cash deposited in the Union Bank . $4000		
3		House in Hanover-street . 2500		
3		Lands for 750 acres in County of Washington, D' of Maine, a ,75 per acre 562,50		
3		Ship Massachusetts . . . 7000		
3		Household furniture . . . 1500		
		Notes receivable,		
		J. Thomson's note, dated Nov. 10 last, payable to my order, at 6 months $350		
2		D. Jones' note, dated Dec. 3d last, payable to my order at 3 months, 410		
		———760		
4		Broadcloth 250 yds. a $3,50 per yd. 875		
4		Linen, 400 yards, a ,80 . . 320		
4		Port wine, 7 hhds. a $45 per hhd. 315		
4		Sugar, 20 hhds. w'g. 240 cwt. a $10,50 2520		
4		Rum, 12 puncheons, a $125 per pun. 1500		
4		T. Lamson, mer. Boston, owes me . 400		
5		A. Locke, carpenter, Salem, owes me 275	22527	50
		"		
1		**Stock Dr. to Sundries** $4490		
	5	To J. Lewis, mer. Boston, due to him $140		
	5	Lemuel Samson, mer. Boston, ditto 800		
	5	James Munson, mer. Boston, ditto 2050		
	5	Jos. Franklin, mer. Boston, ditto 1500	4490	
		2		
7	4	**Charles Lee Dr. to sugar,** For 72 cwt. a $12,50 per cwt. . .	900	
		7		
1	4	**Cash Dr. to rum,** For 9 puncheons, a $135 per pun. . .	1215	
		12		
5	1	**James Lewis Dr. to cash,** Paid him in full	140	
		15		
4	1	**Port wine Dr. to cash,** For 8 hhds. a $42 per hhd. .	336	
		18		
4	7	**Linen Dr. to Andrew Newman,** For 1000 yards, a ,70 per yd. . .	700	
		19		
4	1	**Sugar Dr. to cash,** For 84 cwt. a $10,72,6,4, per cwt.	901	
		20		
5	4	**Coffee Dr. to sugar,** Received 4032 lb. a ,25 per lb. in barter for 84 cwt. sugar, a $12 per cwt. . . .	1008	

ILLUSTRATION 90. Double entry journal example from 1818 Staniford's practical arithmetic...

Item 31. 1819. Benjamin Davies

A NEW

AND

CONCISE SYSTEM

OF

BOOK-KEEPING,

ACCORDING TO THE ITALIAN METHOD

OF

DOUBLE ENTRY.

Adapted to the Commerce of the United States.

BY BENJAMIN DAVIES.

SECOND EDITION, WITH ADDITIONS AND IMPROVEMENTS.

PHILADELPHIA:

PUBLISHED BY BENJAMIN JOHNSON,
No. 31, Market Street.

1819.

ILLUSTRATION 91. Title page from 1819 Benjamin Davies *A new and concise system of book-keeping* ...

Item 31. 1819. Benjamin Davies. *A new and concise system of book-keeping* **... Second edition. Philadelphia: Benjamin Johnson. 66 pgs. (Various pagings) 21.5 cm. SS 47793 (No first edition is known)**

Other American Printings: No other known printings.

Introduction

A new and concise system of book-keeping, according to the italian method of double entry. . . adapted to the commerce of the United States is the second edition of a book by Benjamin Davies printed in 1819. Bentley and Leonard note that the first edition was deposited for copyright in 1813 by Benjamin Johnson, proprietor of the copyright. However, no copies of this edition are known to survive or to have necessarily existed. The title page of the 1819 printing states Second Edition, with Additions and Improvements, Philadelphia, published by Benjamin Johnson, No. 31, Market Street. Illustrations in this printing are all dated 1819.

Benjamin Davies (1774-1806) also wrote a textbook called *A new system of modern geography*, which had editions in 1805, 1813, and 1815. In 1804, in Philadelphia, there was printed a 28 page tract entitled *The petition of benjamin davies and richard north to the general assembly of pennsylvania. . . some account of the City of Philadelphia* was written by Mr. Davies in 1794. Mr. Davies also compiled a monthly publication, the *Philadelphia magazine and review; or monthly repository*, which seems to have only been printed from January to June of 1799. This magazine contained about 30 to 50 pages each month, and stated that its purpose was to further the literature of America since America was developing its own literature and was no longer dependent on England.

A New & Concise System of Book-Keeping

The author states that book-keeping or merchant's accounts is the art of recording with order and accuracy all mercantile trasactions. From this art the merchant can get a complete statement of each branch of his affairs showing profit and loss of each transaction and for his whole business. The merchant will thereby know the true situation of his affairs, whether profitable or not, and thus be able to manage them to the best advantage. It is pointed out that the Italian method of book-keeping by double entry is better than the other modes of bookkeeping. Three books are mainly required: wastebook, journal and ledger. Eight rules are given for posting to the journal. The ledger accounts are either real, personal, or fictitious. In fictitious accounts all articles appear which have relation to Stock, or to Profit and Loss. By Stock is meant the merchant himself, to whom the books belong, for his name never appears.

The mark of the square root is used in the folio column to indicated that the accounts have been journalized. To ascertain the accuracy of the books, it is necessary to make a trial balance of the ledger. When the Profit or Loss is balanced, the balance is carried to the Stock account. The author gives directions for setting up books as to how to draw lines and columns. Definitions and explanations are given of various types of business transactions, for example bartering, bills of exchange, foreign trade, receipts, promissory notes, etc.

The book consists off about 28 pages, of which the first eight pages are explanations. Page 9 begins the examples of the wastebook. The wastebook has Philadelphia, January 1, 1819, at the top. The money columns have D. (dollars) and C. (cents). at the top. The assets are listed first, although the house and farm are listed before cash, then the payables. The accounts mention discounts for quick payment of notes and interest on notes. Money is recorded in the narrative in various types of currency, and it is converted into federal money in the money columns. Sometimes the method of conversion is stated. One excerpt from the Wastebook is called Account of My Family Expenses:

> Finding the keeping of a family expense account in a memorandum book troublesome I shall in the future appropriate about the beginning of each month, a sum supposed adequate to the expenses of a month and reduce or increase the appropriation as experience may prove necessary.

The first appropriation was for $150, and the amount remained about $200 for the entire year.

The items from the wastebook are then posted to the journal. The index to the ledger is shown, and then the ledger is shown. The ledger gives the accounts on one page and the contra accounts are listed on the opposite page. The balancing of the ledger is dated December 31, 1819, and it lists cash first, then bills receivable, merchandise general, accounts (in various people's names), land, and house. The contra accounts are bills payable, accounts (in various people's name), and stock.

There are various accounts where merchandise is shipped on board certain vessels with a listing of the items shipped, the charges for shipping, and the commission percentage paid. One account states goods consigned to J. Winston, merchant, with instructions to vest the net proceeds in tobacco and ship it to Philadelphia. Another account, William Brown, states "being declared insolvent, and his creditors having agreed to a composition of 60 cents in the dollar, I have this day received my dividend on his debt." Other examples include:

> In June, bought of government, land in Illinois, 640 acres, pay 1/4 in ready money, 3 equal yearly payments in installments. In July, bought a House, in Market Street for $20,000 - gave him my house, $6,500, my farm, $5,000, and my bond payable in one year with interest, $8,500.

The book ends giving examples of a Wastebook B and a Journal B showing how to open up books for the next year, January 1, 1820.

Written by L. C. Middleton and Peter McMickle

Item 31. 1819. Benjamin Davies

Philadelphia, November 1st, 1819. 18

Fo.		D.	C.
.1	Sundry accounts Drs. to Lancaster Farm		
.9	Family Expenses for sundry produce received from the tenant - - - - $160 0		
.2	Cash received of ditto - - - 65 0	225	—
.12	Bills of Exchange Dr. to John Oldcastle		
.13	For a bill of exchange bought of him, drawn by Henry Morgan on Peter Greason London, payable 30 days after sight for - - Sterling £310 6 0	1379	11
.12	Thomas Wilson of London Dr. To Bills of Exchange		
.12	For a bill drawn by Henry Morgan on Peter Greason London for £310 6 0 sterling payable at 30 days sight—Remitted per the Rebecca captain Speed	1379	11
	———— December 1st. ————		
.9 .2	Family Expenses Dr. to Cash	100	—
	———— 10th ————		
.7	Robert Fleming Dr. to Port wine		
.6	For 10 pipes containing 900 gallons at $2 50	2250	—
	———— 15th ————		
.11	Market Street House Dr.		
.12	To George Grant for the price of the house valued at	20000	—
.12	George Grant Dr. to Sundry accounts, viz.		
.1	Chesnut street House sold him at - $6500 0		
.1	Lancaster Farm, sold him at - - 5000 0		
.5	Bills payable for my bond payable in one year with interest - - - - 8500 0	20000	—
	———— 20th ————		
.3	Bills Receivable Dr. to Chesnut street House		
.1	For A. Henry's note at 60 days for balance of rent	160	41
	———— 26th ————		
.11	Daniel Drake Dr. to Bills Payable		
.5	For my note to him for balance of account -	575	—
	———— 31st ————		
.3	Bills Receivable Dr. to Thomas Gregory		
.12	For his note at 30 days - - - -	500	—

ILLUSTRATION 92. Journal example from 1819 Benjamin Davies *A new and concise system of book-keeping* ...

5	Dr. Merchandize General				D.	C.		Contra		Cr.		5
1819.							1819.					
Jan. 1	1	To Stock		1	644	75	Jan. 13	2	By Thomas Ellis		6	156	25
" 6	2	" Cash		2	293	—	April 15	6	" William Peters		9	98	—
March 30	5	" John Barnes		9	653	55	May 25	6	" David Jones		11	80	—
June 13	8	" Thomas Wilson		12	1372	45	June 1	8	" Mary Jones		11	77	50
" 17	9	" Cash		2	150	—	" 20	9	" James Peters		10	104	—
" 22	10	" Humphrey Clinker		12	100	—	" 22	10	" Jane Strawberry		12	110	—
		" Profit and Loss		8	659	27			" Humphrey Clinker		12	100	—
									" George Fanshaw		8	65	05
									" Balance, for stock on hand		14	2200	—
					3872	80						3872	80

	Dr. Bills Payable						1819.		Contra		Cr.		
1819.							Jan. 1	2	By Stock for George Grays draft		1	800	—
Jan. 30	3	To Sundry accounts			4200	—	" 8	2	" Richard Wilson		3	1000	—
April 14	5	" Cash paid my note to Robert Turner		2	200	—	" 20	3	" Robert Fleming		7	4200	—
May 10	7	" Sundry Accounts			540	—	Feb. 10	3	" Robert Turner		8	200	—
" 22	7	" Cash paid my note to I. May		2	100	—	March 25	5	" Israel May		9	100	—
" 30	6	" Sundry accounts			800	—	April 15	6	" Spermaceti oil		10	540	—
Aug. 8	11	" Cash paid my note to R. Wilson		2	1000	—	Dec. 15	13	" George Grant		12	8500	—
		" Balance		14	9075	—	" 26	13	" Daniel Drake		11	575	—
					15915	—						15915	—

ILLUSTRATION 93. Two ledger pages from 1819 Benjamin Davies *A new and concise system of book-keeping* ...

Item 32. 1820. Israel Alger.

THE

YOUNG MERCHANT'S MANUAL,

OR

PRACTICAL BOOK-KEEPER:

CONTAINING THE FUNDAMENTAL PRINCIPLES

OF

MERCANTILE SCIENCE;

Upon a System new in Theory and Practice; effectually uniting both, in a plain, and easy

METHOD OF INSTRUCTION,

Calculated to give, in a short time, a competent, scientific, and practical Knowledge

OF

Book-Keeping by Double Entry.

BY I. ALGER, JUN. A. M.
Instructer in Languages and Sciences usually taught in Academies.

BOSTON:
PRINTED FOR THE AUTHOR.
1820.

ILLUSTRATION 94. Title page from 1820 Israel Alger's *The young merchant's manual, or practical book-keeper* . . .

Item 32. 1820. I. [Israel] Alger. *The young merchant's manual, or practical book-keeper*... Boston: Printed for the author. [48] pgs. (Various paging) 32.5 cm. NUC NA0168009

Other American printings: No other known printings, however a second part was published in 1823.

1823. I. [Israel] Alger. *Key to book-keeping; or, a practical illustration of the fundamental principles of mercantile science; being the second part to the young merchant's manual, or practical book-keeper*... Boston: Printed for the author by True & Green 104pgs. (Various pagings) 25.5 cm. NUC NA0168007

Description of *The young merchant's manual*...

Alger was born in 1787 and died in 1825. The title page refers to him as an instructor in languages and sciences usually taught in academies. In the first lesson, book-keeping is defined as "the history of public or private property, in all its change; and of the causes of these changes, and of the increase or decrease of property following from them." Alger's book-keeping system consists of:

1. The books made use of, and their several uses
2. The methods of recording the transactions
3. The methods of balancing the books.

The principal books used in his system are the waste book, journal, and ledger. The waste book, the first day-book, begins with an inventory; every transaction that occurs in the course of business is to be written in this book. Alger defines the term "transaction" as "the giving or passing away." He describes how to record transactions in the waste book.

The journal, the second day-book, which is kept on the right hand page in the waste-book, has two columns, one for the Drs. and the other for the Crs. It is simply an index to the ledger, and the sales book.

The ledger is the chief or grand book of accounts to which the merchant transfers the Dr. and Cr. amount from the journal, so that at any time he may know the true state of any particular accounts, or of the whole of his business with ease. Alger divides the merchant's ledger into three classes:

Item 32. 1820. Israel Alger.

1. Real accounts
2. Personal accounts
3. Summary, intermediate, or imaginary accounts.

Real accounts are "the accounts of effect or things which may be a person's property, and the articles of which, when connected with each other, show instantly a barter or exchange." Personal accounts are accounts of the persons with whom we deal. The summary accounts represent the merchant himself.

The general rules for Dr. and Cr. applying to the three classes of accounts are given. Alger discusses the eight methods of closing the accounts. He then explains in detail characteristics for nineteen accounts.

Two kinds of ledger, double paged ledger and single paged ledger, are explained. Four ways for detecting seven possible errors or mistakes before balancing are suggested:

1. By examination of the posting marks on the journal, with reference to their respective ledger folios.
2. By the particular, and
3. By the general trial balance
4. By the separation of the money columns by months, in the ledger.

Alger explains the auxiliary, or helping books, which are: the cash book, the bill-book, the invoice book, the sales' book, the book of acc'ts, the book of commissions, the book of expenses, the copy book of letters, the book of postage of letters, the book of ship accounts, the receipt-book, and the pocket-book. He states that the first four of these books are indispensably necessary to every merchant. The remaining are employed at the merchant's pleasure or as his business may require.

Written by Wanpen Wasinarom and Steve Ming Wong

3] *Waste, or First Day-Book.* [Second

	DOLLS.	CTS.
Boston, July 26th, 1820.		
Bought at the auction sales, James Henry, agent, at six months, with the condition of the abatement of 1 per cent. per month for ready money,		
5 pipes of port wine, at $333 1-3d per Pipe	1,666	67
———26———		
Bought of James Ker, on my note payable in two months,		
4 Tons Madder, at $12 2-9 per cwt.	977	78
———27———		
Discounted to James Henry, the agent of the sales, my debt for the 5 pipes of port wine,		
The discount is . . . . $ 100 00		
And the sum due 1,566 67		
Paid by my draft on the State Bank	1,566	67
———27———		
Discounted to James Ker, my note payable in two months, at 6 per cent. per annum,		
The discount is . . . . . . $ 9 68		
And the sum due . . . . . 968 10 . . . $977 78		
Paid in ready money	968	10
———28———		
Paid James Taylor the award of the examiners, who viewed the hogshead of madder M. A. by draft on the State Bank.		
My half is . . . . $ 23 33		
John Scott's is 23 33	46	66
———28———		
Paid for the honour of William Kane of New-York, $222 22 his draft on James Henry, protested yesterday for nonpaym't.		
Charges of protest . . . . $ 2 22		
Commission 1-2 per cent. 1 11	225	55
———Aug. February 2———		
Received from William Kane of New-York, an account of the sales of the 4 1-2 tons madder consigned to him 12th current.		
The total sales $1,698 89		
His charges $2 56		
Commission & insurance of credit 4 per cent. . 3 44 6 00	1,692	89
For which he has remitted me a draft of Laine and Co. on King and Co. at 7 days sight, for . . . . $1,853 89.	1,853	89
which includes my former demand of $ 225 55		
———2———		
Received from James Walsh, lent to him $444 44		
Interest for 1 Month, at 6 per cent. 1 85	446	29
———2———		
Paid the expenses of the house for the last month	222	22
Salaries . . . . $ 88 89		
Petty Charges 15 55	104	44

ILLUSTRATION 95. Waste book example in 1820 Israel Alger's *The young merchant's manual, or practical book-keeper . . .*

THE

AMERICAN SYSTEM

OF

PRACTICAL

BOOK-KEEPING,

ADAPTED TO THE

COMMERCE OF THE UNITED STATES,

IN

ITS DOMESTIC AND FOREIGN RELATIONS;

AND

EXEMPLIFIED IN ONE SET OF BOOKS, KEPT BY DOUBLE ENTRY.

DESIGNED FOR THE USE OF SCHOOLS.

To WHICH ARE ADDED,

FORMS OF THE MOST APPROVED MODERN

AUXILIARY BOOKS.

A COPPERPLATE ENGRAVING, TWENTY-ONE BY SIXTEEN INCHES,

EXHIBITING THE FINAL BALANCE OF THE LEGER.

BY JAMES BENNETT,

ACCOUNTANT, LECTURER ON BOOK-KEEPING, AND PRESIDENT OF THE ACCOUNTANTS'
BENEVOLENT SOCIETY OF THE CITY OF NEW-YORK.

NEW-YORK:

PRINTED BY ABM. PAUL, CORNER OF WATER-STREET AND BURLING-SLIP.

1820.

ILLUSTRATION 96. Title page from 1820 James Bennett's *The American system of practical book-keeping . . .*

Item 33. 1820. James Bennett. *The American system of practical book-keeping* **... New York: Printed by Abm. Paul. [20] 72 pgs. (Various pagings) 24 cm. With broadside bound in. NUC NB0313008**

Other American Printings:

1820. James Bennett. *The American system of practical book-keeping* ... New York: Printed by Abm. Paul. [20] 72 [94] pgs. (Various pagings) 24 cm. With broadside bound in. This printing of the first edition contains a 94 page section entitled *Jackson's book-keeping adapted to the coin and commerce of the United States* ... By James Bennett, the section is separately dated 1821. (Not in NUC)

1820. James Bennett. The American system of practical book-keeping . . . New York: Printed by Abm. Paul. [20] 84 pgs. (Various pagings) 24 cm. With broadside bound in. This printing has 12 extra pages that was part of the Jackson section mentioned above. NUC NB0313009

1824. James Bennett, A.& M. *The American system of practical book-keeping* ... Sixth edition. New York: Collins & Hannay. With broadside bound in. NUC NB0313010

1824. James Bennett, A.& M. *The American system of practical book-keeping* ... Seventh edition. New York: Collins & Hannay. [24] [64] pgs. (Various pagings) 24 cm. With broadside bound in. NUC NB0313011

1826. James Bennett, A.& M. *The American system of practical book-keeping* ... Eighth edition. New York: Collins & Hannay. [24] [64] pgs. (Various pagings) 24 cm. With broadside bound in. NUC NB0313012

1826. James Bennett, A.& M. *The American system of practical book-keeping* ... ninth edition. New York: Collins & Hannay. (Unpaged) 23.5 cm., in 4 series. With broadside bound in. NUC NB0313013

1828. James Bennett, A.& M. *The American system of practical book-keeping* ... Tenth edition. New York: Collins & Hannay. With broadside bound in. NUC NB0313014

1828. James Bennett, A.& M. *The American system of practical book-keeping* . . . Eleventh edition. New York: Collins & Hannay. With broadside bound in. NUC NB0313015

1829. James Bennett, A.& M. *The American system of practical book-keeping* . . . twelfth edition. New York: Collins & Hannay. With broadside bound in. NUC NB0313016

1831. James Bennett, A.& M. *The American system of practical book-keeping* . . . Fourteenth edition. New York: Collins & Hannay. [32] 72 pgs. With broadside bound in. NUC NB0313018

1833. James Bennett, A.& M. (Attorney and Counsellor at Law). *The American system of practical book-keeping* . . . Fifteenth edition. New York: Collins & Hannay. [32] 72 pgs. 25.5 cm. With broadside bound in. NUC NB0313019

1835. James Bennett, A.& M. (Attorney and Counsellor at Law). *The American system of practical book-keeping* . . . Sixteenth edition. New York: B. & S. Collins. 104 pgs. 25 cm. With broadside bound in. NUC NB0313020

1837. James Bennett, A.& M. (Attorney and Counsellor at Law). *The American system of practical book-keeping* . . . Eighteenth edition. New York: Collins, Keese & Co. With broadside bound in. NUC NB0313021

1839. James Bennett, A.& M. (Attorney and Counsellor at Law). *The American system of practical book-keeping* . . . Nineteenth edition. New York: Collins, Keese & Co. With broadside bound in. NB0313022

1842. James Arlington Bennett, LL.D. *The American system of practical book-keeping* . . . Twenty-first edition. New York: Collins, Brother & Co. 104 pgs. 27 cm. With broadside bound in. NUC NB0313023

1843. James Arlington Bennett, LL.D. *The American system of practical book-keeping* . . . Twenty-second edition. New York: Harper & brothers 128 pgs. 27 cm. With broadside bound in. NUC NB0313024

1848. James Arlington Bennett, LL.D. *The American system of practical book-keeping* . . . Twenty-eighth edition. New York: M. H. Newman & Co. 160 pgs. 25.5 cm. With broadside bound in. NUC NB0313025

1851. James Arlington Bennett, LL.D. *The American system of practical book-keeping* . . . Twenty-ninth edition. New York: M. H. Newman & Co. With broadside bound in. NUC NB0313026

1852. James Arlington Bennett, LL.D. *The American system of practical book-keeping* . . . New York: M. H. Newman & Co. 160 pgs. With broadside bound in. NUC NB0313027

1854. James Arlington Bennett, LL.D. *The American system of practical book-keeping* . . . Thirty-first edition. New York: Ivison & Phinney. 160 pgs. 26 cm. With broadside bound in. NUC NB0313029

1855. James Arlington Bennett, LL.D. *The American system of practical book-keeping* . . . Thirty-first edition. New York. With broadside bound in. NUC NB0313030

1857. James Arlington Bennett, LL.D.. *The American system of practical book-keeping* . . . Thirty-first edition. Philadelphia: J. B. Lippincott & Co. 160 pgs. 25.5 cm. With broadside bound in. (Not in NUC)

1862. James Arlington Bennett, LL.D.. *The American system of practical book-keeping* . . . Forty-first edition, improved. New York. 126 pgs. 25.5 cm. With broadside bound in. NUC NB0313031

Introduction

James Bennett's *The American system of practical book-keeping* . . . was the first American authored text totally devoted to accounting to achieve widespread distribution and popularity. In 1815, Bennett deposited for copyright a similar title but no copy of this early work is known to exist. It may be that this was a manuscript which Bennett used in his lectures on bookkeeping between 1815 and 1820.

The edition of 1820 carries an 1820 copyright and is probably the first edition published for general distribution. Early printings of this edition also include a 78 page section entitled (William) *Jackson's bookkeeping: adapted to the coin and commerce of the United States*. This section was not included in later editions.

Item 33. 1820. James Bennett

James Bennett was born in 1788. He is listed in the New York City directories from 1818 to 1822 as an accountant and from 1824 to 1835 as a teacher of bookkeeping. In several editions of his book he described himself as:

Professor to the Accountants Society of New York
Late Professor to the Accountants Society of Pennsylvania
Late President of the Accountants Society of New York

Nothing is known about these early accounting societies and it has been suggested that these organizations may have included only his students. In the early 1840's, he changed his name to James Arlington Bennett and listed himself as an Attorney and Counselor at Law.

About book-keeping, the author states:

Of all the numerous aids necessary for a safe, satisfactory, and successful commerce, *Book-keeping.* or a methodical, easy, and concise plan of recording every transaction, even the most minute, and of exhibiting, on a slight inspection, the actual state of business, whether prosperous or adverse, is undoubtly the most important. Without some expeditous method of obtaining this knowledge, especially in complicated mercantile pursuits, the merchant might dream of increasing wealth, when on the edge of the vortex that is ready to ingulph himself and his connexions in ruin. . . .

Book-keeping is the art of recording mercantile transactions in a summary, scientific, and perspicuous form, according to the order of time when they happen, without omission or unnecessary repetition of articles and names. This branch of education, so important to the success, the satisfaction, and the reputation of commercial men, it appears has been cultivated with less felicity and care than many others of less utility and extant. It has been taught in seminaries of learning in a very injudicious manner, and on plans entirely different from what takes place in real business. It is hoped that this evil will find a speedy remedy.

Description of *The American system of practical book-keeping*...

The essence of Bennett's system is a hybrid of the day book and journal. The day book, with a detailed description of each transaction, is entered on the left-hand pages of the book of original entry. Journal entries are entered on the right-hand pages opposite the day book descriptions. The author says:

> This system will be found to be an important improvement on that published in the Edinburg Encyclopedia, so justly and generally admired. It requires only two *principal books*, as the *Day-Book* incorporates the Journal with it, and renders it an index to the Leger. This reduces the labour of writing in the Journal, compared with the old plan, perhaps nineteen in twenty parts.

The date of the transaction was in the left margin of the day-book which also corresponded to the date of its opposite journal entry. Each journal entry had a debit column and a credit column. For further convenience and to save errors each column on the page could be added to prove that the entries were made accurately. He felt that if these columns were equal, no other errors could remain undetected on the books.

The only other book that this system required was the leger, "the chief or grand book of accounts, to which all others were subservient." Each leger account had a debit and a credit side. The merchant opened these accounts as he found it necessary and useful in conducting his business. From these accounts he could determine his net gain or loss and a correct statement of his affairs in general.

A general leger balance was usually taken every six to twelve months. A trial balance, where all the debit and credit columns of the leger accounts were listed, was prepared to determine if the leger books were balanced and correct. If errors were made in recording transactions and amounts, the bookkeeper should not scratch out the mistake, but reenter it on the other side.

Bennett listed three classes of accounts:

(1) His effects or property............ Real Accounts
(2) His debts due to, or by him......Personal Accounts
(3) His gains or losses.................Imaginary Accounts

He also discussed twelve other auxiliary books, the first four of which he said were indispensable to most merchants: the case book, bill-book, invoice-book, sales-book, book of accounts current, book of commissions, book of charges, copy book of letters, book of postage of letters, book of ships' accounts, receipt-book, and the pocket-book of memorandums.

Throughout the book very specific examples were given which illustrated the day-book and the journal, the leger, and several of the auxiliary books; also, several of the most useful forms of documents were shown.

Bennett was particularly concerned about the possibilities of plagiarism and in many editions he devotes several introductory pages to a discussion of the copyright laws.

On February 25, 1817, Bennett copyrighted *A balance chart: exhibiting a complete and final balance of the accounts in a merchant's leger kept by double and single entry*. This handsome broadside appeared as a fold-out in every edition of his book. The original engraving was executed by Asaph Williard, Ralphi Rawdon, and Freeman Rawdon of the Albany Firm of Williard and Rawdon.

Bennett's book ran into many editions, each only a little different from its predecessor. The final edition, the forty-first, was last published in New York in 1862 shortly before his death the following year.

Written by Peter McMickle

CONTENTS.

	Page		Page
Introduction	7	Form of an Invoice-Book	77
Explanation of the principal Books	ib.	—— of a Sales Book	79
Explanation of the Classes of Accounts; of the General Rules for Dr. & Cr. and of the Auxiliary Books	9	—— of a Commission Sales Book	81
		—— of an Account Sales	83
A Course of Lectures, as delivered by the author in the city of New-York, embracing *Domestic and Foreign Trade Proper, Commission Business, Bills of Exchange, and Company Concerns and Accounts*	12	Two Methods of averaging an Account Sales	84
		Rates of Coins for estimating Duties	ib.
		Method of making out an Account Current	89
		Form of a Postage Book	90
		—— of a Check Book	ib.
Of Posting the items to the Leger	19	—— to be used by Master Mechanics and Superintendants of every kind of work	91
Questions for the Curious	20	Description of the Public Funds in Great Britain	ib.
Day-Book A, in which are exemplified a copious variety of business transactions	22	Three tables for receiving and paying the gold coins of Great Britain, Portugal, France, and Spain	92
Journal A, in which no error can exist without detection	23	Three tables showing the weight of any required sum of English, Portuguese, French and Spanish gold	ib.
Additional Journal Forms for the use of those who may not think proper to unite the Day-Book and Journal	53	Form of a Bottomry Bond	93
		—— of a Bottomry Bill	94
Trial Balance and method of detecting and correcting errors	55	—— of a Respondentia Bond	95
Leger A, in which each account has its definition and method of closing under it	57	—— of an Instrument of hypothecation of ship and cargo	97
Value of foreign Coins in the Money of the United States	ib.	Stipulation for the return of a ship	98
		Form of a Charter-Party	99
Curious and useful exemplification of the Imaginary Accounts	69	—— of a Shipping Paper	100
		—— of a Bill of Sale of a registered ship	102
Method of opening the new Books	70	—— of a Bill of Sale of an enrolled ship	103
Method of opening a Set of Books in a Concern where the Partners are active	70, 71	Useful calculations relating to the purchase and sale of Bills and Bank Stock	ib.
Mercantile Precedents	72	A copper-plate engraving nearly two feet square exemplifying the final Balance of a Merchant's Leger	ib.
Form of a Bill-Book	74, 75		
Method of keeping a Cash-Book	76		

CONTENTS OF JACKSON'S BOOK-KEEPING.

1. Day-Book A, in which is exemplified Domestic and Foreign Trade Proper	109	Of Sweden and Norway	165
		—— Germany	166
2. Journal A, which serves as a Merchandise Account	120	—— Bohemia	169
		—— Hungary	171
3. Leger A, which is posted by the page	126	—— Switzerland	ib.
1. Day-Book B, in which is exemplified Commission Business, Domestic and Foreign	133	—— Holland	172
		—— the Netherlands	174
2. Journal B, exemplifying a method by which the Commission Merchant can determine his Gain or Loss in Business at the foot of each page	144	—— France	ib.
		—— Spain	177
		—— Portugal	180
3. Leger B, posted by the month	150	—— Italy	181
		—— The Two Sicilies	183
MONEYS, EXCHANGES, WEIGHTS, AND MEASURES		—— the Levant and Ports up the Mediterranean	184
		—— Barbary	185
Of the United States	159	—— Canton, Pekin, &c.	187
—— Great Britain and Ireland	160	Moneys of Turkey, Persia, Coromandel, Bengal and Japan	186, 187
—— Russia	161	Naturalization of Aliens	ib.
—— Prussia and Poland	162	Advertisement of Bennett's Lectures on Book-Keeping and Mathematics	188
—— Mecklenburg and Lubeck	163		
—— Denmark and Holstein	164		

ILLUSTRATION 97. Table of contents from 1820 first printing of Bennett's *The American system of practical book-keeping* . . .

ILLUSTRATION 98. Day-book and journal example from 1820 James Bennett's *The American system of practical book-keeping*.

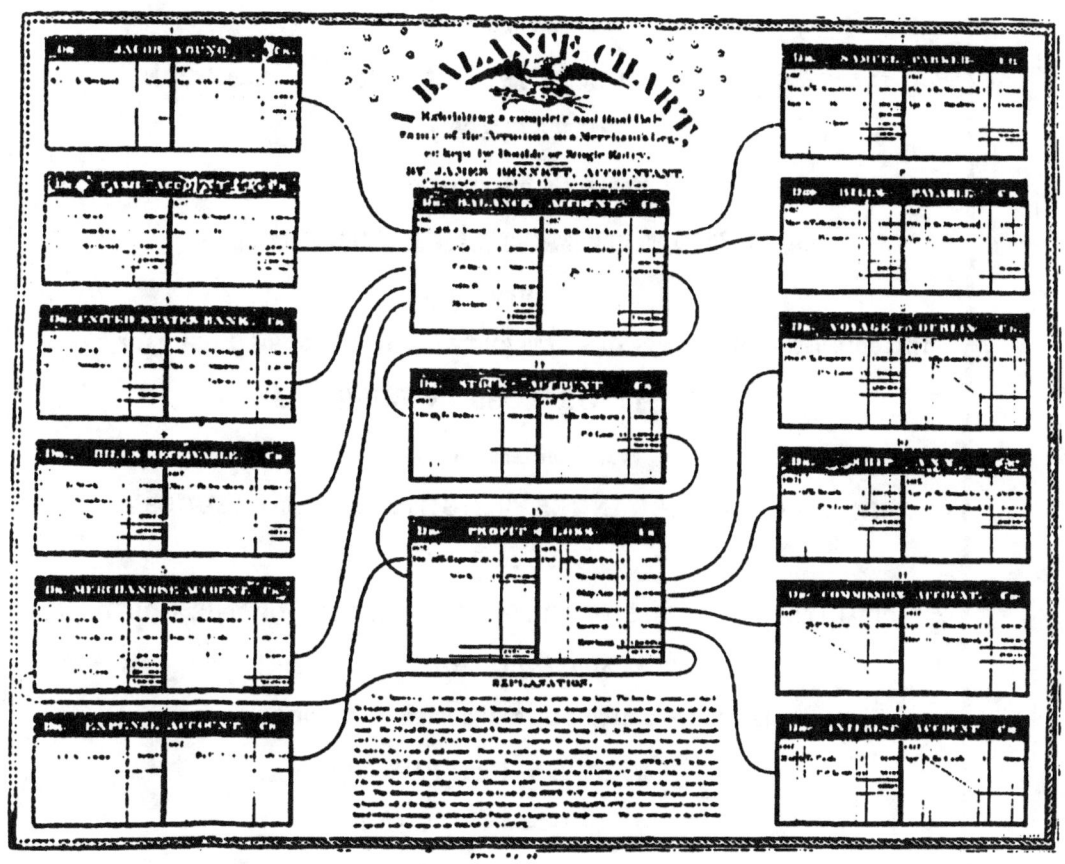

ILLUSTRATION 99. Broadside from 1820 Bennett's *The American system of practical book-keeping* . . . (greatly reduced).

Item 33. 1820. James Bennett

JACKSON'S
BOOK-KEEPING,

ADAPTED TO THE

COIN AND COMMERCE OF THE UNITED STATES,

AND COMPREHENDING

ALL THE IMPROVEMENTS IN THE MODERN PRACTICE

OF THE ART;

WHEREIN IS EXEMPLIFIED

A METHOD OF KEEPING A JOURNAL

BY WHICH

THE COMMISSION MERCHANT CAN DETERMINE, AT THE FOOT OF EACH PAGE,

HIS PROFIT OR LOSS IN BUSINESS;

TO WHICH ARE ADDED,

THE MONEYS, EXCHANGES, WEIGHTS, AND MEASURES,

OF THE

PRINCIPAL TRADING CITIES OF THE FOUR QUARTERS OF THE WORLD,

AS NOW ESTABLISHED,

COMPARED WITH EACH OTHER, AND WITH THOSE OF THE

UNITED STATES.

BY JAMES BENNETT,

AUTHOR OF THE AMERICAN SYSTEM OF PRACTICAL BOOK-KEEPING FOR SCHOOLS.

NEW-YORK:

PRINTED BY ABM. PAUL, CORNER OF WATER-STREET AND BURLING-SLIP.

1821.

ILLUSTRATION 100. Title page of *Jackson's book-keeping* bound in some printings of Bennett's first edition of 1820.

For Product Safety Concerns and Information please contact our EU
representative GPSR@taylorandfrancis.com
Taylor & Francis Verlag GmbH, Kaufingerstraße 24, 80331 München, Germany

www.ingramcontent.com/pod-product-compliance
Lightning Source LLC
Chambersburg PA
CBHW071815300426
44116CB00009B/1334